Genealogist's Handbook for Irish Research

Marie E. Daly

with Judith Lucey

AmericanAncestors.org

Copyright © 2016 by the New England Historic Genealogical Society.

All rights reserved. No part of this publication may be reproduced or transmitted in any form or by any means, electronic or mechanical, including photocopying, recording, or any information storage or retrieval system, without permission in writing from the copyright holder, except for the inclusion of brief quotations in a review.

ISBN-13: 978-0-88082-346-3

Library of Congress Catalog Card Number: 2016941749

Design by Carolyn Sheppard Oakley and Ellen Maxwell.

Cover photo: © Linda Caldwell | Dreamstime.com

Maps by Patti Isaacs

Contents

Preface and Acknowledgments v

Part 1: Getting Started

1   Embarking on the Genealogical Voyage 3

2   Using the Census and Vital Records 11

Part 2: Linking Your Immigrant Ancestors to Ireland

3   Using North American Church Records....................29

4   Researching Your Ancestors' Records
of Immigration, Citizenship, and Travel....................43

5   Researching Your Ancestors through
Gravestones, Newspapers, and Business Records.......61

6   Looking Further Back: Early Irish
Immigration to North America 75

7   Identifying Irish Place Names
and Administrative Divisions 85

Part 3: Using Irish Records

8   Finding Your Ancestors in Irish
Church Records and Civil Registrations...................101

9   Using Records of Property
and Valuation in Ireland.......................................123

10   Making the Most of Irish Online
Census and Land Valuation Records......................133

Part 4: Online Resources...155

Illustration Credits 161

Index 165

Preface and Acknowledgments

In 1976, I was looking for an inexpensive vacation in a foreign land, and chose Ireland. Being a fourth generation Irish American, I knew little about my Irish roots or the country. My trip turned out to be a revelation from the moment I stepped off the plane. Even the air, redolent with peat smoke, smelled different. A visit to the National Museum of Ireland in Dublin introduced me to a magnificent ancient heritage that dated back thousands of years. For the first time, I heard traditional Irish music–not the "Mother Machree" tunes of St. Patrick's Day in Boston–and was astounded by a vibrant culture I had never had known but to which I was somehow connected.

When I returned home, I asked my father about his family. Who was your father? —Matthew Daly. Who was your grandfather? —I don't know. "Dad," I asked, "how can you not know the name of your grandfather?" He had died before my father was born; the connection between generations had been lost. My father and I then went to town hall to get my grandfather's birth record, and on it we discovered the names of his grandparents, Matthew Daly and Mary Callan. With that initial success, I was off and running. In those days, genealogy involved winding through many reels of microfilm, signing up on wait lists to access the microfilm readers at crowded National Archives, and climbing ladders to access Massachusetts vital records ledgers housed at the Department of Vital Statistics. I got my first computer in 1983, but it was many years before the Internet came on the scene. I made contact with other Irish American family researchers in the Boston area, and from them I learned about research sources and techniques. In 1983, I helped found The Irish Ancestral Research Association (TIARA) and served as their first president. In that year also, I attended the first of many genealogical conferences – the Federation of Genealogical Societies Conference in Hartford, Connecticut—and I still have the souvenir mug to prove it.

In the following decade, the Internet revolutionized genealogical research. Advances in digital technology allowed great quantities of records to be reproduced and indexed in searchable databases, putting genealogical data within reach of family historians all over the world and advancing our research. As a result, we now needn't climb ladders to locate records but can find many of them from our home computers—and new record sets are becoming available online all the time.

To help researchers find sources of information about their Irish ancestors, some excellent guidebooks have been published; among the best of these is John Grenham's *Finding Your Irish Ancestors*. With these expert guidebooks to identify the many possible sources, including the many available online, you might imagine that tracing Irish ancestors is as quick and easy as the process shown on television. And yet over the years, Judy and I have given presentations to, and consulted with, myriad Irish American genealogists who have encountered hurdles they have not been able to overcome. Usually the brick wall is the exact place of an ancestor's origin in Ireland.

Unlike a search for colonial New England ancestors, which can lead to fruitful collections of information about many forebears, Irish research does have some inherent hurdles and frustrations. There's the matter of many people having similar or the same names. In addition, Irish censuses were largely destroyed in a fire, and other records can be scanty. For Irish Americans, the quest is less about quantity and more about understanding who our ancestors were, locating their places of origin, and discovering what life was like for them in a country and culture so different from twenty-first-century America.

Given these challenges, with the proper tools you can sometimes break down those brick walls: knowing how to widen your searches, looking not only at your individual ancestors but the others around them; gaining knowledge of the history of your ancestor's community; and discovering the network of the ancestor's family and friends. In other words, you need not just access to records but a set of strategies for research and interpretation.

This book arose from the many materials we have developed over the years to help people with Irish research. In it, we aim to show you the approaches that will increase your chances for success. By using the examples of two families—the Fitzgerald family of Boston, Massachusetts, and the McClements family of Brighton, Michigan—we demonstrate the sources, methods, and tactics that will lead researchers to specific origins in Ireland. Further, we give you the tools to extend your research into Irish records. With some good detective work, you might be able to locate your family in Ireland, determine where they lived, and even "see" the land or house on Google.

Using This Book

This book is divided into four basic sections:

In Part 1, Getting Started, we cover basics of genealogical research—which is the same for all types of genealogical research.

In Part 2, Linking Your Immigrant Ancestors to Ireland, we discuss the most fruitful sources for finding Irish origins and also the research techniques that will improve the odds of success.

In Part 3, Using Irish Records, we explain the sometimes confusing Irish place names and administrative divisions and then delve into the kinds of Irish records that will help you learn even more about your ancestors.

Finally, Part 4 is a summary table of the many online resources available to help you in your research. Compiling an up-to-date list was a bit like sipping water from a fire hose: every time we thought we had a complete list, a new, family-tree-shaking addition to records was announced. Although we have made every attempt to ensure that URLs are up to date, please regularly check AmericanAncestors.org/Irish-handbook for updates to the summary list.

Throughout the book, we have included real-life examples, to-do lists and other summaries of actions to take, and images of many kinds of records. Our goal is for this handbook to be a launching pad into the great and wonderful universe of Irish genealogy!

Acknowledgments

First and foremost, I want to thank my colleague Judith Lucey, NEHGS Archivist, for her assistance with planning the book and for contributing Chapter 7, Identifying Irish Place Names and Administrative Divisions, and Chapter 9, Using Records of Property and Valuation in Ireland. Morrison deS. "Toby" Webb, NEHGS Trustee, generously contributed the two-page box on Irish Quaker research on pages 108–109.

Martha Bustin wielded her editorial skills on our draft manuscript, turning it into a helpful guidebook. Publications Director Penelope Stratton helped shepherd the project through from an idea to a completed project. Thanks also to my colleague Eileen Curley Pironti, Researcher for the Newbury Street Press and a fellow Irish expert, for reviewing drafts of the manuscript, and to my colleague Valerie Beaudrault for proofreading. Andrew Pierce and Paul Milner generously provided peer reviews.

Publications Coordinator Ellen Maxwell helped adapt the design for this book, and Creative Director Carolyn Sheppard Oakley designed the front cover. Thanks are due to typographer Marlene Stemple, cartographer Patti Isaacs, and indexer Steve Csipke.

Finally, many thanks to President and CEO D. Brenton Simons, who has provided continued support; to former Chief Operating Officer Thomas Wilcox, who encouraged Judy and me to explain "how you do what you do" to help find someone's family in Ireland; and to the many people Judy and I have coached over the years, whose hurdles and problems helped us develop our own best practices in Irish genealogy.

Marie E. Daly
Spring 2016

PART 1
Getting Started

Some thirty-five million Americans claim Irish ancestry, according to the 2010 U.S. federal census.[1] While the largest percentage resides in the Northeast, the Irish American population stretches from Maine to California and from Alaska to Florida. Their Irish forebears were among America's pioneers who supported the country's struggle for independence; in fact, three signers of the Declaration of Independence—George Taylor, Matthew Thornton, and James Smith—were born in Ireland. Americans with Irish ancestry hailed from many corners of our culture ranging from the military—General John Sullivan, General Philip Sheridan, and Commodore John Barry, father of the U.S. Navy—to writers and playwrights—F. Scott Fitzgerald, William Kennedy, Flannery O'Connor, Mary McCarthy, and Eugene O'Neill. Irish Americans fought on both sides of the Civil War, and their contribution to the Union was a significant factor in the outcome of the war. As many as twenty-two U.S. presidents have Irish ancestors. In these and countless other ways, Irish immigrants and their children have been integral to the political, cultural, commercial, and educational affairs of the nation. With the ancestries of so many Americans rooted in Ireland, we have written this book to help our fellow family historians learn about their origins in the Old Country.

---

[1] http://trends.truliablog.com/category/demographics/

 Chapter 1
Embarking on the Genealogical Voyage

People have long connected questions about identity—*Who are we? What distinguishes us?*—with questions about genealogy—*Who were our forebears? Where are we from? What is our history?* In Ireland, the *senachies,* or traditional storytellers and historians, memorized the genealogies of their clansmen, trailing back a thousand years. Recitation and song played big parts in preserving the names of ancestors and powerfully affirming a continuity between those who lived long ago and those like ourselves who came later. Gradually writing, printing, and now the digital medium have supplemented or even supplanted the roles formerly played by collective memory and oral history. As you begin your research and fill out your basic family-history documents, you are part of a venerable tradition of preserving information that might otherwise be lost or forgotten.

Start with What You and Your Relatives Know

Most family research begins at the same point, with oneself, and proceeds back in time. To gather and organize genealogical data, researchers rely on two basic documents: the *five-generation chart* and the *family group sheet*. You will want to start your genealogical journey by filling in these two documents.

On the first, the five-generation chart (see Figure 1.1), you will record your name, the names of your parents, grandparents, great grandparents, and great-great grandparents, and any known dates and places of birth, marriage, and death. (The charts can range from four to thirty-two generations, but for our purposes we will use a five-generation chart, which goes back to great-great grandparents.) The goal is to complete the document with as many pieces of information as you can, as far back as you can, using what you know about your family from personal knowledge, interviews with relatives, and any research you may have done to date. When you get to certain lines, you may not know a name or you may be lacking specific dates and places. Don't worry. You can fill in the blanks later with data from historical records.

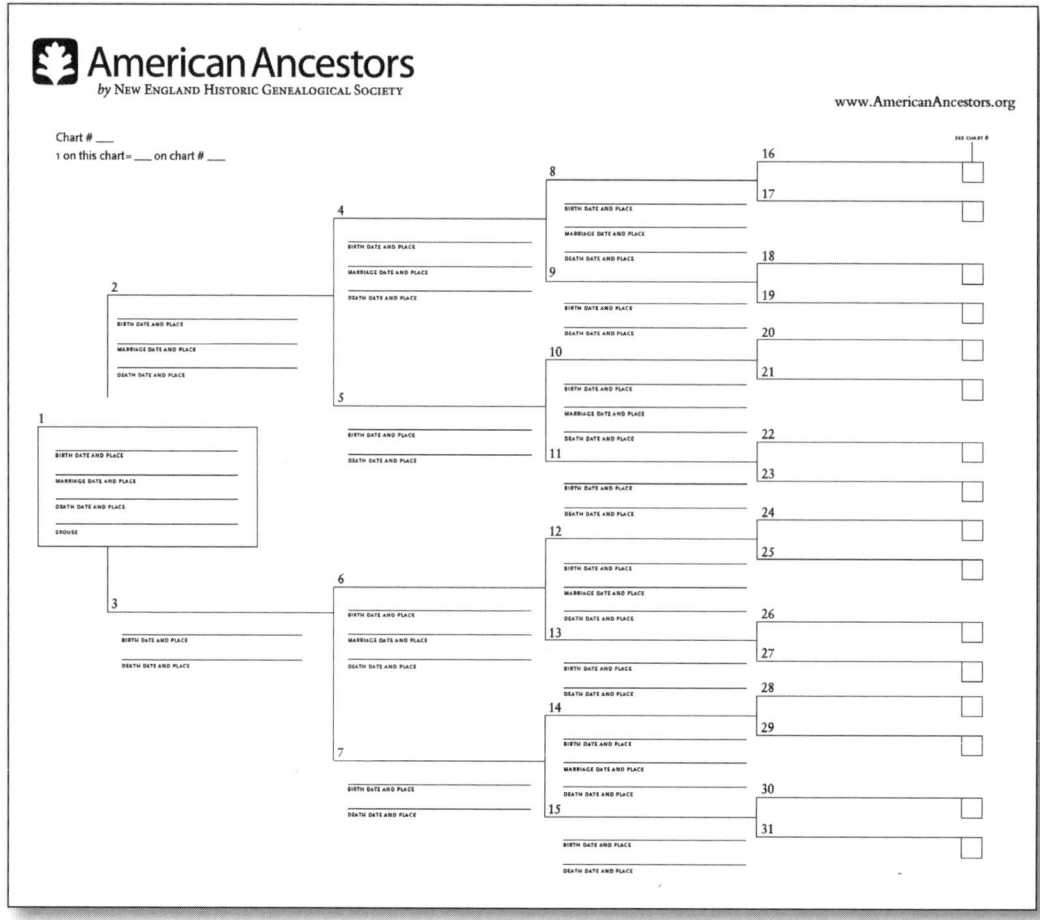

Figure 1.1. Sample of five-generation chart.
Available at AmericanAncestors.org/education/learning-resources/download.

Start by writing your name in the #1 position, and enter the date and place of your birth and marriage. Put your father's name in the #2 position and your mother's name in the #3 position. Your paternal grandfather (father's father) goes in #4, and your paternal grandmother (father's mother) goes in #5. Likewise, your maternal grandfather (mother's father) goes in #6, and your maternal grandmother (mother's mother) goes in #7. And so on.

Next, you will want to complete family group sheets. On this second type of basic genealogical document, you record the names of a set of parents, their dates, and the places of birth, marriage, and death. The form then records the names of the children in birth order, and their dates and places of birth, marriage, and death, as well as the names of their spouses. Fill in the names of your father and mother at the top, as well as their data. Then fill in data about yourself and your brothers and sisters in the spaces below, starting with the oldest child first. Now do the same for your two sets of grandparents, and list your parents, aunts and uncles as the children of your grandparents. (See Figure 1.2, page 5.)

American Ancestors
by New England Historic Genealogical Society

Family Group Sheet

Write dates as Day, Month, Year
example: 1 Jan 1904

Father
Given Name(s) | Last Name
Born | Place
Died | Place
Married | Place
Father's Father (first, middle, last)
Father's Mother (first, middle, maiden)
Other Marriages (first, middle, last)

Mother
Given Name(s) | Last Name
Born | Place
Died | Place
Mother's Father (first, middle, last)
Mother's Mother (first, middle, maiden)
Other Marriages (first, middle, last)

Child #1
Sex | Given Name(s) | Last Name
Born | Place
Died | Place
Spouse (first, middle, last)
Married | Place

Child #2
Sex | Given Name(s) | Last Name
Born | Place
Died | Place
Spouse (first, middle, last)
Married | Place

Child #3
Sex | Given Name(s) | Last Name
Born | Place
Died | Place
Spouse (first, middle, last)
Married | Place

Page 1
www.AmericanAncestors.org

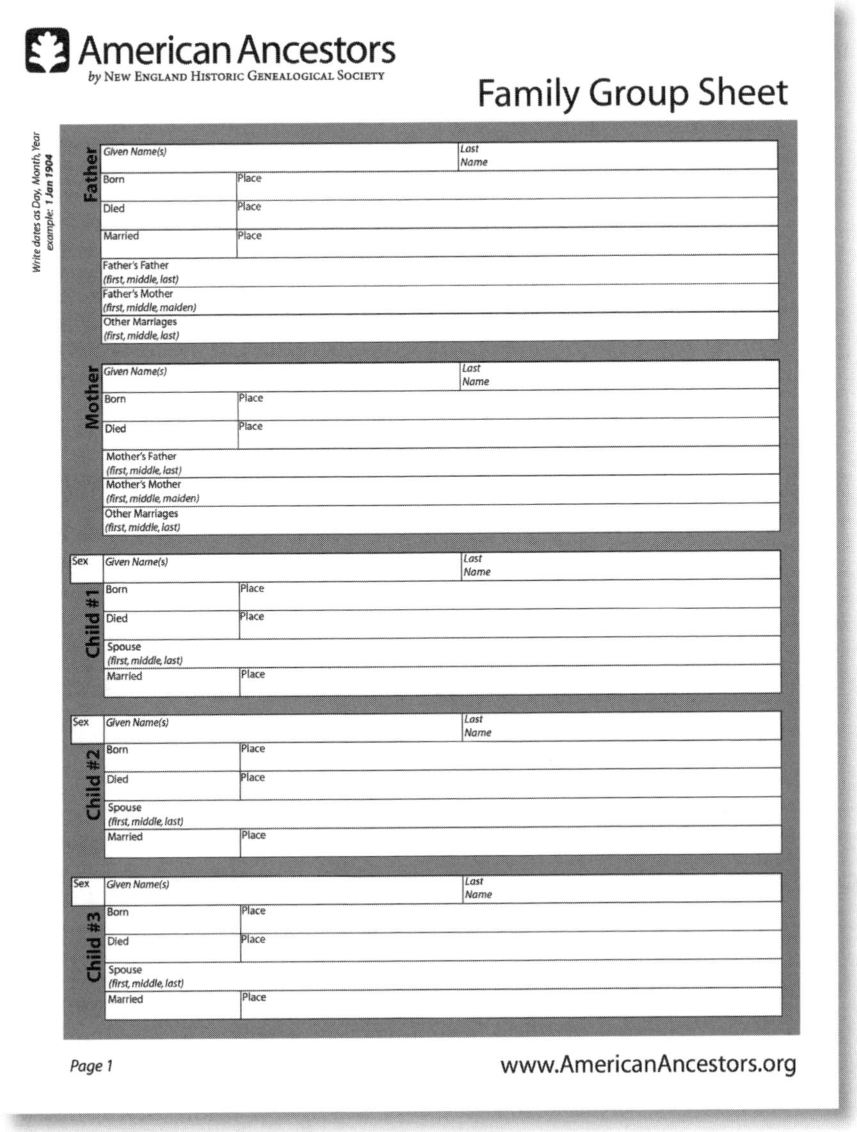

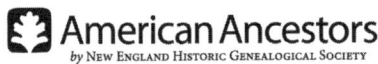

Figure 1.2. Sample of family group sheet.
Available at AmericanAncestors.org/education/learning-resources/download.

The information about your aunts and uncles can be considered *collateral* research, which often enables you to overcome brick walls when resources are not available or do not provide enough detail. The importance of collateral research will be illustrated in Chapter 8 with the case study of the McClements family of Brighton, Michigan.

Computer programs such as RootsMagic and Reunion now handle these basic genealogical forms. You just enter the data in the program, and you can then print out the pedigree chart and the family group sheet from the program. You can also save digitized results of your searches on your computer and attach the results to your computer program's family files. Alternatively, or in addition, you may wish to create a folder or a three-ring binder for each family, and store the pedigree charts, family group sheets, research logs, documents, and the results of your research in these folders or binders.

Conduct Oral History Interviews

As you get started in your genealogical research, seek the help of other family members, such as your parents, grandparents, aunts and uncles, cousins, and even family friends and neighbors. Talk about your family history around the Thanksgiving dinner table, summer barbecue, or whenever or wherever your family tends to gather. Getting other people involved in your quest brings your family together and encourages an appreciation of your shared experiences. In addition to questions about names, dates, and places, ask them about their childhood days, where they worked and worshipped, how they played, and what they learned at school.

You may encounter someone who does not want to remember or recount personal stories, perhaps due to tribulations in the past. Sometimes an issue that lacks controversy to you, such as a divorce, rushed wedding, or illegitimate birth that occurred many years ago, is a scandal or a painful memory in your relative's mind. Don't pester anyone. People are entitled to their privacy. Turn to someone else or to another topic instead.

> **To-Do List**
> - Fill in a five-generation chart and family group sheets.
> - Interview relatives.
> - Scrutinize family photos and documents.
> - Learn the stories that make up your family's life.

Ask your relatives to bring out the old photo albums and go through them together. The photographs may help jog their memories and elicit stories. If people digress from the direction of your questions, let them wander. They may bring up serendipitous information that you had never thought to ask about. In addition to photo albums, other family keepsakes may provide launching pads for your interview–scrapbooks, letters, family bibles, prayer books, missals, Mass cards, ordination and funeral cards, household objects, antiques, and furniture. Perhaps your great grandfather's Civil War belt or your grandmother's recipe box will lead your relatives to reflect on their lives in an earlier time.

Document your interview as soon as possible after your visit with your relative. Recording the interview is ideal, but some people object to being recorded or will be less forthcoming once they know the "record" button has been pressed. Do not, however, record anyone without their permission. If you are not recording, take what notes you can during the interview, though you may find that process distracting. At the very least, make a clear record of the important genealogical facts you have learned in the interview, such as locations, names, and dates. After the interview, write down all the information you can while it is fresh in your mind. Document the name of the person interviewed, the date, time, and place where the interview occurred. If you have recorded the interview, transcribe the recording as soon as possible afterward.

Interview Irish-born Relatives

Some Americans are fortunate to have living Irish-born relatives who can give them important details about their origins in Ireland. Interviewing these relatives is crucial in preserving the family history, since historical records cannot provide as much information as the immigrant. In addition to the usual questions about family history, focus on determining the location of the family in Ireland; the existence of parents or grandparents alive in 1911, who would therefore be included in that year's Irish census; the maiden names of the women family members; and details of your ancestor's migration experience, such as date of immigration, port of entry, citizenship status, and visits home, if any. All will be discussed in more depth later, but let's now look briefly at why each of these four interview topics is particularly important to explore as you embark on your genealogical voyage.

> **To-Do List**
> - Determine location of your family in Ireland.
> - Identify parents or grandparents alive in the early twentieth century.
> - Ascertain maiden names of wives and mothers.

Because Irish names can be very common, knowing a specific location where your ancestor lived will help you identify him or her in records. *Location* of the exact origin in Ireland is imperative in using historical records in Ireland. Concentrate on learning the place where your immigrant relative was born and lived (not necessarily the same place). If your Irish-born relative came from a big city, such as Dublin or Cork City, ascertain if possible, from the person you are interviewing, the street address or neighborhood in which the family lived and what church the family attended. The family may have migrated to the city from a rural parish in previous years. Pinpointing the nineteenth-century rural origins of urban families is essential to tracing the family back in previous generations.

Focus on getting back to the early twentieth century, a time period when Irish records are readily available online. Your research will be greatly helped if you can learn any information about *parents and grandparents* of the immigrant who can be identified in online records.

Maiden names are important pieces of evidence in singling out your family in Ireland. Irish surnames can be very common, even within a single parish. Maiden names of a wife or mother will help differentiate your John Doherty or Patrick Sullivan from all the others.

Learning about the *migration experience* to America can yield vital clues about our ancestors' families and origins. Ask your Irish-born relative about the journey to America. Did he or she travel via England or Canada? When and where did he or she disembark in the United States? Inquire about the citizenship status of your relative, and when and where he or she become an American citizen. Ask about visits home, if any, including return dates and entry ports. Passenger arrival lists of the twentieth century can reveal significant facts about visiting ancestors, even years after their initial immigration date.

Cite Your Sources

Many family historians have experienced the frustration of reading a compiled genealogy that has not provided reliable evidence or clear, complete source information to back up its assertions. These omissions leave the reader wondering if the claims being made are true or just wishful thinking. When you gather material for your family history, make sure you write down the details of all the records you consult. Enter the citations into your own files or computer. Most genealogical computer programs have functions for entering source data. Be sure to take advantage of these useful features, since the programs will automatically generate footnotes for the reports you print out.

When you photocopy records from a published book, make an additional photocopy of the title page of the book. Then staple that copy of the title page to your copy of the record. When you obtain a vital record at a records office, online, or from microfilm, make a printout. Write in pencil the title of the record, date, and the volume and page number on the backside of the copy. When you save an image of a record, include the volume and page in the file name. Programs such as Evernote and Microsoft OneNote can capture a web page from the Internet and save the citation for later reference.

Many citation styles exist for the presentation of source notes. For a good option that is widely used in genealogical works, see the format presented in *The Chicago Manual of Style*. (*See also Guide to Genealogical Writing* for tips on formatting your footnotes.) Whatever style you use, it is important to be consistent.

Example:

Hasia R. Diner, *Erin's Daughters in America: Irish Immigrant Women in the Nineteenth Century* (Baltimore: Johns Hopkins University Press, 1983), 25.

Think of citing your sources as similar to what you did when writing a term paper for English 101. The basic rationale for careful citation practices is the same in both cases: You need to make it possible for your reader to retrace your steps as a researcher and to evaluate the reliability of your sources. Therefore, in your finished family history you will want to provide a source note for each fact you include, communicating where you found your information. The key to successful citation is to keep good records about all sources you consult, through all the phases of your research.

Keep a Research Log

To stay organized, prevent duplication of effort, and lay the groundwork for easy source citation, you will want to keep a research log. The log should include all sources checked, even ones that proved unproductive. You can also use a research log to review problems, weigh evidence, and develop a plan for your research. A log will record the name of the individual researched, the date of the entry, the researcher's name, the place of research, and the document's author, title, publisher, call number, and date of publication. You can include a comment or observation field where you can evaluate the evidence and record plans for further research.

You can integrate the log with your filing system by including a column for a file, binder, or document number. Organize your filing system by family and individuals. Each family folder or binder should have its own set of research logs, which become like a table of contents to the family folder.

When you use oral history in your research, write down or transcribe the interview, documenting the date and time, place of interview, name of interviewer, and the person interviewed. The record can then be entered into the research log.

You can create your own form for the log using readily available programs, such as Microsoft Word or Excel. For more information about research logs and how to use them, see the many learning resources, including a downloadable research log, at AmericanAncestors.org/education/learning-resources. (See Figure 1.3, below.) The Family History Library website has downloadable research log forms and a wiki explaining research logs in detail at https://familysearch.org/learn/wiki/en/Research_Logs.

American Ancestors
by New England Historic Genealogical Society

Research Log

Repository: ______________________ **Date:** ______________________

Source Information (title, author, publisher, publication date, etc.)	**Call Number** (film number, URL, etc.)	**Objective**	**Results**

www.AmericanAncestors.org

Figure 1.3. Sample research log.
Available at AmericanAncestors.org/education/learning-resources/download.

Summary

As you begin to research your Irish ancestry in earnest, your mission is to interview, collect, and organize any relevant information, using a five-generation chart, family group chart, and research log. You will want, if possible, to determine the location of your family in Ireland, identify parents or grandparents alive in 1911, learn the maiden names of wives and mothers, and find out all you can about your family members' immigration stories and paths to citizenship. Beyond this gathering of precious information, however, you will be talking to family members and family friends about the past, recording their memories and stories of what life was like, and capturing information about past decisions and occurrences that affect and reverberate through present and future generations. In making this valuable time to listen, record, and remember, you are making an important stand against forgetting and taking the crucial long view on preserving family history. As John Ruskin said in another context, about architecture, "When we build, let us think that we build forever. Let it not be for present delight nor for present use alone. Let it be such work as our descendants will thank us for."

Further Reading

- Barnickel, Linda. *Oral History for the Family Historian: A Basic Guide.* Carlisle, Pa.: Oral History Association, 2006.
- *The Chicago Manual of Style.* 16th ed. Chicago: University of Chicago Press, 2010. Available online by subscription at www.chicagomanualofstyle.org.
- Hart, Cynthia, and Lisa Samson. *The Oral History Workshop: Collect and Celebrate the Life Stories of Your Family and Friends.* New York: Workman, 2009.
- Mills, Elizabeth Shown. *Evidence Explained: Citing History Sources from Artifacts to Cyberspace.* 2nd ed. Baltimore: Genealogical Publishing Company, 2009.
- Stratton, Penelope L., and Henry B. Hoff, CG, FASG. *Guide to Genealogical Writing: How to Write and Publish Your Family History.* Boston: NEHGS, 2014.
- Sturdevant, Katherine Scott. *Bringing Your Family History to Life through Social History.* Cincinnati: Betterway Books, 2000.

 Chapter 2
Using the Census and Vital Records

You have filled out a five-generation chart as far back as you can, prepared family group sheets, and interviewed family members. The next step is to advance your research by using the historical records, especially the census and vital records. Consulting archival records to learn more about your ancestors can be like following an intriguing trail that winds back in time. In your oral history, try to get back to at least the last available federal census (currently the 1940 census). For many people, reaching to this point will mean getting back to their grandparents' generation.

Start with Federal Census Records

The U.S. federal government began collecting census data in 1790 and continued the collection of population and other schedules every ten years. The 1890 census was destroyed in a fire. Before 1850, the census records provide head-of-household only, and a table of the sex and ages of the household members. Starting in 1850, the census documents the names, ages, and occupations of all household members. Each census asked different questions, and a genealogical researcher learns how to make use of what each census provides. In some years, the value of real estate and personal estate was recorded. This data can point you to other records, such as probate records and deeds. The census in 1870 had a check-off box indicating if the person listed was a U.S. citizen. This information can lead you to naturalization records for your immigrant ancestors. Starting in 1880, census takers collected not only the birthplace of individuals, but the birthplaces of their parents. This data can lead you back to the birthplaces of your immigrant ancestors. In 1900, the number of years married, the number of children born, and the number of children living were collected. Beginning in 1900, census takers recorded year of immigration and citizenship status, using the abbreviations *Na* for naturalized, *Pa* for someone with first papers, and *Al* for alien. The 1920 census indicates not only citizenship status, but also the year of naturalization. The data in the census records from 1900 through 1940 can therefore point you toward passenger arrival lists and naturalization records.

1790–1840	Includes name of head-of-household only, with sex and ages of other household members
1850	Begins including name, ages, birthplaces, occupations of all in household
1860	Adds value of real estate and personal estate
1870	Continues value of real and personal estate; adds check box to indicate citizenship
1880	Adds birthplaces of parents; adds street address in many cities
1900	Adds street address, years married, number of children born, number of children living; records year of immigration and citizenship status
1920	Records year of naturalization
1940	Records residence in 1935

Figure 2.1. Chart showing addition of key questions to U.S. federal census.

You can search census records online at AmericanAncestors.org, Findmypast.com, Ancestry.com, or FamilySearch.org, as well as at other sites. Each site differs regarding search criteria and the way variant spellings are indexed. If you don't find a record on one site, don't give up: try another.

Use "± 2 years" (or ± 3, 4, or 5 years) in date fields, when searching census records online and entering the approximate age an ancestor would have been in that year. Many of our Irish immigrant ancestors were born in rural communities, where agricultural and religious calendars prevailed. Often they did not know exactly when they were born, how old they were, or the year they immigrated. In addition, immigrants may have lied about dates and ages for various reasons. Perhaps they were intimidated by the government collecting data about them. A woman who was older than her husband might shave years off her age. An immigrant might say he arrived at an earlier date, so that he could claim he was under the age of 18 years when he arrived, and therefore did not have to make a declaration of intent. A local ward boss might try to recruit as many voters as possible and entice people to lie about their arrival dates so that they could become citizens and vote in an upcoming election. For these reasons, you will want to input search criteria as "±" 2 to 5 years when searching at sites such as Ancestry.com.

Start with the most recent federal census that you can for the person you are researching, and work your way back in time. Look for your parents or grandparents in the 1940 census. Find them in census records as children living with their parents.

As an example, let us look at the census records of the future President John Fitzgerald Kennedy (Figure 2.2). He was born in 1917 in Brookline, Massachusetts. He can be found in the 1940 census living with his parents and all eight siblings in Eastchester, New York. Since his father, Joseph P. Kennedy, was the U.S. Ambassador to the United Kingdom, the family may have been living in London, England, at the time, but they may have maintained a legal residence in New York.

Kennedy, Joseph P.	Head	M	W	50	M	No	C-5	Massachusetts	Same house
—, Rose	Wife	F	W	48	M	No	C-4	Massachusetts	Same house
—, Joseph Jr.	Son	M	W	24	S	Yes	C-5	Massachusetts	Same house
—, Rosemary	Daughter	F	W	21	S	Yes	C-1	Massachusetts	Same house
—, John	Son	M	W	23	S	Yes	C-3	Massachusetts	Same house
—, Kathleen	Daughter	F	W	20	S	Yes	C-4	Massachusetts	Same house
—, Eunice	Daughter	F	W	18	S	Yes	H-4	Massachusetts	Same house
—, Patricia	Daughter	F	W	15	S	Yes	H-2	Massachusetts	Same house
—, Robert	Son	M	W	14	S	Yes	7	Massachusetts	Same house
—, Jean	Daughter	F	W	12	S	Yes	5	Massachusetts	Same house
—, Edward	Son	M	W	8	S	Yes	2	Massachusetts	Same house
Ham, Loretta	Maid	F	W	45	S	No	C-4	New York	Mt Vernon W
Ambrose, Margaret	Cook	F	W	39	S	No	8	Eire	Same house
Dunn, Elizabeth	Secretary	F	W	25	S	No	C-4	Massachusetts	Boston

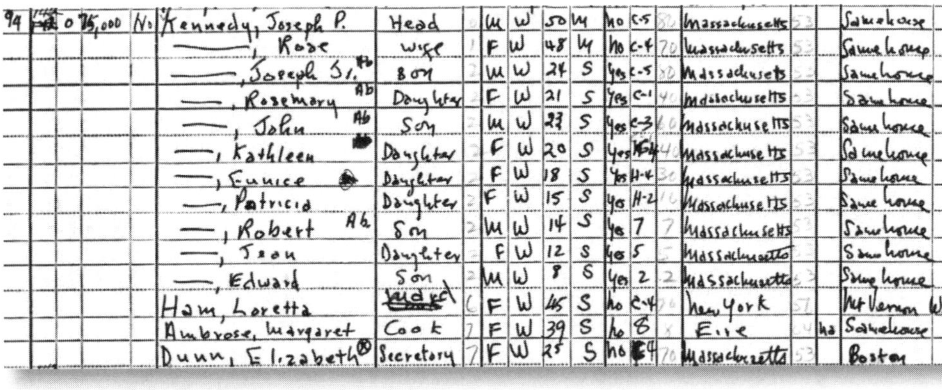

Figure 2.2. Family of John Fitzgerald Kennedy, 1940 Census, Eastchester, Westchester County, New York.

The census reveals the age of John Kennedy, 23, so that his year of birth can be calculated, 1917. It also identifies the names, ages, and birthplaces of his parents, so that you can work your way back to the previous generation. The 1940 census also asked at what the residence did the individual live five years previously. The Kennedys lived in the same house, but previously members of their household staff had lived in Boston and in Mt. Vernon, New York.

Work Your Way Back in Time in the Census Records

Note that all but Edward Kennedy were over the age of 10 years and therefore should be recorded in the 1930 census (Figure 2.3). Although many of the children had common given names, Eunice had a less common name. *To minimize the number of results in a search, choose a family member with a less common given name.* A search for a Eunice Kennedy, born in Massachusetts in 1922, "± 2 years," turns up only one result—the correct one. The 1930 census asked the parents how old they were when they married. Rose Kennedy was 24 years old when she married in 1915, which was fifteen years previously. So she was 39 years old in 1930, and she had been 24 years old in 1915 when she married. With this information, you can then look for the 1915 marriage record of the parents, Joseph and Rose.

Kennedy, Joseph P	Head	O	250000	R	No	M	W	41	M	26
—, Rose	Wife - H				V	F	W	39	M	24

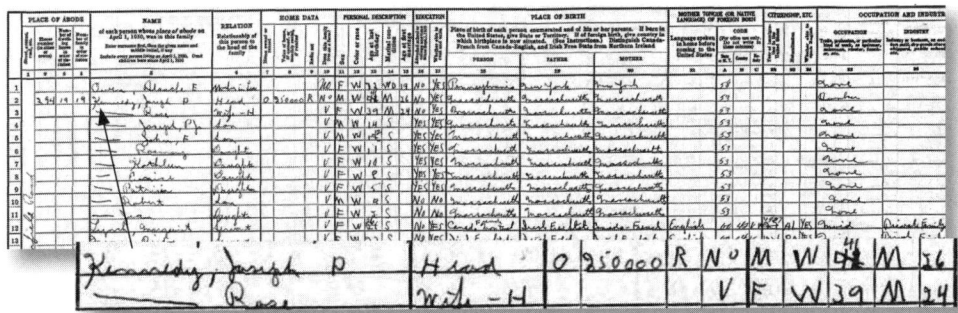

Figure 2.3. Family of John Fitzgerald Kennedy, 1930 Census, Bronxville, Westchester County, New York.

Detail, 1930 census showing age when married (Rose was 24 years old).

The Kennedys had been born in Massachusetts, but some of their household employees had been born in Ireland. For these people, the 1930 census reported the year of immigration and their citizenship status. (See Figure 2.4.) Here it is important to know, as mentioned earlier, that *Al* means alien; *Pa* means someone with first papers; and Na (not shown) means naturalized.[1] With this information you can look for passenger arrival lists, or in the case of the Canadian servant, a Canadian border-crossing document.

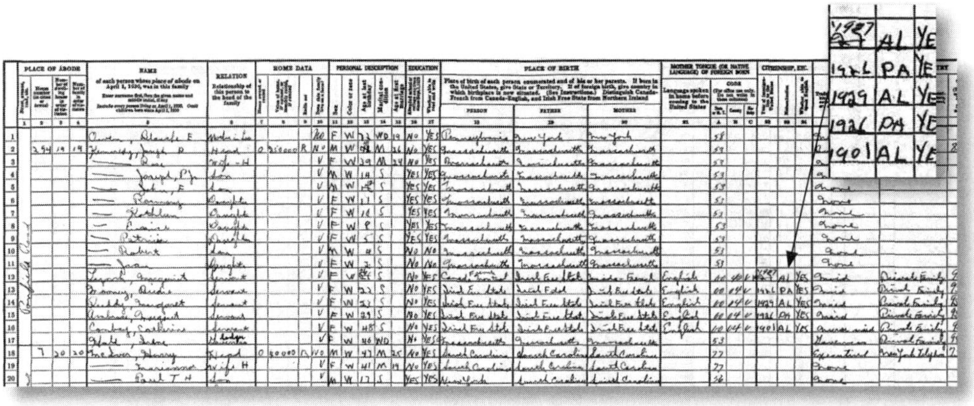

Figure 2.4. Detail of 1930 census, showing year of immigration and naturalization status.

Keep working back ten years in census records to a date before the couple was married. The 1920 census (Figure 2.5) provides not only the year of immigration and citizenship status, but also the year the immigrant became a naturalized citizen. The Kennedys had been born in Massachusetts, but their neighbors, Joseph and Lillian Fullerton, had been born in Canada. The census indicated that they had immigrated in 1881 and had become U.S. citizens in 1914. Before 1922, women derived their citizenship status from their husbands, and so Lillian automatically was naturalized when her husband was. This information can help you look for the naturalization petition of an immigrant. As an example, see the naturalization petition of Joseph Hea Fullerton shown in Figure 2.6.

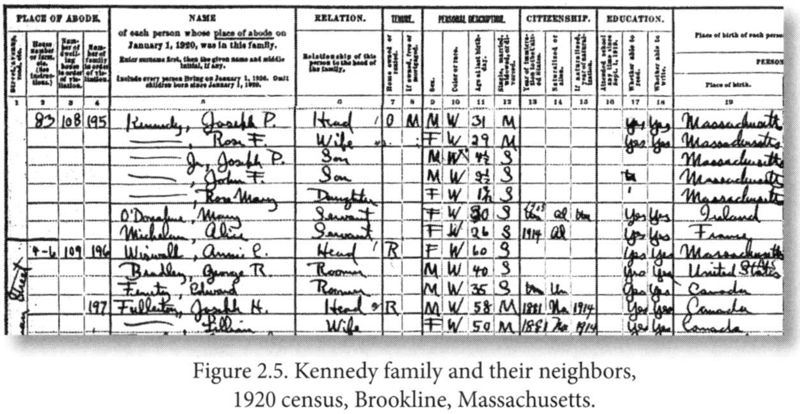

Figure 2.5. Kennedy family and their neighbors,
1920 census, Brookline, Massachusetts.

---

[1] Naturalizations, National Archives, http://www.archives.gov/research/naturalization/naturalization.html.

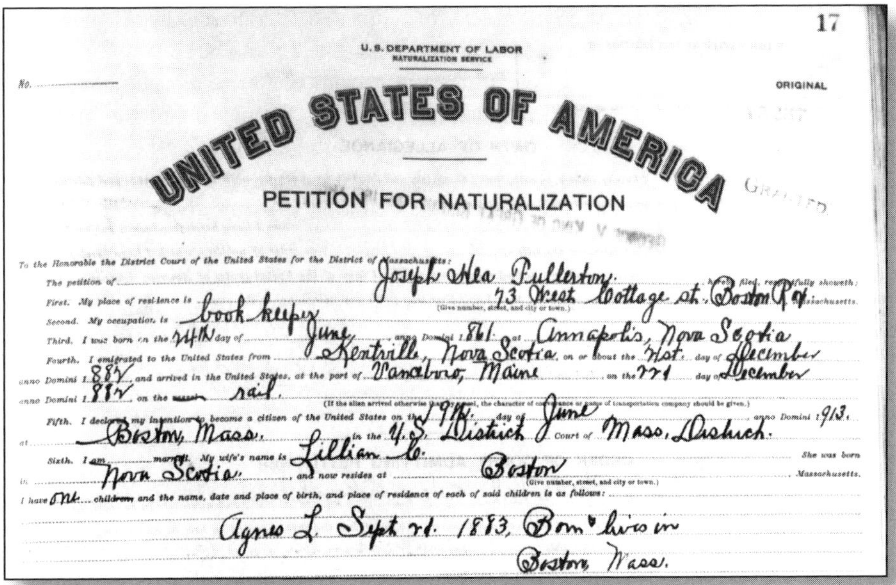
17

U. S. DEPARTMENT OF LABOR
NATURALIZATION SERVICE

No. ....

ORIGINAL

UNITED STATES OF AMERICA

PETITION FOR NATURALIZATION

To the Honorable the District Court of the United States for the District of Massachusetts:

The petition of Joseph Hea Fullerton. hereby filed, respectfully showeth:

First. My place of residence is 73 West Cottage St. Boston R. Massachusetts. (Give number, street, and city or town.)

Second. My occupation is book keeper

Third. I was born on the 24th day of June anno Domini 1861 at Annapolis, Nova Scotia

Fourth. I emigrated to the United States from Kentville, Nova Scotia on or about the 21st day of December anno Domini 1884, and arrived in the United States, at the port of Vanceboro, Maine on the 22d day of December anno Domini 1884, on the vessel rail.

Fifth. I declared my intention to become a citizen of the United States on the 9th day of June anno Domini 1913, at Boston, Mass. in the U.S. District Court of Mass. District.

Sixth. I am married. My wife's name is Lillian E. She was born in Nova Scotia, and now resides at Boston (Give number, street, and city or town.) Massachusetts.

I have one children and the name, date and place of birth, and place of residence of each of said children is as follows:

Agnes L. Sept 21. 1883, Born & lives in Boston, Mass.

Figure 2.6. 1915 naturalization petition of Joseph Hea Fullerton, neighbor of Kennedys in Brookline in 1920.

Look for Records of Births, Marriages, and Deaths

Based upon the ages in the census records and information about the year of marriage, next look for birth, marriage, and death records. State-wide and town records can vary widely from one place to another, especially in regards to the earliest possible records and also the type of information included.

Birth records can sometimes give the maiden names of the mothers. The census records had shown that John F. Kennedy was born in 1917 in Massachusetts and that his parents were Joseph and Rose Kennedy. They also indicated that Joseph and Rose were living in Brookline, Massachusetts, just three years after John F. Kennedy's birth. But a search of the birth records leads to the discovery that Joe and Rose did not register the birth of their son, John Fitzgerald Kennedy, right away, and his birth was recorded in the *delayed registrations books.* However, the 1915 birth of JFK's older brother, Joseph, is recorded in the birth record (Figure 2.7), which show that the parents of Joseph were Joseph Kennedy and Rose Fitzgerald.

To-Do List

- Keep working back ten years in census records.
- Don't enter too much information in search fields.
- Minimize the number of results by searching on a family member with a less common name.
- Marriage records can help.

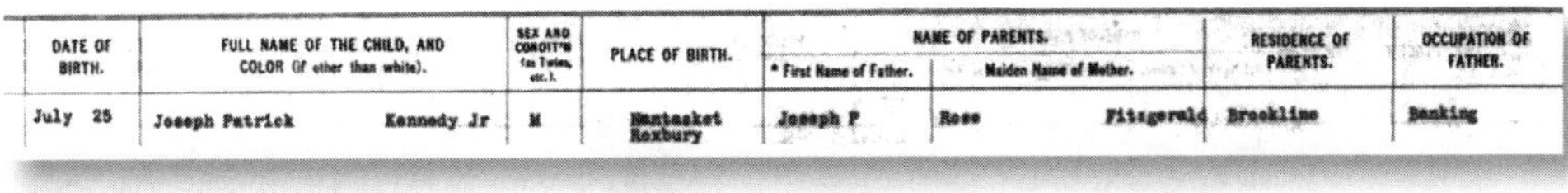

DATE OF BIRTH.	FULL NAME OF THE CHILD, AND COLOR (if other than white).	SEX AND CONDIT'N (as Twins, etc.).	PLACE OF BIRTH.	NAME OF PARENTS. * First Name of Father.	Maiden Name of Mother.	RESIDENCE OF PARENTS.	OCCUPATION OF FATHER.
July 25	Joseph Patrick Kennedy Jr	M	Nantasket Roxbury	Joseph P	Rose Fitzgerald	Brookline	Banking

Figure 2.7. Birth record of Joseph Patrick Kennedy, Jr., July 25, 1915.

Marriage records can be useful in working your way back to a previous generation. First determine when the recording of civil vital records began for the state in which you are researching, since these vary from one state to another. In some states, the marriage record includes the names of the parents of the bride and groom, and if you are lucky, the maiden name of the mother. In other places, such as Ireland and England, the civil marriage record includes the names of the fathers of the bride and groom. Marriage can be among the most reliable records for determining the names of parents because the information is originating from the brides and grooms. On the other hand, the information on death records is coming from the bereaved family and undertakers, who can be less accurate.

In the case of Joseph P. Kennedy and Rose Fitzgerald, their record of their 1914 marriage in Boston lists their residences, the names of their parents, and the name of the priest who married them. See Figure 2.8.

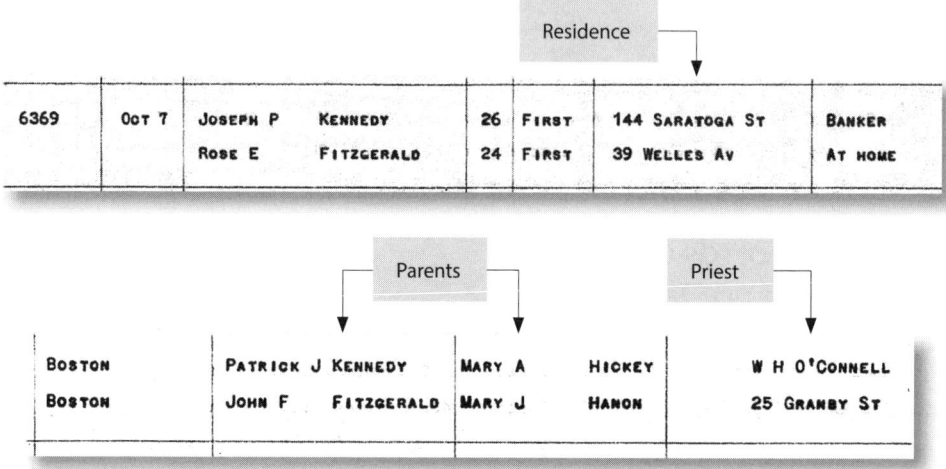

Figure 2.8. Marriage record of Joseph Kennedy and Rose Fitzgerald, October 7, 1914, Boston, Massachusetts.

So the parents of Joseph Kennedy were Patrick J. Kennedy and Mary A. Hickey, and the parents of Rose Fitzgerald were John F. Fitzgerald and Mary J. Hanon. They were married in a small chapel by Cardinal William O'Connell, whose residence was on Granby Street near Kenmore Square in Boston.[2]

The informant on marriage records is often the priest or minister who performed the marriage. Using city directories, census records, or Catholic directories, you can often determine the church where the marriage was performed. This information can then lead to church records of marriages and baptisms.

There was a significant amount of underreporting of marriage records to civil authorities. The clergy informants did not always strictly adhere to civil requirements. So many genealogists are frustrated in their searches for civil marriage records. Church records can make up for the absence of civil records, but the

---

[2] Marriage announcement, *Boston Daily Globe* (1872–1922), Oct. 8, 1914; Proquest Historical Newspapers Boston Globe (1872–1927), p. 3.

church records may not contain the same information and often do not include the names of the parents.

Death records can also provide the names of the parents of the deceased. However, the informants on death records are the bereaved family, undertakers, hotel employees, neighbors, or municipal employees. The deceased person is not around to correct erroneous information on the death certificates. Nevertheless, these records may be the only ones available to you as a family historian. You will need to cross reference the information from death records with other sources, such as census records if available, to verify their accuracy.

Return to Earlier Census Records and Vital Records

Once the names of the parents of the bride and groom have been discovered, you can look in census records for the couple as singles living with their parents. The goal of this census research is to work back to an earlier generation, possibly the immigrant generation.

According to the marriage record, Rose was 24 years old when she married Joseph P. Kennedy, which would place her birth around 1890, and she was the daughter of John F. Fitzgerald and Mary J. Hanon. The next step is to find Rose living with her parents before her marriage. Since the 1890 census was destroyed in a fire, the next census to document Rose would have been the 1900 census. You can plug in the search criteria for a Rose Fitzgerald, born in Massachusetts in 1890, "± 2 years,"

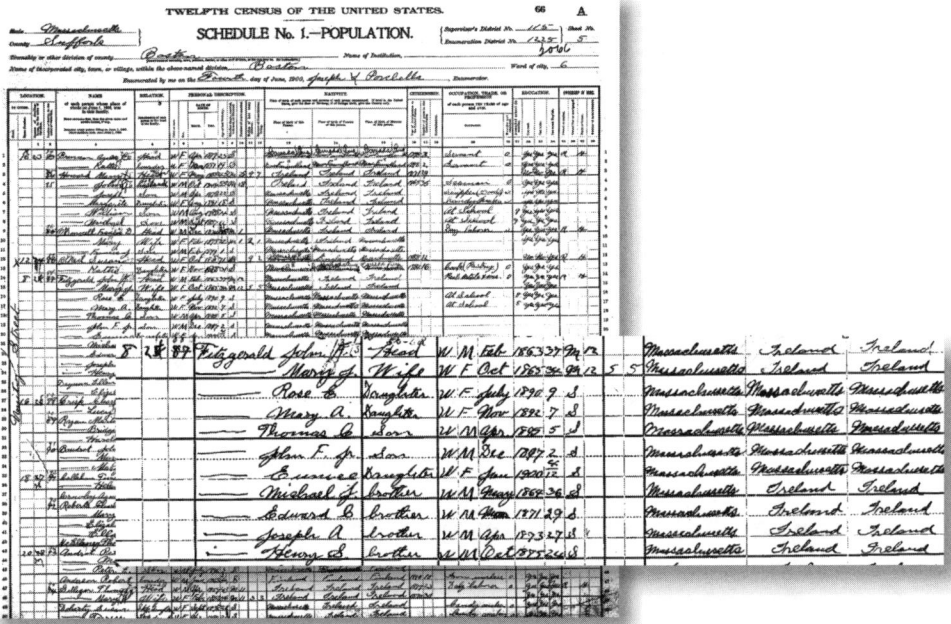

Figure 2.9. Family of John F. Fitzgerald, 1900 Census,
Ward 6, Boston, Massachusetts

and living in Boston. *Do not put the exact birthplace in the search field* because the census documents only the state of birth. By entering only the state of birth, you will avoid a common error, one that often leads a researcher looking for a particular ancestor to hit a "brick wall," or dead end. In this case, the results (Figure 2.9) show a Rose Kennedy, daughter of John F. and Mary J. Fitzgerald. The census records that Rose was born in July 1890 in Massachusetts. The family lived at 8 Unity Street, in the North End of Boston. The 1900 census shows that Rose's mother had five children, who were all still living in 1900. The census also reveals that John F. Fitzgerald and Mary J. had been married twelve years previously. So you can now search for their marriage record, estimating the year to be about 1888.

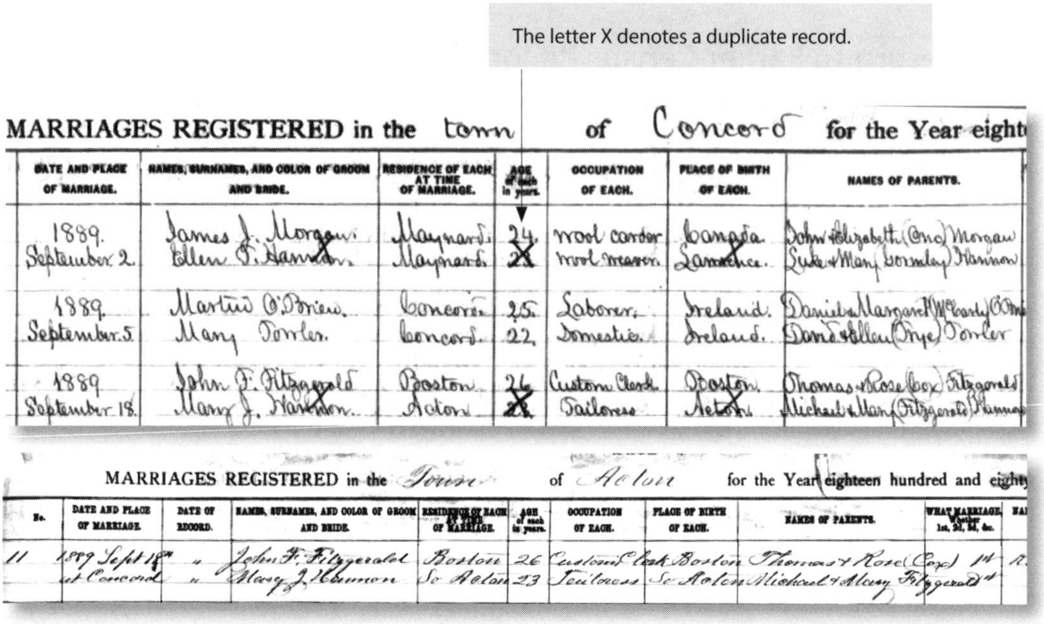

Figure 2.10. *Top:* Marriage record of John F. Fitzgerald and Mary J. Hannon, Concord, Massachusetts, September 18, 1889. *Bottom:* Marriage record of John F. Fitzgerald and Mary J. Hannon, Acton, Massachusetts, September 18, 1889.

A search for a marriage of a John Fitzgerald who married a Mary J. Hanon in about 1888 turns up two entries in two separate towns, neither of which was Boston. This marriage record illustrates a common occurrence when one marriage is recorded in two different places, in this case, Concord and Acton, Massachusetts. (See Figure 2.10.) Sometimes the double entries occur because the bride and groom were from two different towns. In this case, the duplication occurred because the bride lived in South Acton, but the Catholic church where they were married was located in Concord.

Research Back to the Immigrant Ancestor

Using North American census records, vital records, and church records, keep working back in time until you reach the immigrant ancestor. Look for records that identify the parents of your ancestor or that place your ancestor, as a child, living with his or her parents. Once you find these records, note the birthplaces of the parents.

The marriage record of John F. Fitzgerald and Mary J. Hannon shows that the parents of John F. Fitzgerald were Thomas Fitzgerald and Rose Cox. The record also shows that John F. Fitzgerald was 26 years old in 1889 and had been born in Boston. Therefore, he was born in about 1863 in Boston. This information can lead to his birth record and to census records showing him living with his parents. His birth record in Boston vital records (Figure 2.11) shows he was born on 11 February 1863 at 30 Ferry Street, which is in the North End, in Boston. His parents, Thomas and Rose, had been born in Ireland. So one immigrant ancestor of President John Fitzgerald Kennedy was Thomas Fitzgerald.

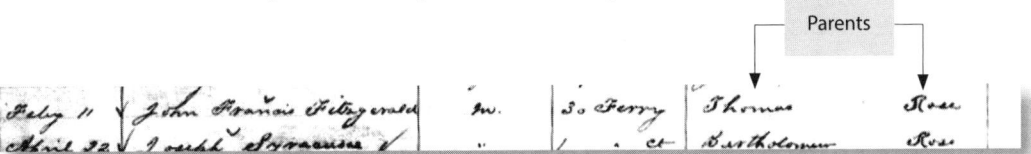

Figure 2.11. Birth record of John Francis Fitzgerald,
Boston, Massachusetts, February 11, 1863

The next step is to look for John F. Fitzgerald as a child living with his parents. Since he was born in 1863, he would have been 7 years old in the 1870 census. *When you are searching census records online, do not enter too much information.* For instance, although you know that John Fitzgerald was born in Boston, do not enter Boston in the "born in" field. As noted earlier, the census recorded the state only. If you put Boston in the search field, you will get no hits. Say you do a search in the 1870 census for a John Fitzgerald, born in 1863, "± 2 years," in Massachusetts, lived in Boston, Suffolk County, Massachusetts. When you start to enter Boston in the "lived in" search field, Ancestry.com will suggest the county and the state. Allowing Ancestry to automatically enter the county and state works most of the time, but be aware that county boundaries and histories vary over time. If you were to search for someone in Charlestown, Massachusetts, in 1870, and used the Ancestry suggestion of Charlestown, Suffolk, Massachusetts, you would get no hits. Charlestown, which is now a neighborhood in Boston, was a separate town in 1870, and it was located in Middlesex County. Furthermore, if you put Charlestown, Middlesex County, Massachusetts, in the "lived in" field, the results will include all of Middlesex County. In that case, type Charlestown in the key word field to get only the Charlestown hits.

A search for John Fitzgerald, born in 1863, "± 2 years," born in Massachusetts, who lived in Boston, Suffolk County, Massachusetts—with all fields checked "exact"— turns up seven hits. But only one was the son of Thomas and Rosey. John was the second oldest child among the eight children of Thomas and Rosey Fitzgerald of Ward 2, Boston. The 1870 census indicates that Thomas and Rosey Fitzgerald had been born in Ireland. See Figure 2.12.

The 1870 census can be useful to family researchers with immigrant ancestry. In column 19, there is a check-off box for "Male citizen of U.S. of 21 years and upwards." Column 19 is checked off for Thomas Fitzgerald. So the census implies that Thomas Fitzgerald, who was born in Ireland, was a naturalized citizen of the United States. With this information, you can then look for the naturalization petition of a Thomas Fitzgerald, born approximately 1835, "± 5 years," in Ireland, who naturalized before 1870.

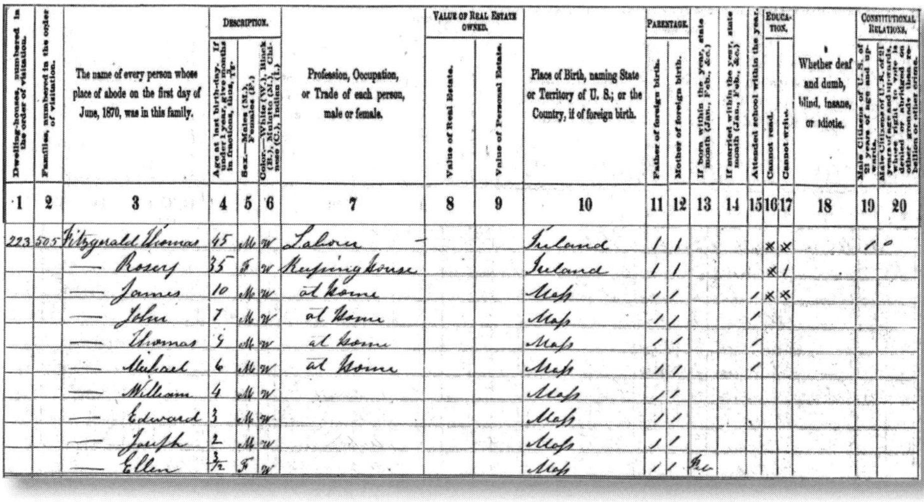

Dwelling-houses	Families	Name	Age	Sex	Color	Profession, Occupation, or Trade	Value of Real Estate	Value of Personal Estate	Place of Birth	Father of foreign birth	Mother of foreign birth	If born within the year, state month	If married within the year, state month	Attended school within the year	Cannot read	Cannot write	Whether deaf and dumb, blind, insane, or idiotic	Male Citizens of U.S. of 21 years of age and upwards	Male Citizens of U.S. of 21 years whose right to vote is denied
1	2	3	4	5	6	7	8	9	10	11	12	13	14	15	16	17	18	19	20
223	505	Fitzgerald Thomas	45	M	W	Laborer			Ireland	/	/				×	×		/	o
		— Rosey	35	F	W	Keeping house			Ireland	/	/				×	/			
		— James	10	M	W	at Home			Mass	/	/			/	×	×			
		— John	7	M	W	at Home			Mass	/	/			/					
		— Thomas	9	M	W	at Home			Mass	/	/			/					
		— Michael	6	M	W	at Home			Mass	/	/			/					
		— William	4	M	W				Mass	/	/								
		— Edward	3	M	W				Mass	/	/								
		— Joseph	2	M	W				Mass	/	/								
		— Ellen	1/12	F	W				Mass	/	/	Feb							

Figure 2.12. Family of Thomas and Rosey Fitzgerald,
1870 federal census, Ward 2, Boston Massachusetts.

Research Back to the Immigration Date

The 1870 census shows that Thomas and Rosey Fitzgerald had a 10-year-old son, James. Therefore, James was born around 1860 in Massachusetts. With this information, you can search for the family in the 1860 census, specifically searching for a Thomas Fitzgerald, born in Ireland, who lived in Boston. The census shows Thomas and Rosa Fitzgerald had a 2-month-old child, James. In addition, there was a 2-year-old child, Michael, who did not appear in the 1870 census. (See Figure 2.13.) The Michael in the 1870 census had been born in 1864. This Michael was born around 1858 and was probably the oldest child, and he had probably died between 1860 and 1864. The parents, Thomas and Rosey, had named their next son Michael.

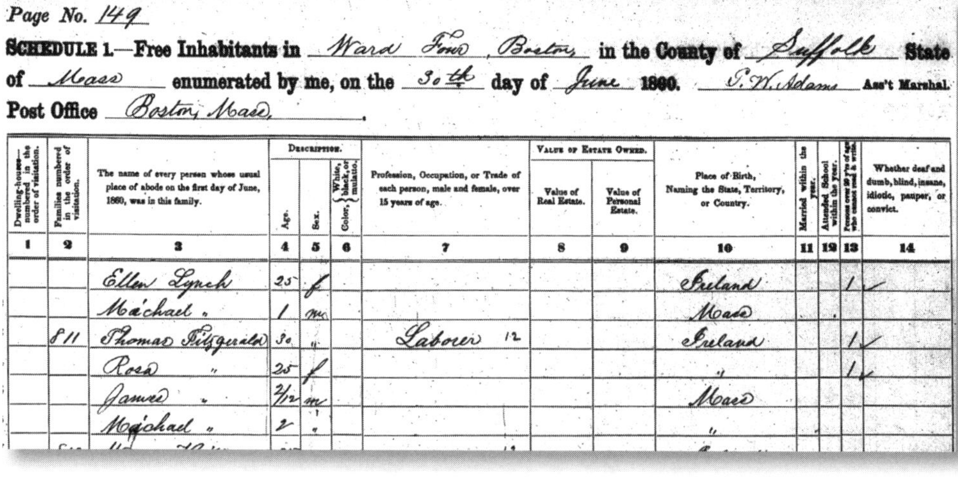

Page No. 149
SCHEDULE 1.—Free Inhabitants in Ward Four, Boston, in the County of Suffolk State of Mass enumerated by me, on the 30th day of June 1860. S. W. Adams Ass't Marshal.
Post Office Boston, Mass.

Dwelling-houses	Families	Name	Age	Sex	Color	Profession, Occupation, or Trade	Value of Real Estate	Value of Personal Estate	Place of Birth	Married within the year	Attended School within the year	Persons over 20 y'rs of age who cannot read & write	Whether deaf and dumb, blind, insane, idiotic, pauper, or convict
1	2	3	4	5	6	7	8	9	10	11	12	13	14
		Ellen Lynch	25	f					Ireland			/	
		Michael "	1	m					Mass				
	811	Thomas Fitzgerald	30	"		Laborer 12			Ireland			/	
		Rosa "	25	f					"			/	
		James "	2/12	m					Mass				
		Michael "	2	"					"				

Figure 2.13. Family of Thomas and Rosa Fitzgerald,
1860 federal census, Ward 4, Boston, Massachusetts.

The census shows that all of the children of Thomas and Rose had been born in Massachusetts. This fact suggests that Thomas and Rose were married in the New World, not in Ireland. To estimate the approximate year of marriage, count back one or two years from the birth of the oldest child, but be prepared to consider dates outside those parameters.

At FamilySearch.org, a search for a marriage in Massachusetts of Thomas Fitzgerald, from 1855 to 1860, with a spouse named Rose, yields one result: the 1857 Boston marriage of Thomas Fitzgerald and Rose Cox (Figure 2.14). Thomas was the son of Michael Fitzgerald, and Rose was the daughter of Philip Cox. The informant for the marriage was Rev. Geo. F. Haskins of Boston.

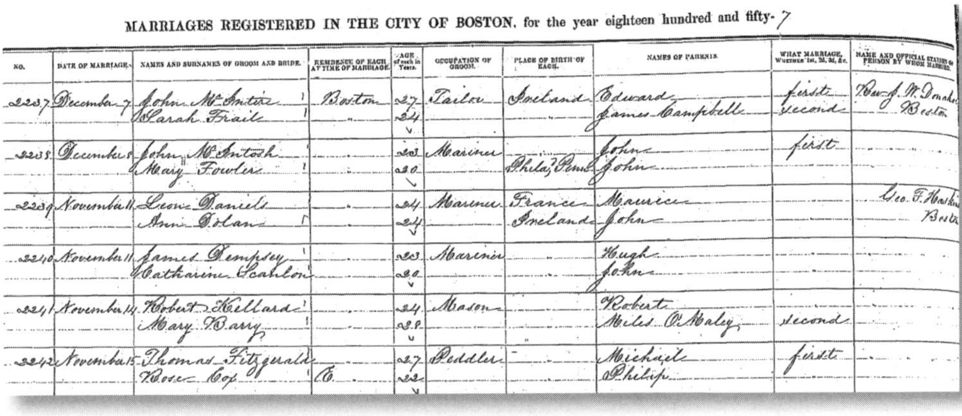
MARRIAGES REGISTERED IN THE CITY OF BOSTON, for the year eighteen hundred and fifty-7

No.	Date of Marriage	Names and Surnames of Groom and Bride	Residence of each at time of Marriage	Age of each in Years	Occupation of Groom	Place of Birth of each	Names of Parents	What Marriage, whether 1st, 2d, 3d, &c.	Name and official station of person by whom married
2237	December 7	John McIntire Sarah Frail	Boston	27 24	Tailor	Ireland	Edward James Campbell	first second	Rev. J. W. Donahoe Boston
2238	December 8	John McIntosh Mary Fowler		23 20	Mariner	 Phila, Penn	John John	first	
2239	November 11	Leon Daniels Ann Dolan		24 24	Mariner	France Ireland	Maurice John		Geo. F. Haskins Boston
2240	November 11	James Dempsey Catharine Scanlon		23 20	Mariner		Hugh John		
2241	November 14	Robert Kellard Mary Barry		24 28	Mason		Robert Miles O'Maley	second	
2242	November 15	Thomas Fitzgerald Rose Cox	C.	27 22	Peddler		Michael Philip	first	

Figure 2.14. Marriage Record of Thomas Fitzgerald and Rose Cox, Boston, Massachusetts, November 15, 1857.

The informants on marriage records are frequently the priest, minister, rabbi, justice of the peace, or town clerk who married the couple. With this information, you can research the informant in city directories. The 1857 Boston city directory lists Rev. George F. Haskins at St. John Roman Catholic Church on Moon Street, which was in the North End of Boston—this was likely the church, as we know the family lived in the North End. St. John the Baptist Church was established in 1843, and became St. Stephen Church in 1863.[3]

This marriage record reveals the identity not only of the immigrant ancestor of Rose Fitzgerald Kennedy, but also the names of the fathers in Ireland. Also note that Thomas Fitzgerald and Rose Cox named their oldest son Michael, which can be seen now to have been the name of the paternal grandfather. Many, but not all, Irish families followed a naming pattern in which the oldest son was named after the paternal grandfather and the oldest daughter was named after the maternal grandmother. But census records can be misleading as to the identity of the oldest child. The 1860 census shows that the oldest child of Thomas and Rose Fitzgerald was Michael, aged 2 years, and the next child was James, aged 2 months. But in 1870, the oldest child is James. Moreover, there is a 6-year-old Michael. From this data, it is fair to theorize that the oldest child, Michael, died between 1860 and 1864.

---

3 Archives of the Archdiocese of Boston, http://www.bostoncatholic.org/Offices-And-Services/Office-Detail.aspx?id=12304&pid=1484.

Once you determine the date of marriage, you will want to look for your ancestor as a single person, living possibly with other family members. This practice may help identify relatives that expand the focus, and thus potential success, of your research. State census records were often compiled on the five-year intervals between federal census records. The existence and availability of state census records vary widely from one state to another. For Massachusetts, state census records for 1855 and 1865 are searchable at AmericanAncestors.org, FamilySearch.org, and Ancestry.com. A search for Thomas Fitzgerald in the 1855 Massachusetts state census, a time period before Thomas was married, shows a 16-year-old Thomas Fitzgerald living with an Edward and Ellen Fitzgerald, and the relationship to the head-of-household is not defined. (See Figure 2.15.)

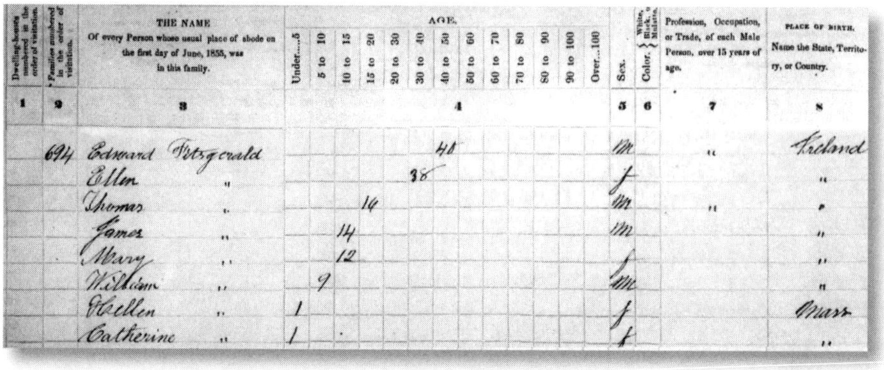

Dwelling-houses numbered in the order of visitation. 1	Families numbered in the order of visitation. 2	THE NAME Of every Person whose usual place of abode on the first day of June, 1855, was in this family. 3	AGE. 4	Sex. 5	Color. White, Black, or Mulatto. 6	Profession, Occupation, or Trade, of each Male Person, over 15 years of age. 7	PLACE OF BIRTH. Name the State, Territory, or Country. 8
	694	Edward Fitzgerald	40	M		"	Ireland
		Ellen "	38	F			"
		Thomas "	16	M		"	"
		James "	14	M			"
		Mary "	12	F			"
		William "	9	M			"
		Ellen "	1	F			Mass.
		Catherine "	1	F			"

Figure 2.15. Thomas Fitzgerald as found in the 1855 Massachusetts state census, Ward 1, Boston, Massachusetts.

The census record is somewhat ambiguous about the family and their relationship to each other. But you can file it under "possible" hits and continue looking for information about Thomas. The age and the place (Ward 1 was the North End of Boston) fits the information already gathered about Thomas from his marriage record. Do not discard evidence that does not quite fit your information about your ancestor. Make note of the information and weigh the evidence as you collect more information.

You have now identified an Irish immigrant ancestor of President John Fitzgerald Kennedy and also determined the name of the father back in Ireland. Since the surname Fitzgerald is common in Ireland, you need to find more information about the parents of Thomas Fitzgerald, especially the name of his mother.

Death records can also be useful in identifying the parents of the immigrant, although they are less reliable than marriage records. The immigrant is not around to correct the misinformation supplied by his or her children. In this case, the marriage record gives only the name of the father. But the 1885 death record of Thomas Fitzgerald shows that his parents were Michael and Ellen. (See Figure 2.16.)

The death record provides the given name of his mother, but not her maiden name. Since Fitzgerald is such as common name, identifying the maiden name of the mother is essential in locating this family in Ireland.

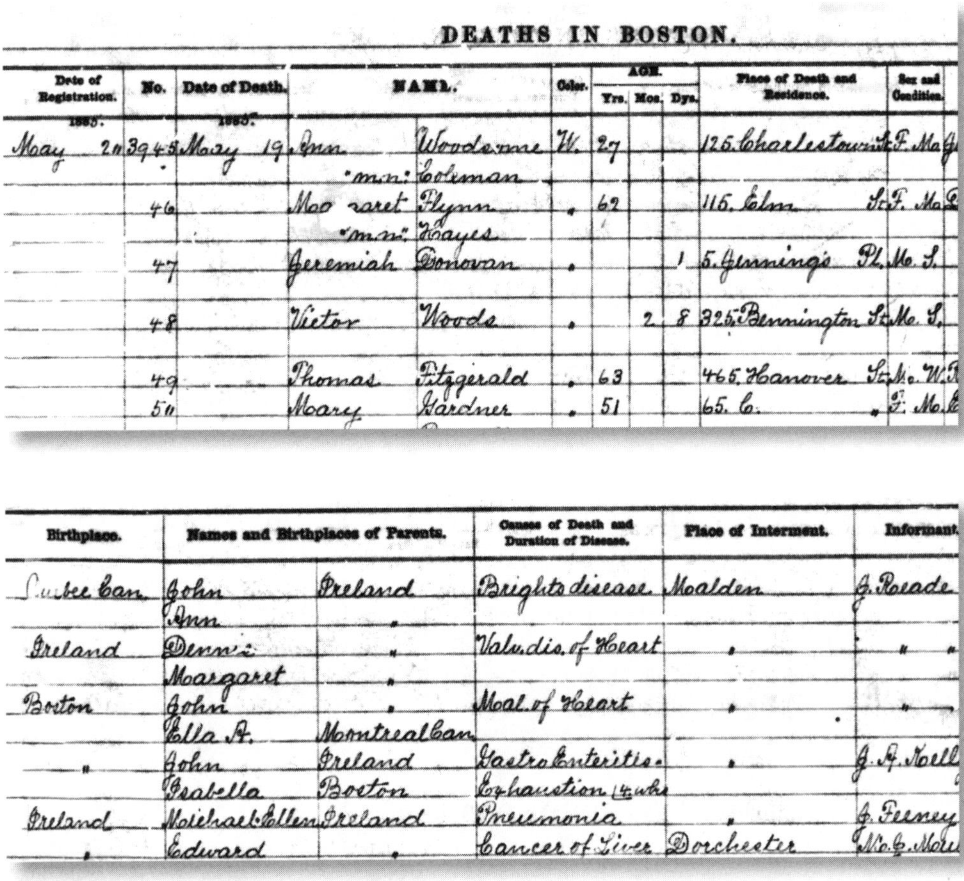

DEATHS IN BOSTON.

Date of Registration.	No.	Date of Death.	Name.		Color.	Age Yrs.	Mos.	Dys.	Place of Death and Residence.	Sex and Condition.
1885. May 20	3945	1885. May 19	Ann	Woodsome "mn: Coleman	W.	27			125 Charlestown St.	F. M.
	46		Margaret	Flynn "mn: Hayes	"	62			116 Elm St.	F. M.
	47		Jeremiah	Donovan	"			1	5 Jennings Pl.	M. S.
	48		Victor	Woods	"		2	8	325 Bennington St.	M. S.
	49		Thomas	Fitzgerald	"	63			465 Hanover St.	M. W.
	50		Mary	Gardner	"	51			65 E.	F. M.

Birthplace.	Names and Birthplaces of Parents.		Causes of Death and Duration of Disease.	Place of Interment.	Informant.
Quebec Can.	John Ann	Ireland "	Brights disease	Malden	J. Reade
Ireland	Dennis Margaret	" "	Valv. dis. of Heart	"	"
Boston	John Ella A.	" Montreal Can.	Mal. of Heart	"	"
"	John Isabella	Ireland Boston	Gastro Enteritis Exhaustion	"	J. A. Noell
Ireland	Michael & Ellen Edward	Ireland "	Pneumonia Cancer of Liver	" Dorchester	J. Feeney Mc. G. [illegible]

Figure 2.16. Thomas Fitzgerald, Boston Death Record, May 19, 1885.

Widen the Focus of Research

Faced with a lack of vital records detailing the parents of Thomas Fitzgerald, your strategy in such a case would be to widen your research focus to include siblings and other relatives. Our Irish ancestors were generally parts of networks of friends and relatives from the Old Country. Irish families rarely had just one child and instead often included numerous children. It was common in the nineteenth century for an Irish couple to have a child every two years. When you see a four- or five-year gap in the ages of children, you should consider the possibility that a child was born in the intervening years and died before the census data was gathered.

If your ancestor lived in a small town, you can search the census records by leaving the name fields blank, entering Ireland for birthplace, and the town in the "lived in" field. This practice will result in an alphabetical list of all the Irish in the town. Look for others with the same

To-Do List

- Work back in censuses and vital records to the immigrant ancestor.
- Identify the parents of the immigrant ancestor.
- Widen the search to include siblings and other relatives.

surname. Make note of the most frequently occurring surnames. Often small towns had clusters of Irish immigrants who originated from the same area in Ireland, and many of these immigrants were siblings and cousins. Even if you strike out with your ancestor, you can research other immigrants in the town. In addition, if you choose another immigrant with the same surname you should look at others on the same page, and the pages before and after. You may discover your ancestor was indexed incorrectly, or omitted in the index.

In large cities like Boston, New York, or Philadelphia, this approach of looking at other immigrants will not work because the population was too large and diverse. Therefore, in the case of Thomas Fitzgerald, vital records may hold the key in the search for his siblings. In the *Massachusetts Deaths, 1841–1915* database on FamilySearch.org, you can pursue the research by leaving the name fields blank, but entering the names of the parents, Michael Fitzgerald and Ellen, and specifying the death place as Boston, Massachusetts, and the birth place as Ireland. Search results come back with four death records. Three are for children of Michael Fitzgerald and Ellen Wilmot: Ellen Fitzgerald Olson, Hannah Fitzgerald Miller, and Bridget Fitzgerald Williams. The fourth was for Patrick Fitzgerald, son of Michael Fitzgerald and Ellen Noonan. This finding narrows the name of Thomas Fitzgerald's mother to two possibilities: Ellen Wilmot or Ellen Noonan. Your task will be to tie these names to Thomas Fitzgerald through church baptisms or marriages, a process which will be discussed in Chapter 3, Using North American Church Records to Widen Your Search.

Don't Make Assumptions

Brick walls in Irish genealogical research can also arise from certain assumptions people make about their ancestors. In doing so, they automatically ignore important records or take questionable information as truth.

Assumption #1: My ancestor was too poor

A common assumption refers to an ancestor's economic status and what records they may or may not have generated: "My ancestor was too poor to have a probate," or "My family was too poor to leave a paper trail." We cannot measure our nineteenth-century ancestors with a twenty-first-century yardstick. Even when families did not own real estate, a probate could still be generated to provide for personal property. In addition, guardianships for their children may also be available.

Beyond an inventory of property, probate records provide valuable information about the ancestor's origins and family network. For example, the 1838 probate record of Thomas Kennedy of Boston shows his estate was valued at $452. He didn't have a big estate, but he left $50 to his mother, Nancy Kennedy of Ballynure, County Antrim.[4] While the chance of finding such records may be slightly smaller, you cannot rule out records until you have looked. By not looking, you are guaranteeing failure.

---

[4] Suffolk County Probate Records, will of Thomas Kennedy, 1838, docket no. 31784.

Assumption #2: My ancestor came alone and had no siblings

The likelihood of this statement is very slim. In the nineteenth century, the average Irish family had six children; passage to America was often paid by friends and relatives from the Old Country; and our ancestors settled in American towns where they had contacts. While siblings and other family connections don't always jump off the page, they do exist.

Assumption #3: Oral history cannot be wrong

Many family stories come down to us about our ancestors. While these can be very helpful clues or research leads, we should not believe them blindly. We need to thoroughly research each claim to test its validity and always be willing to pursue other paths or ideas when faced with contradictory evidence. Think outside the box!

Summary

Once you have filled out a five-generation chart back as far as you can based upon family oral history, you can begin your research using records. Start with the 1940 census and work your way back in time. Use census records to estimate the year of birth and marriage, the year of immigration, and citizenship status. Then look for vital records of births, marriages, and deaths to identify previous generations. Marriage records in particular can identify the parents of the bride and groom and are more reliable than death records, since the information is originating with the bride and groom. Using census records and vital records, work your way back in time until you get to the immigrant ancestor. Follow the immigrant ancestor back as close as possible to the date of immigration, and if possible, identify the names of the parents back in Ireland.

Further Reading

- Buggy, Joseph. *Finding Your Irish Ancestors in New York City.* Baltimore: Genealogical Publishing Company, 2014.

- Clifford, Karen. *The Complete Beginner's Guide to Genealogy, the Internet, and Your Genealogy Computer Program.* Baltimore: Genealogical Publishing Company, 2001, revised 2011.

- Fulton, Lindsay. *Portable Genealogist: Using the Federal Census: 1790–1840* and *Portable Genealogist: Using the Federal Census: 1850–1940.* Boston: NEHGS, 2015.

- Grenham, John. *Tracing Your Irish Ancestors: The Complete Guide.* 4th ed. Dublin: Gill & Macmillan, 2012.

- Paton, Chris. *Tracing Your Irish Family History on the Internet: A Guide for Family Historians.* Barnsley, U.K.: Pen & Sword Family History, 2013.

- Ryan, James G. *Irish Records: Sources for Family and Local History.* Salt Lake City: Ancestry, 1997.

- Paton, Chris. *Irish Family History Resources Online,* 2nd ed. St. Agnes, S.A.: Unlock the Past, 2015.

PART II
Linking Your Immigrant Ancestors to Ireland

Where in Ireland did your ancestors come from? What was their point of origin? These questions are deceptively simple, but the answers can be elusive. Since many Irish surnames are common and widely distributed, you must have a specific locale in Ireland to be able to carry out further research in Irish records. Knowing the names of the immigrant's parents, including mother's maiden name, is important in differentiating your ancestor from the many others with the same name. If your ancestor had an unusual name, identifying the names of the parents may be less crucial. But for most family historians, determining the names of the parents is essential in linking individuals to Ireland. This part of the book examines ways to link your immigrant ancestors to Ireland.

- **Using North American church records to widen your search.** Eventually you will encounter a brick wall: records just don't exist or they omit vital details such as the names of parents. By widening your search, you increase the chances that at least one of the individuals associated with your ancestor has the information you seek. Church records are an important source for identifying and locating those individuals.

- **Searching in North American records that document the exact birthplace in Ireland.** Records such as naturalization petitions, declarations of intent, immigration records, and travel documents—as well as gravestone inscriptions, newspapers, and business records—may provide the kind of detailed information that allows you to locate our ancestor's place of origin.

- **Looking farther back to Irish immigration in the seventeenth and eighteenth centuries.** If your ancestors arrived in North America before the nineteenth century, you will find fewer available records with many details. Early newspapers, local histories and the associated biographical dictionaries, and archival collections of letters of early immigrants may prove useful. An important technique is to research your ancestors in the context of their communities, since group and chain migrations played a vital role in the development of these places.

By looking at these methods, types of records, and steps in the research process, the next four chapters will help you link your ancestor to Ireland.

Chapter 3
Using North American Church Records

To successfully link your ancestor back to Ireland, you must extend your American research to include siblings, parents, other relatives, and friends. Once you identify the circle of relatives and friends, you then research their origins in Ireland, in addition to your direct ancestors. By increasing the number of people you are researching, you increase the odds of finding a linking document to an exact place in Ireland. Church records—baptism, marriage, and other sacramental records—often provide more information than civil records and thus can provide the links to associates of our ancestors.

For example, according to the 1864 civil birth record of Michael Fitzgerald, son of Thomas and Rose, he was born at 23 Clark Street, Boston, Massachusetts (see Figure 3.1). This street was located adjacent to St. Stephen's Roman Catholic Church on Hanover Street in the North End of Boston. Although this civil birth record provides you with the date of birth and place of residence of Michael Fitzgerald and his family, Michael's baptism record shows even more information, specifically the names of the godparents of Michael—Edmund Fitzgerald and Bridget Fitzgerald (Figure 3.2). As we will see in subsequent chapters, *this link will prove pivotal in locating the origins of the Fitzgerald family in Ireland.* By doing some research on Edmund Fitzgerald, we learn that he was Thomas's uncle and a witness listed on Thomas's naturalization petition. Further, Edmund placed a "missing friends" advertisement in the *Boston Pilot* newspaper, indicating the parish of origin: a key piece of information. Researching Bridget Fitzgerald, who was Thomas's sister, we

Figure 3.1. 1864 Civil Birth Record of Michael Fitzgerald.

find her death record, which gives us yet another piece of critical information: the maiden name of her and Thomas's mother, Ellen Wilmot.

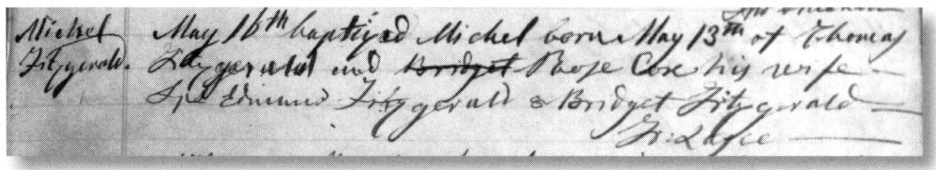

Figure 3.2. Baptism of Michael Fitzgerald, brother of John Fitzgerald, showing Edmund Fitzgerald and Bridget Fitzgerald as sponsors, St. Stephen's Roman Catholic Church, May 16, 1864.

Church records of baptisms and marriages can be of tremendous use for other reasons. In many cases, the collection of civil records of births, marriages, and deaths did not start until late in the nineteenth century. Even when these records do exist, under-registration was widespread, especially for births. Children were usually born at home, and it was up to the parents to report the birth of the child. Being newcomers in American communities, many immigrants were reluctant to cooperate with local bureaucrats, especially where anti-immigrant sentiments were prevalent. In some large cities like Boston, city employees canvassed door-to-door twice a year asking what children had been born in the previous sixth months. Occasionally, this practice resulted in children who had been born in Ireland being recorded in America shortly after their arrival. When you see records arranged not chronologically, but rather by street address, this array suggests a periodic collection of births. Even this more complete recording of births had some gaps, since the family might not be home at the time of the collection or might have moved to another address that had already been covered. So for many reasons, vital records in Irish American communities were under-reported or completely lacking.

In the nineteenth century, however, many Catholics believed that unbaptized children who died would go to a place called limbo, instead of heaven. This belief was not an official doctrine of the Church but rather was based on ideas advanced by some theologians.[1] In a practice dating from the Counter-Reformation period of the sixteenth and seventeenth centuries, and perhaps even from early medieval times, unbaptized infants in Ireland were not allowed to be buried in consecrated ground. Instead, they were buried in separate cemeteries, called *cillini*.[2] Given parents' eagerness to avoid these dire consequences, newborns were usually baptized within a day or two of birth. Not until the late nineteenth century did baptisms start to occur at ages 1 or 2 months. If the parish priest or minister was a careful recorder, baptism records can be an excellent and complete source for birth

---

[1] International Theological Commission, "The Hope of Salvation for Infants Who Die Without Being Baptized," at www.vatican.va/roman_curia/congregations/cfaith/cti_documents/rc_con_cfaith_doc_20070419_un-baptised-infants_en.html. In this 2007 report, the Vatican abolished the concept of limbo.

[2] Emma Pankey, "The Tradition of Separate Burials in Ireland: Cillini and Place," College of Liberal Arts, Department of Anthropology, University of New Hampshire, Spectrum, Second Issue, Fall 2012, available at cola.unh.edu/sites/cola.unh.edu/files/student-journals/spectrumFall2012_Pankey.pdf.

records; in many cases, the actual date of birth was recorded along with the date of baptism.

The informants for civil marriage records were often the priests or ministers who performed the marriage, so the collection of civil marriage data depended on the cooperation of local clergy. In many instances, the clergy neglected to submit marriage records to civil authorities. As a result, under-registration of marriages was common. *If you are unable to find a civil record of your ancestors' marriage, do not assume that they did not marry.* There may be a church record, but not a civil record, of their marriage. For many cities and towns, church records can compensate for the lack of civil registrations. However, most church records did not usually include the names of the parents of the bride and groom, whereas many civil records did. Obtaining the civil record of marriage—if it is available—is preferable because often it will include the names of the parents.

Type of Record	Information Included
Marriage	• Date of marriage • Names of bride and groom • Names of witnesses
Baptism	• Date of baptism • Date of birth (sometimes) • Name of child • Names of parents (frequently including mother's maiden name) • Names of godparents
First communion	• Date of first communion • Name of child
Confirmation	Generally kept not in parishes but in episcopal registers (bishop's registers). Don't usually record individual names.
Ordination	Kept in episcopal registers, since ordinations are performed by bishops.
Sick call	• Name of sick person • Address of sick person (frequently) • Notation of confession and receipt of Eucharist
Death	Records rarely kept, but on occasion burial records (which are more often included with cemetery records) document certain information: • Name and age of person • Date of burial • Date of death

Table 3.1. Information included in Catholic Church records.

Canon law of the Catholic Church has specific requirements for marriage, baptism, and other records, depending on the kind of record. As a researcher, you should be aware that all seven types of records exist—but also note that some will yield more genealogical information than others. See Table 3.1 for a summary of the seven types of records.

Where to Find Church Records

Both Catholic and Protestant church records can be locally held, centralized into archives at diocese or other administrative offices, or preserved in private and public libraries. Always check at the diocesan level first when looking for the sacramental registers of a church. If a church has been closed, its records may have been transferred to the diocese. Some records have been microfilmed or published and are available in libraries. Only as a last resort should you contact the local parish priest, minister, or administrator. These people lead busy lives ministering to their congregations and often do not have the time nor the interest to assist family historians. Furthermore, because some may have been offended by rude or persistent inquirers in the past, courtesy and patience will gain you more cooperation. Sometimes you can identify an interested parishioner who is willing to look up the information for you.

Figure 3.3. Old St. Peter's Roman Catholic Church, New York City.

In some parishes, records have been transferred to a central repository, such as an archdiocesan or church archives, and clergy who have transferred from another parish are unaware of such a transfer. In some parishes, church personnel may try to explain the situation of missing registers by stating they had been burned in a fire. To avoid a negative research experience, first research the history of the parish, the status of the records, and the location and holdings of a diocesan archives before approaching local parish officials.

Locating Catholic Church records in America

The web portal Cyndi's List maintains a list of Catholic Church archives, libraries, and repositories at cyndislist.com/catholic/libraries. You can consult this list for the diocese of interest to determine the status of sacramental registers. For printed guides, check *U.S. Catholic Sources: A Diocesan Research Guide* by Virginia Humling.[3] This book lists the addresses of Catholic dioceses, the areas covered in the dioceses, the location of sacramental records and newspapers, and fees. For New York City, *Finding Your Irish Ancestors in New York City,* by Joseph Buggy, lists information on all of the Catholic par-

---

[3] Virginia Humling, *U.S. Catholic Sources: A Diocesan Research Guide* (Salt Lake City: Ancestry, 1995).

ishes of the dioceses of New York (including Manhattan and Staten Island) and Brooklyn.[4]

Locating Protestant church records in America

When Irish immigrants came to America in the seventeenth and eighteenth centuries, many joined the predominant churches of the communities in which they settled. For early New England, this would have been the Congregational Church; and for southern communities, it would have been Baptist congregations. Some Catholics may have preferred to join Episcopal churches in communities where the choice was between a Calvinist church and an Episcopal church. For instance, a number of Irish surnames appear in the early burials of Christ Church [Episcopal] in Philadelphia,[5] and King's Chapel, Boston.[6] If they migrated in groups large enough to support their own church, they retained the religious preference of their upbringing. The largest groups were Presbyterians, Episcopalians (Anglicans), Catholics, and Quakers.

Due to the fragmentation of religious groups, the changing composition of European immigration from colonial times to the twentieth century, and westward migration in America, locating records and repositories of Protestant church records can be challenging. For each state, the population makeup by religion differed. Presbyterians tended to go to Pennsylvania, the Carolinas, and Virginia. Anglicans were more common in New York and Virginia. Many records are still in local churches, while older records and records of closed churches reside in church diocesan archives, state libraries and archives, and university archives. One of the first places to look for church records is the catalog of the Family History Library. By searching for the community or county of interest, and then choosing the subheading of church records, you can see if the church records have been microfilmed, published in print form, or digitized. The Works Progress Administration (WPA) published inventories of church records for each state, and many of these books are available in libraries throughout the country. For the sake of brevity, the following subcategories reflect the most common states and denominations Irish tended to populate.

A good way to locate church records held in state, local, and historical archives is to search on the ArchiveGrid website of OCLC (Online Computer Library Center).[7] For instance, a search for Presbyterian records shows a number of entries for Ohio parishes at Bowling Green State University; for upstate New York at Cornell

---

[4] Joseph Buggy, *Finding Your Irish Ancestors in New York City* (Baltimore: Genealogical Publishing Co., 2014).

[5] Michael J. O'Brien, "Records of Burials at Christ Church, Philadelphia," The Journal of the American Irish Historical Society 13 (1914).

[6] Michael J. O'Brien, "Memorials of the Dead in Boston, Being Copies of Some Tombstone Inscriptions in Copp's Hill and Kings Chapel Burying Grounds," *The Journal of the American Irish Historical Society* 13 (1914).

[7] OCLC is a non-profit computer library service. ArchiveGrid, at https://beta.worldcat.org/archivegrid/ is a collection of more than 2 million archival material descriptions, including catalog records from OCLC and finding aids harvested from the web. It contains archival collections held by thousands of libraries, museums, historical societies, and archives.

University; and for Kentucky at the University of Kentucky. ArchiveGrid displays the results in a list view and a summary view. By clicking on summary view, you can narrow your search by places. You can also perform a Boolean search on a place, such as Albany *and* Episcopal, to narrow your search to a specific place.

Episcopal Church records

Episcopal Church records of baptism, marriages and burials are usually kept at the individual church where the event took place. For closed churches, the records may be kept in diocesan archives or as manuscripts in local collections. Many historical registers of Episcopal churches are preserved in state libraries and archives, such as the New York State Archives, the Kentucky State Archives, or the Virginia State Library Archives. Other records are located in the New Jersey Historical Society and the Kentucky Historical Society. Others have been maintained in theological school libraries, such as Harvard Divinity School and Andover Theological Seminary. Using ArchiveGrid is probably the best way to locate Episcopal church records in America.

Presbyterian records

The Presbyterian Historical Society in Philadelphia serves as the national archives for the Presbyterian Church in America. The society, located at 425 Lombard Street, is open to the public on weekdays, and encourages visitors to consult their website in advance of a visit, at history.pcusa.org. The website lists church records surveys for Illinois, Maryland, New York, Pennsylvania, New Jersey, and North Carolina, but warns that the list is not comprehensive. The site also features *Hall's Index of American Presbyterian Congregations* and *Church Record Surveys* holdings that are relevant to genealogical research. Some Presbyterian records have ended up at university archives. For example, the early records of the Federal Street Church in Boston (now called Arlington Street Church) are located at the Harvard Divinity School Library, but the records were copied and published in the *New England Historical and Genealogical Society Register,* and are now searchable online in the Boston Church Records database on the NEHGS website, AmericanAncestors.org.

Baptist records

Unless your ancestor was a minister, a missionary, or a graduate of a theological seminary, Baptist church records will not be helpful for your genealogical research. Church members did not practice infant baptism, marriage was not regarded as a sacrament, and only a few churches have placed their records in archival facilities.[8]

Quaker records

To locate a monthly meeting for a particular area, you can consult *Monthly Meetings in North America: A Quaker Index,* 4th ed., by Rev. Thomas C. Hill (Cincinnati: Thomas C. Hill, 1998). The Family History Library has a large collection of Quaker records on microfilm and has digitized records for many of the Quaker meeting records in its library, including ones for Delaware, Georgia, Illinois, Indiana,

---

[8] American Baptist Historical Society, abhsarchives.org/for-researchers/genealogy.

Massachusetts, Michigan, New Jersey, New York, Ohio, Oklahoma, Pennsylvania, South Carolina, and Virginia.

Ancestry.com has created a searchable database of Quaker meeting records, 1681 to 1935, collected from four Quaker college archives. These include the Friends Historical Library, Swarthmore College, Swarthmore, Pennsylvania; North Carolina Yearly Meeting Minutes, Hege Friends Historical Library, Guilford College, Greensboro, North Carolina; Indiana Yearly Meeting Minutes, Earlham College Friends Collection and College Archives, Richmond, Indiana; and Quaker Meeting Records, Haverford College, Haverford, Pennsylvania. The database is available to individual subscribers only, not to institutional subscribers. The collection is sizable; for instance, a search for Philadelphia births yielded more than 3,500 records.

Methodist records

Methodist church records are generally kept at the local church level. If a church has closed, the records may be sent to a regional depository of the annual conference archives. A list of the Jurisdictional Commissions on Archives and History is available on the website of United Methodist Church General Commission on Archives and History at www.gcah.org.

How to locate the church your ancestor attended

Small towns

To locate a church in a small town, research the history of the town and the establishment of churches in the town. Did the town's inhabitants travel to another town to attend services? Was the town a satellite of a city parish? Did a priest from the city parish come out to say Mass once a month? Determining the history of the parish can come from several sources. First of all, many churches have a history of their congregation online, so finding the history can be as simple as accessing Google. Town, local, and county histories often relate the history of the churches in the community. City directories have useful sections that list the churches in town and the ministers and priests who led them. Some nineteenth-century diocesan histories have been digitized and are available on Google Books or at Archive.org. These histories can be useful in learning the history of parishes and determining if a town's church was originally a satellite of an older church. Two examples of online histories are the following:

- *The Catholic Church in the United States of America, Undertaken to Celebrate the Golden Jubilee of His Holiness, Pope Pius X.* v. 1-3, available at Archive.org and on Google Books.[9]

- *The History of the Catholic Church in the New England States* by Very Rev. Wm Byrne, D. D. et al., available at Archive.org.[10]

---

[9] *The Catholic Church in the United States of America, Undertaken to Celebrate the Golden Jubilee of His Holiness, Pope Pius X. v. 1-3* (New York: Catholic Editing Company, 1912).

[10] Very Rev. Wm. Byrne, D. D. et al., *The History of the Catholic Church in the New England States* (Boston: Hurd & Evert, 1899).

As dioceses developed, new parishes were established in towns that previously had been part of another parish. Baptisms for your family can therefore be entered in numerous parishes over time, with the oldest in a nearby city. The family of one of the authors, Marie Daly, lived in Belmont, Massachusetts, after arriving in America in 1851. At that time, Belmont was part of the town of Watertown. The earliest marriages and baptisms for the family have been found in St. Peter's Church, Cambridge. When St. Agnes's Church in Arlington was built in 1870, Belmont Catholics rode a horse-drawn cart to that church. But some entries for the family can also be found in St. Patrick's, Watertown, the adjacent community. St. Joseph's Church in Belmont was built in 1898. Entries have been found in the records of four churches, three of which were in neighboring towns. Knowing the development of the churches in Belmont and surrounding towns helped locate the parish registers.

Another example is the history of the Catholic Church in Vermont. Many Irish immigrants who entered the United States through Quebec came through Vermont. The Vermont French-Canadian Genealogical Society has been publishing the Catholic Church records for all of Vermont, including non-French parishes. They are available at NEHGS; the American-Canadian Genealogical Society, Manchester, New Hampshire; the Family History Library, Salt Lake City; Allen County Public Library, Fort Wayne, Indiana; and the New York City Public Library. Initially, St. Mary's Cathedral (now Immaculate Conception) in Burlington was the only Catholic church, and entries in the baptismal register, which begins in 1830, cover all of Vermont.[11]

Cities

Locating the church your ancestor attended in a city with multiple parishes is a little more challenging than in a small town. If you find a civil marriage record, the informant can often be the priest or minister who married the couple. Remember to look for marriage records not only of your direct ancestor, but also his or her siblings. City directories and later census records can also identify the address of your ancestor, and you can then determine the nearest church. City directories usually have sections that list churches by denomination, their addresses, and the clergy who staff them. Be sure to select a directory published close to the time of the record. So once you have the informant on the marriage record, or a street address for your ancestor, you can then refer to the city directory for the church location.

In large cities, churches were established over time as the population grew. So understanding the history of the diocese and the city is essential to determining which parish church your ancestor attended. In the North End of Boston in the 1850s, for example, there were two Catholic churches: St. Mary's, established in 1834, and St. John the Baptist's, established 1843, which became St. Stephen's in 1862. Since the Fitzgerald family lived on or just off Hanover Street, they attended the closest church, St. John the Baptist's, later renamed St. Stephen's.

---

[11] *St. Mary's Cathedral Baptism Repertoire, St. Mary's Catholic Church, Burlington, Vermont, 1830-1858* (Burlington, Vt.: Vermont French-Canadian Genealogical Society, 2006).

If your ancestor lived in the Manhattan borough of New York City in the early nineteenth century, he or she may have been recorded in the records of St. Peter's Church, the oldest Catholic church in the state of New York. The records of this church are available on microfilm at the New York Public Library. They include not only Manhattan but also the early records of outlying towns, such as White Plains. The earliest baptisms from 1787 to 1800 were published in the *National Genealogical Society Quarterly*.[12]

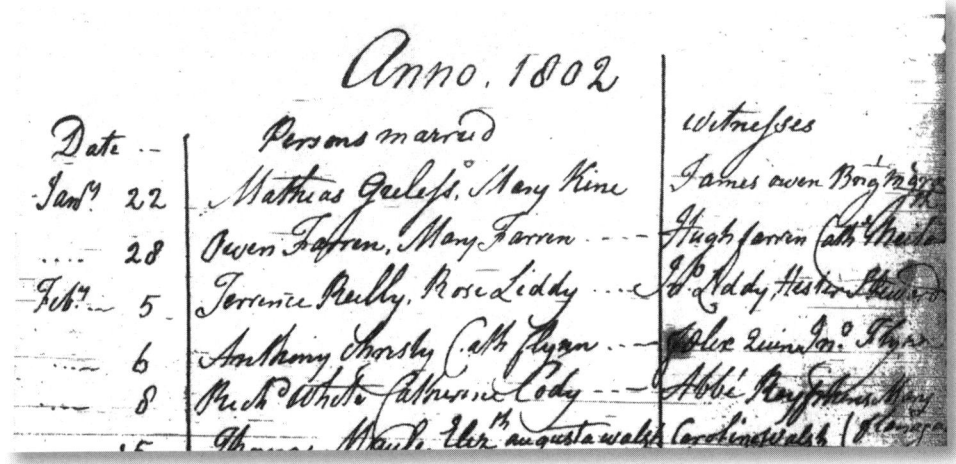

Figure 3.4. Marriage records,
St. Peter's Roman Catholic Church, Manhattan, 1802.

Other Types of Church Records

Records of communion, confirmation, and burial

Records of first communions and confirmations can help identify your ancestor, but they will probably not add greatly to your knowledge of him or her. If a graveyard is connected with the church, burial records may be mixed into the baptisms and marriages or in a separate register. But in large cities, burial grounds were often located outside the urban area, and records were kept by undertakers, sextons, or cemetery administrators. If the cemetery had a religious affiliation, the records may have been deposited with diocesan archives or an independent cemetery association.

---

[12] Constance Denise Sherman, "Baptismal Records of St. Peter's Church, New York City, 1787-1800," *National Genealogical Society Quarterly* 68, No. 1 (March 1980): 21–30; No. 2 (June 1980): 129–136; and No. 3 (Sept. 1980): 203–212.

Marriage dispensations

When a couple who were related by blood *(consanguinity)* or by affinity (in-laws) wished to marry, they needed to obtain a dispensation from the diocesan bishop. Marriages up to and including 4th degree were prohibited. But dispensations for 4th degree (e.g., first cousins) could have been granted. The parish marriage registers often recorded the dispensation, the reason, and the degree to which the relationship existed, such as a dispensation for 4th degree consanguinity. Dispensations for consanguinity can be useful in constructing family trees, since the common ancestor can be identified or estimated. One good source is *Bishop Loughlin's Dispensations, Diocese of Brooklyn, 1859–1866: Genealogical Information from the Marriage Dispensation Records of the Roman Catholic Diocese of Brooklyn: Kings, Queens, and Suffolk Counties, New York* by Joseph M. Silinonte.[13] Figure 3.5 shows the degrees of consanguinity. [14]

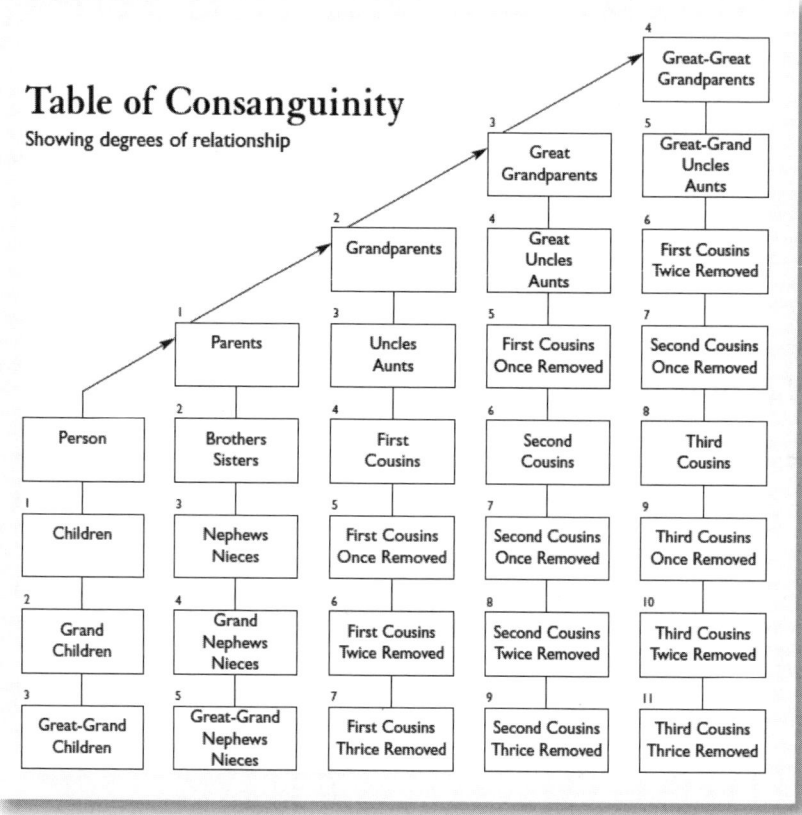

Figure 3.5. Table of consanguinity, showing degrees of relationship.

---

[13] Joseph M. Silinonte, Bishop Loughlin's Dispensations, Diocese of Brooklyn, 1859–1866: Genealogical Information from the Marriage Dispensation Records of the Roman Catholic Diocese of Brooklyn: Kings, Queens and Suffolk Counties, New York (Toronto: Becker Associates, 1996).

[14] Table of Consanguinity Showing Degrees of Relationship, Wikimedia Commons, upload. wikimedia.org/wikipedia/commons/2/28/Table_of_Consanguinity_showing_degrees_ of_relationship.png

Other dispensations were granted for marriages that were performed within a "forbidden time," such as Lent or Advent. One of the most common reasons was for the dispensation of one or more of the marriage banns. Couples were required to publicly proclaim their intention to marry, often for three successive weeks. Dispensations for banns were common in rural areas served by traveling priests or where the bride and groom lived far from the church. In these cases, waiting three weeks for the banns to be read was unfeasible.

Parochial school records

Religiously affiliated schools kept records of students, teachers, and administrators. These records can be locally held, at a diocesan archives or religious order archives. You need to determine from the parish history who ran the school. For example, was it an order of nuns or brothers? Many Catholic schools were taught by the Sisters of Notre Dame de Namur, the Sisters of Saint Joseph, Sisters of Charity of New York, Sisters of Charity of the Blessed Virgin Mary, the Christian Brothers, and other orders. Many of these orders maintain provincial archives in various regions around the country, and some have online archival finding aids, such as the Sisters of Notre Dame de Namur New England Archives.[15]

To-Do List
- Identify priest or minister from civil marriage records.
- Use city directories to locate clergy and church.
- Research history of church and diocese.
- Contact diocese before local church.

Orphanage records

With high mortality rates of nineteenth-century American cities, many children lost both parents and were truly orphaned. Other children may have lost one parent, but the remaining parent was not able to care for his or her children. In these cases, the children may have been placed in an orphanage temporarily. Other children were simply abandoned, left on the doorsteps of churches and convents. Orphanage records can be useful when you can find and access them, but in many cases, access to the public is restricted. In New York City, the Sisters of Charity ran the New York Foundling Hospital. Many orphaned children were sent west on "orphan trains" to be placed with rural families. Some of

Figure 3.6. Children at New York Foundling Hospital, 1888.

---

[15] Sisters of Notre Dame de Namur New England Archives, https://sndnewengland.wordpress.com/finding-aids/.

the records can be accessed at the New York Historical Society, and the finding aid can be accessed online at dlib.nyu.edu/findingaids/html/nyhs/foundling/.[16] Steve Morse has a good site listing resources for researching orphans not only in Brooklyn, but also other boroughs and towns at bklyn-genealogy-info.stevemorse.org/Orphan/index.html. If the orphanage is still operating, the records will most likely still be held by the institution. For closed orphanages, records of many Catholic institutions are maintained by archdiocesan archives, such as the Philadelphia Archdiocesan Historical Research Center.

Summary

Church records often provide crucial information about Irish American communities when civil registrations are nonexistent or under-reported. Even when civil births are available, the names of godparents in baptism records and the witnesses at weddings help connect our ancestors to a network of friends and relatives. Baptisms and marriages are the most genealogically useful types of sacramental records for determining birth and marriage information. Church records can be locally held or preserved in diocesan or other archives. Some records have been microfilmed and are available at public libraries and the Family History Library. Locating the church your ancestor attended can be challenging in developing communities that were included in regional parishes or served by travelling clergy. In small towns, a history of the town may shed light on where Irish immigrants attended church, perhaps in neighboring towns. In large cities, the street address of immigrant ancestors and the location of churches will help determine which church your ancestor attended. Although less common, records of schools, orphanages, dispensations, ordinations, and other sources can help to shed light on the lives of your ancestors.

Further Reading

- Axelson, Edith F. *A Guide to Episcopal Church Records in Virginia*. Athens, Ga.: Iberian Pub. Co., 1988.

- Buggy, Joseph. *Finding Your Irish Ancestors in New York City*. Baltimore: Genealogical Publishing Co., 2014.

- *Catholic Church Records of the Pacific Northwest*. St. Paul, Ore.: French Prairie Press, 1972.

- Humling, Virginia. *U.S. Catholic Sources: A Diocesan Research Guide*. Salt Lake City: Ancestry, 1995.

- Kirkham, E. Kay. *A Survey of American Church Records: Major and Minor Denominations before 1880–1890: Religious Migrations of Some of the Major Denominations*. Logan, Utah: Everton Publishers, 1978.

- Lord, Robert H., John E. Sexton, and Edward T. Harrington. *History of the Archdiocese of Boston in the Various Stages of Its Development, 1604 to 1943*. New York: Sheed & Ward, 1944.

---

[16] Guide to the Records of the New York Foundling Hospital, 1869–2009, MS 347, dlib.nyu.edu/findingaids/html/nyhs/foundling.html.

- Lucey, William Leo. *The Catholic Church in Maine.* Francestown, N.H.: M. Jones Co., 1957.

- O'Connor, Thomas H. Boston Catholics: *A History of the Church and its People.* Boston: Northeastern University Press, 1998.

- O'Toole, James M. *Guide to the Archives of the Archdiocese of Boston.* New York: Garland Pub., 1982.

- Piet, Mary A., and Stanley G. Piet. *Early Catholic Church Records in Baltimore, Maryland, 1782 through 1800: From the Original Records of "Old St. Peter's Pro-Cathedral: Baptisms, 1782 through 1800, Marriages, 1783 through 1800, Burials, 1783 through 1800."* Westminster, Md.: Family Line, 1989.

- Sullivan, James S. *A Graphic, Historical, and Pictorial Account of the Catholic Church of New England, Archdiocese of Boston.* Boston: Illustrated Pub. Co., 1895.

- Thompson, Joseph J. *The First Chicago Church Records, 1833–44: Including a Chronology of Churches in Northeastern Illinois, 1833–60.* Baltimore: Gateway Press, 1988.

Chapter 4
Researching Your Ancestors' Records of Immigration, Citizenship, and Travel

This chapter looks at United States citizenship records, border-crossing records, passenger arrival lists, and passport applications. These documents can help you determine your immigrant ancestor's exact origin in Ireland. As you begin to research the date of your ancestor's arrival and a possible naturalization date, U.S. census records remain the best place to start. But given the inherent unreliability of dates and places appearing in the census records, you will need to use them primarily as springboards into the next phase of your research: a search of the records of U.S. citizenship, border crossings, passenger arrival lists, and passport applications.

For determining an immigrant's detailed place of origin, examining the records of citizenship and travel is essential.

Finding these records can take a little effort. The first step is to figure out if and when your ancestor applied for citizenship. To review some key points from Chapter 2 about using census records, U.S. federal census records often reveal a person's date of immigration and citizenship status. The 1900, 1910, and 1930 census records show the year of immigration and the citizenship status. The 1920 census also provides the year of naturalization. Census records contain three codes used to indicate citizenship status: *Na* for naturalized; *Pa* for someone who has filed papers (specifically, a *declaration of intent*); and *Al* for alien. You will need to consider the years of immigration, as given on census records, as potentially unreliable. Often the immigrant was not the person answering the questions, but rather his or her spouse or even a landlord or a neighbor. The census data recording the year of immigration was gathered often decades after the year of actual immigration, when the person's memory might have become foggy. Furthermore, the immigrant may have lied to the census taker, perhaps out of fear of deportation. Therefore, you should use the information only as a guide.

Examine Immigration and Citizenship Records

Recapping previous points, we return to a look at the 1870 census, which has a check-off column to indicate citizenship. For example, in the 1870 census John F. Kennedy's immigrant ancestor Thomas Fitzgerald was checked off in column 19 as a male citizen of U.S. of 21 years of age and upwards. (See Figure 4.1.) With this information in hand, we can look for a pre-1870 naturalization record.

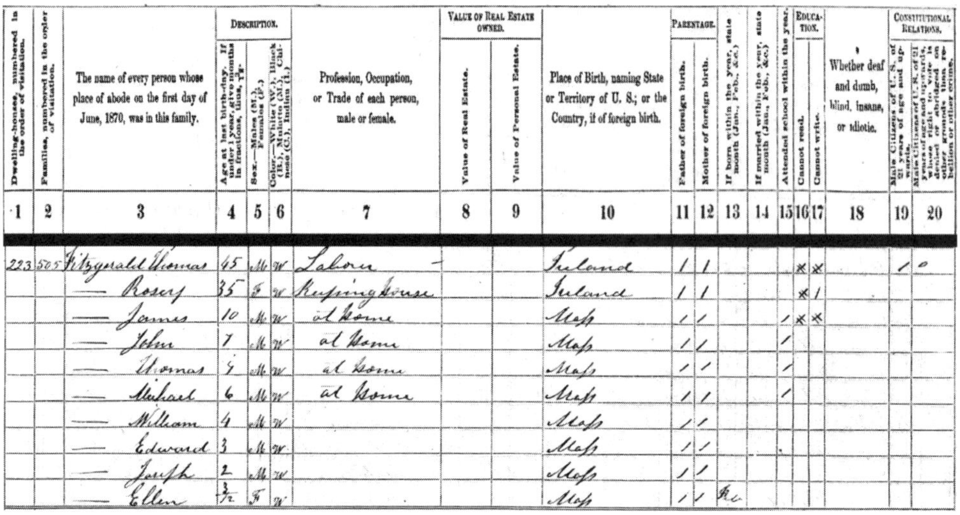

Dwelling-houses, numbered in the order of visitation.	Families, numbered in the order of visitation.	The name of every person whose place of abode on the first day of June, 1870, was in this family.	Description: Age at last birth-day. If under 1 year, give months in fractions, thus, 3/12.	Sex.—Males (M.), Females (F.)	Color.—White (W.), Black (B.), Mulatto (M.), Chinese (C.), Indian (I.)	Profession, Occupation, or Trade of each person, male or female.	Value of Real Estate Owned: Value of Real Estate.	Value of Personal Estate.	Place of Birth, naming State or Territory of U. S.; or the Country, if of foreign birth.	Parentage: Father of foreign birth.	Mother of foreign birth.	If born within the year, state month (Jan., Feb., &c.)	If married within the year, state month (Jan., Feb., &c.)	Attended school within the year.	Education: Cannot read.	Cannot write.	Whether deaf and dumb, blind, insane, or idiotic.	Constitutional Relations: Male Citizens of U. S. of 21 years of age and upwards.	Male Citizens of U. S. of 21 years of age and upwards, whose right to vote is denied or abridged on other grounds than rebellion or crime.
1	2	3	4	5	6	7	8	9	10	11	12	13	14	15	16	17	18	19	20
223	505	Fitzgerald Thomas	45	M	W	Laborer			Ireland	/	/				×	×		/	
		— Rosey	35	F	W	Keeping House			Ireland	/	/				×	/			
		— James	10	M	W	at Home			Mass	/	/			/	×	×			
		— John	7	M	W	at Home			Mass	/	/			/					
		— Thomas	9	M	W	at Home			Mass	/	/			/					
		— Michael	6	M	W	at Home			Mass	/	/			/					
		— William	4	M	W				Mass	/	/								
		— Edward	3	M	W				Mass	/	/								
		— Joseph	2	M	W				Mass	/	/								
		— Ellen	3/12	F	W				Mass	/	/	Fe							

Figure 4.1. Thomas and Rosey Fitzgerald, 1870 census, Ward 2, Boston, Massachusetts.

Pre-1906 naturalization petitions and declarations of intent

Records of citizenship and *denization* (grant of partial rights to resident aliens) date back to colonial times. But early Irish settlers were considered British subjects, and thus they were citizens of the British colonies in America. Therefore, you will not find pre-Revolutionary period naturalization records for seventeenth- and eighteenth-century Irish immigrants. (For more on seventeenth- and eighteenth-century immigration, see Chapter 6.)

Naturalization records date back to 1790, and, up to 1906, someone from another country could apply for U.S. citizenship in a variety of courts: federal district and circuit courts, county superior and supreme courts, municipal courts, police courts, and courts of common pleas. After a minimum of two years' residency, an immigrant, to this point considered by the state as an *alien,* could file a declaration of intent and, after a minimum of five years' residency, could petition the court for citizenship. (For a brief period of time in the 1850s, the residency requirement was extended to seven years.) The documents generated by these two steps are called declarations of intent and naturalization petitions.[1] Once the court granted

[1] Naturalization Records, National Archives, www.archives.gov/research/naturalization/naturalization.html.

the petition, a naturalization document that was taken home was generated. This record does not usually provide much information.

Note that women usually did not apply for citizenship, since they derived their citizenship status from their husbands—at least until 1922. They automatically became U.S. citizens when their husbands did. If their husband was already a U.S. citizen, a woman gained citizenship on her marriage date. Infrequently, a woman, such as an unmarried businesswoman, would apply for citizenship,

As a genealogist, you should treat the dates of birth and arrival on naturalization records with skepticism. Nineteenth-century Irish were coming from rural communities where agricultural and religious calendars were common. Many did not know exactly when they were born, and many provided the dates of March 17 or July 12 (St. Patrick's Day or Orangeman's Day, respectively) as their dates of birth. Furthermore, they may have been motivated for political reasons to lie about their dates of birth or arrival. If the immigrant arrived in America when he was under the age of 18 years, he did not have to make a declaration of intent before petitioning for citizenship. If a ward boss was trying to recruit immigrants to vote in an upcoming election, he may have encouraged the immigrant to fudge his birth date or arrival date, so that the immigrant would skip the declaration of intent and go directly for a petition.

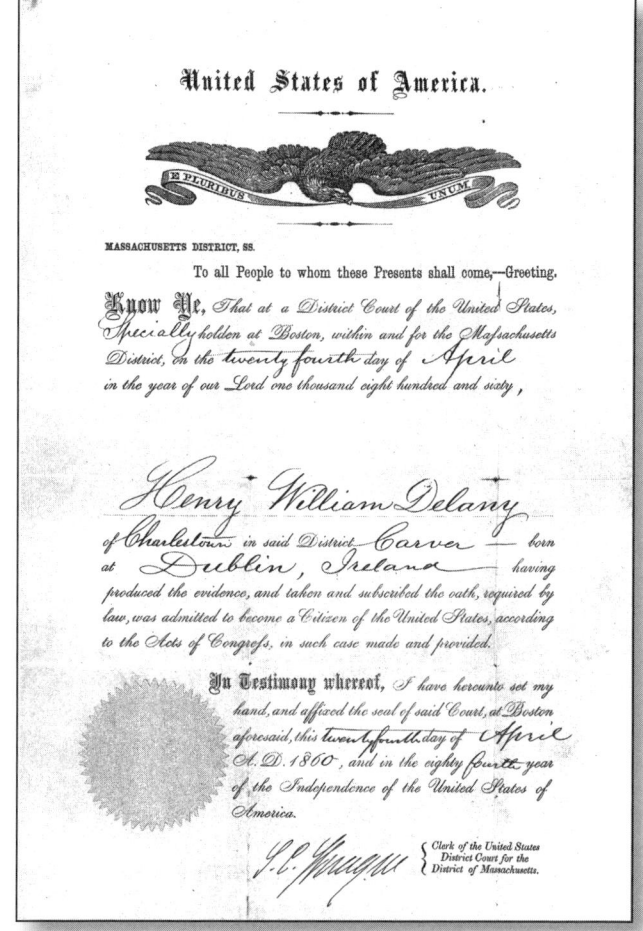

Figure 4.2. 1860 naturalization record of Henry Delaney of Charlestown, Massachusetts, native of Dublin.

Sometimes the declaration of intent or the petition for naturalization will show the parish or townland of birth. Detailed birthplaces on citizenship records occur more frequently in New England states, except for Connecticut. But even if the records list county only, they can be helpful, since Irish church records can be searched in online databases—provided the names of the Irish parents are known (see Chapter 8).

The Family History Library website, FamilySearch.org, has many county and some federal naturalization records available as databases. The website also has an excellent online Research Wiki that provides links to Wiki pages detailing individual court records by state.[2] For many states, the courts recorded only the country of nativity, not the county of origin in Ireland. Each county and state used different forms. Occasionally, the court record listed the county of origin, and even less frequently a parish or townland. For federal court records that are not online, such as those from New York City, you should check the website of the regional National Archives repository for the area where the immigrant lived.

You will find other useful pieces of information on naturalization petitions, even if you strike out on exact origin. If the immigrant made a declaration of intent, the date and court of the declaration was often listed on the petition. These details allow you to then look for the declaration, in hopes that it will contain more exact information about the immigrant's origin. Also, the names of the witnesses can be important. In many instances, at least one witness was a friend or relative from the Old Country. Since the witness was a U.S. citizen, you can next look for the naturalization record of the witness as well.

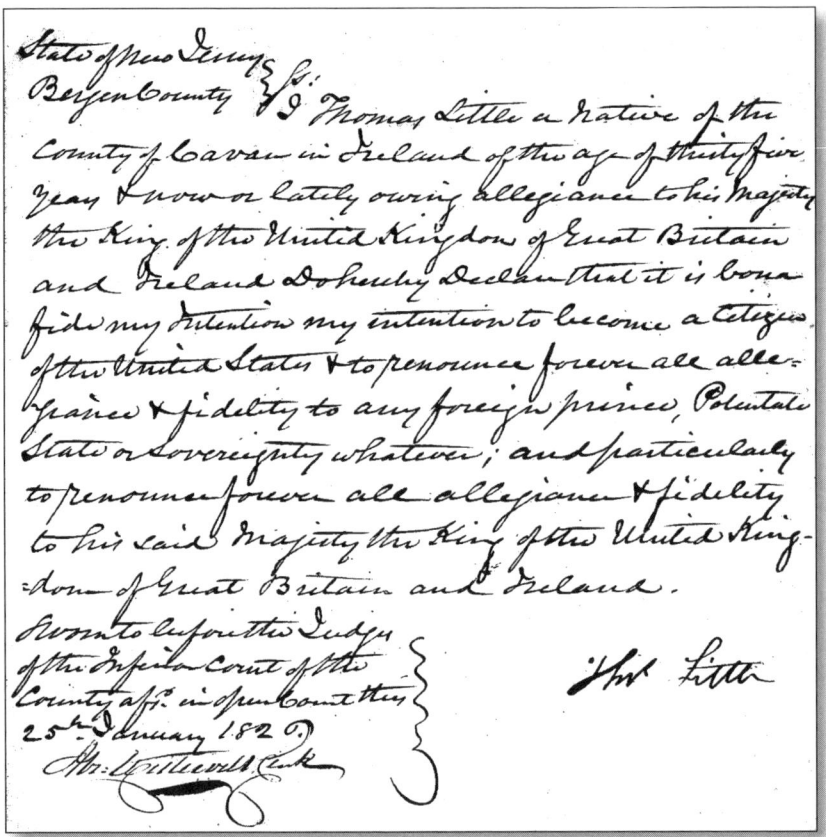

Figure 4.3. 1829 Declaration of Intent, Thomas Little, Bergen County, New Jersey.

---

[2] United States Naturalization and Citizenship Research Wiki, FamilySearch.org/learn/wiki/en/United_States_Naturalization_and_Citizenship.

Indexes of pre-1906 New England naturalization petitions

Working with the Immigration and Naturalization Service (INS), the Works Progress Administration (WPA) copied New England naturalization petitions with a dexigraph camera (an early photocopier) and created a card index. The dexigraph copies included not only federal court petitions, but also county and local court records petitions. They also indexed the copies by a system called Soundex, which congregates like sounding names together. The index cards were microfilmed and digitized by the Family History Library, and the images of the cards are available on FamilySearch.org and Ancestry.com. The cards are arranged first by Soundex code, then by given name, then given name and middle name initial, then by residence, then by birth date. When searching, it is wise to check "exact" next to as many fields as possible.

For example, to search for a Thomas Fitzgerald of Boston, born ca. 1825, you would enter his name, a date of birth range from 1820 to 1830, a naturalization date range of 1845 to 1870 (since he indicated he was a U.S. citizen in the 1870 census), and the naturalization place as Massachusetts. Do not enter the birthplace as Ireland, since many courts recorded Irish birthplaces as Great Britain. Also, FamilySearch.org and Ancestry.com do not index the specific town of residence or where naturalized. If you had entered "Boston, Massachusetts" in the naturalization place, FamilySearch.org would have come back with no results, whereas by entering just Massachusetts, eleven results come back. You will have to look at each result to determine the town of residence. Out of the eleven results, three were for Thomas Fitzgeralds who lived in Boston. How do you choose among these three Thomas Fitzgeralds? Compare the information in the petition to what you know about the immigrant from oral history and written records. Examine the occupation, arrival date, port of entry, naturalization date, and names of the witnesses. In the case of Thomas Fitzgerald, an oral history and a family Bible claimed he was from Limerick.

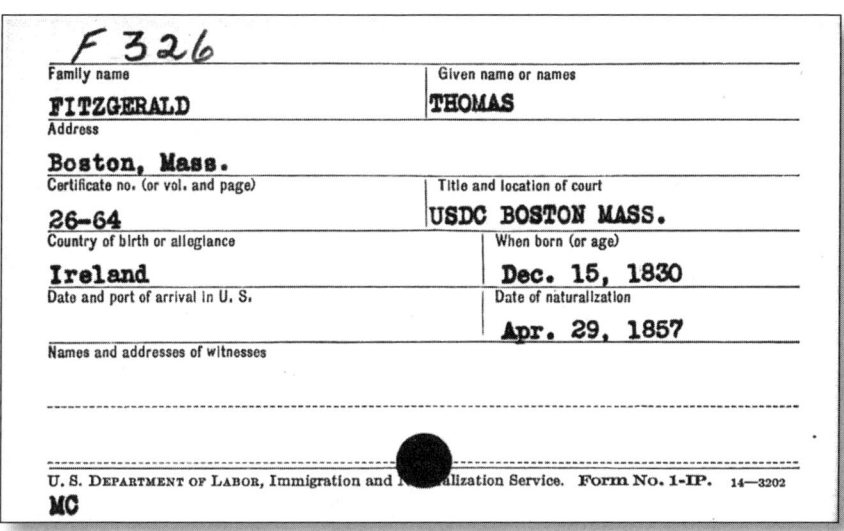

Figure 4.4. WPA naturalization index card.

With the information indicated on the index card, you can then look for a naturalization petition for Thomas Fitzgerald in the database *New England, Petitions for Naturalization, 1787–1906*, on FamilySearch.org. This material currently is a browsable, not searchable, database. Browse for the record by going to the main search page and typing the name of the database in the "Collection Title" field under "Find a Collection." Elect to browse images, then select Massachusetts, then U.S. District Courts, then volume 26. Since each record is two pages in length, you have to double the page number in the image number field to locate the record. Even then you have to slowly find your way to page 64. Although the database is difficult to navigate, it is easier than your only other option: to write to the National Archives New England Region and pay for a copy.

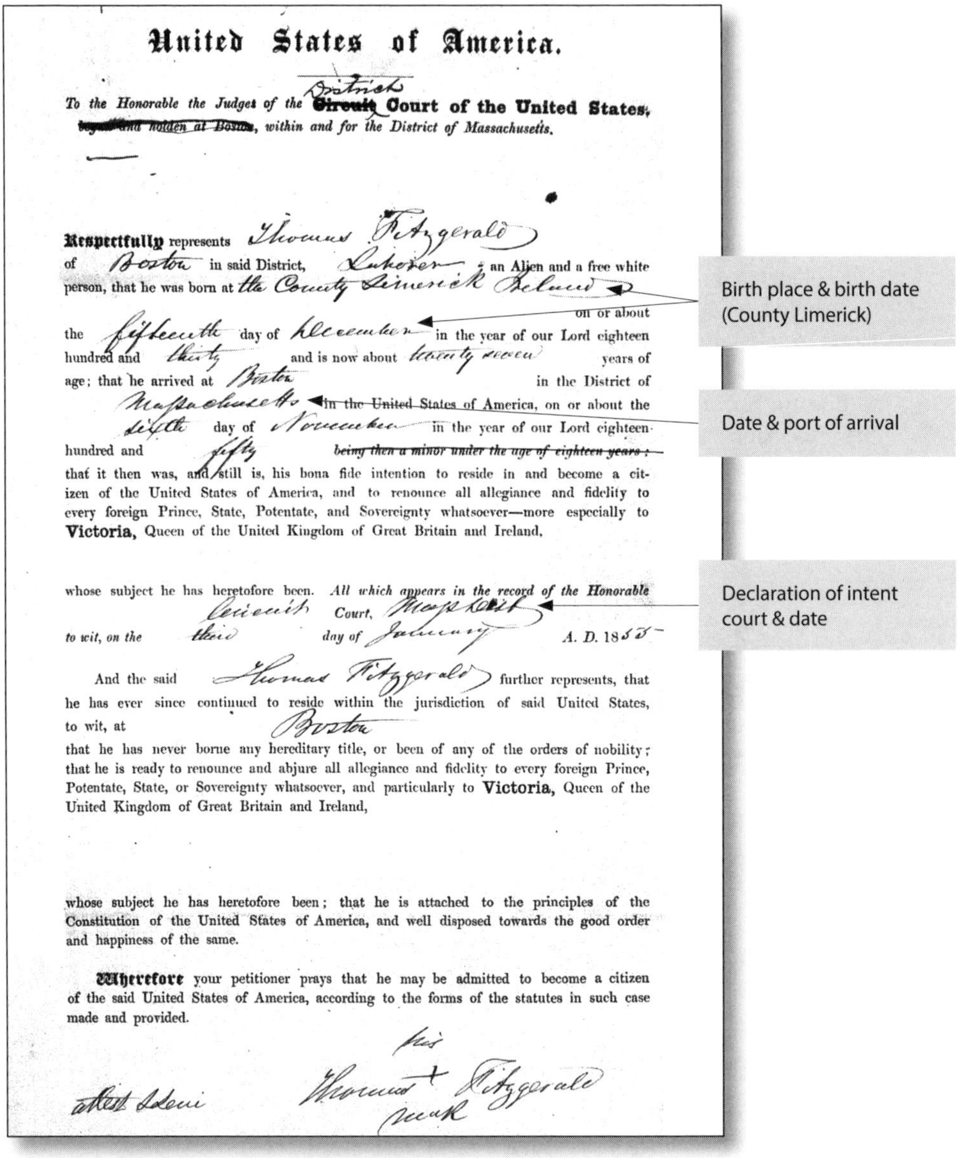

United States of America.

To the Honorable the Judges of the ~~Circuit~~ District **Court of the United States,** ~~begun and holden at Boston~~, *within and for the District of Massachusetts.*

Respectfully represents Thomas Fitzgerald of Boston in said District, Laborer an Alien and a free white person, that he was born at the County Limerick Ireland on or about the fifteenth day of December in the year of our Lord eighteen hundred and thirty and is now about twenty seven years of age; that he arrived at Boston in the District of Massachusetts ~~in the United States~~ of America, on or about the sixth day of November in the year of our Lord eighteen hundred and fifty ~~being then a minor under the age of eighteen years~~; that it then was, and still is, his bona fide intention to reside in and become a citizen of the United States of America, and to renounce all allegiance and fidelity to every foreign Prince, State, Potentate, and Sovereignty whatsoever—more especially to **Victoria**, Queen of the United Kingdom of Great Britain and Ireland,

whose subject he has heretofore been. *All which appears in the record of the Honorable* Circuit *Court*, Mass Dist *to wit, on the* third *day of* January *A. D.* 1855

And the said Thomas Fitzgerald further represents, that he has ever since continued to reside within the jurisdiction of said United States, to wit, at Boston that he has never borne any hereditary title, or been of any of the orders of nobility; that he is ready to renounce and abjure all allegiance and fidelity to every foreign Prince, Potentate, State, or Sovereignty whatsoever, and particularly to **Victoria**, Queen of the United Kingdom of Great Britain and Ireland,

whose subject he has heretofore been; that he is attached to the principles of the Constitution of the United States of America, and well disposed towards the good order and happiness of the same.

Wherefore your petitioner prays that he may be admitted to become a citizen of the said United States of America, according to the forms of the statutes in such case made and provided.

Thomas his + mark Fitzgerald

attest

Figure 4.5. Naturalization petition of Thomas Fitzgerald, U.S. District Court, Boston, Vol. 26, p. 64 [part 1].

Note the difference between the date of birth on the naturalization petition (see Figure 4.5), 1830, and Thomas's age on the 1870 census, which would have placed his birth in about 1825. A discrepancy like this one is not unusual for Irish immigrants and is a reason for searching "±5 years." The petition also states that he arrived in the port of Boston on 6 November 1850. A search of *Massachusetts Passenger and Crew Lists 1820–1963* at Ancestry.com yielded no results that corresponded with this date. Again, a discrepancy of this nature is not unusual.

Although often ignored by genealogists, the second page of the naturalization petition can contain important pieces of information. In the case of Thomas Fitzgerald, one of the witnesses was his uncle, Edmond Fitzgerald (see Figure 4.6). As we will see later, this clue will prove important.

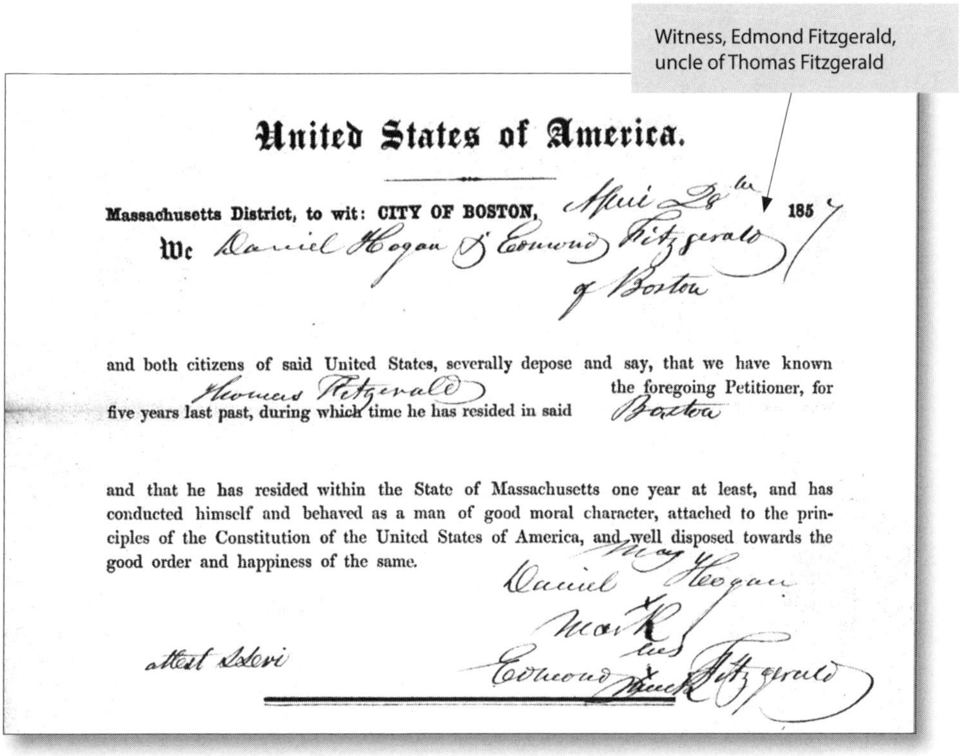

United States of America.

Massachusetts District, to wit: CITY OF BOSTON, April 28th 1857

We Daniel Hogan & Edmond Fitzgerald of Boston

and both citizens of said United States, severally depose and say, that we have known Thomas Fitzgerald the foregoing Petitioner, for five years last past, during which time he has resided in said Boston

and that he has resided within the State of Massachusetts one year at least, and has conducted himself and behaved as a man of good moral character, attached to the principles of the Constitution of the United States of America, and well disposed towards the good order and happiness of the same.

Daniel Hogan

Edmond Fitzgerald

attest

Figure 4.6. Detail of second page of naturalization petition of Thomas Fitzgerald, U.S. District Court, Boston, Vol. 26, p. 64.

Declarations of intent

After an immigrant had been in the United States for a minimum of two years, he or she could file a declaration formally stating the intention to become a citizen. The declaration was ordinarily the first step in the process of naturalization. Note, however, that an applicant could skip this step and petition the courts directly, in the following circumstances:

1. Starting in 1824, if the immigrant was under the age of 18 years when he arrived in the United States.

2. After 1862, if the immigrant was an honorably discharged veteran of the U.S. Army (with the provision extended to Navy and Marine Corps in 1894) who served during the Civil War and was resident in the United States for at least one year.

3. In 1918, if the immigrant was in the U.S. military during World War I. If he was, the immigrant was immediately naturalized in a military camp or a court nearby, without declaration of intention, certificate of arrival, or proof of residency.[3]

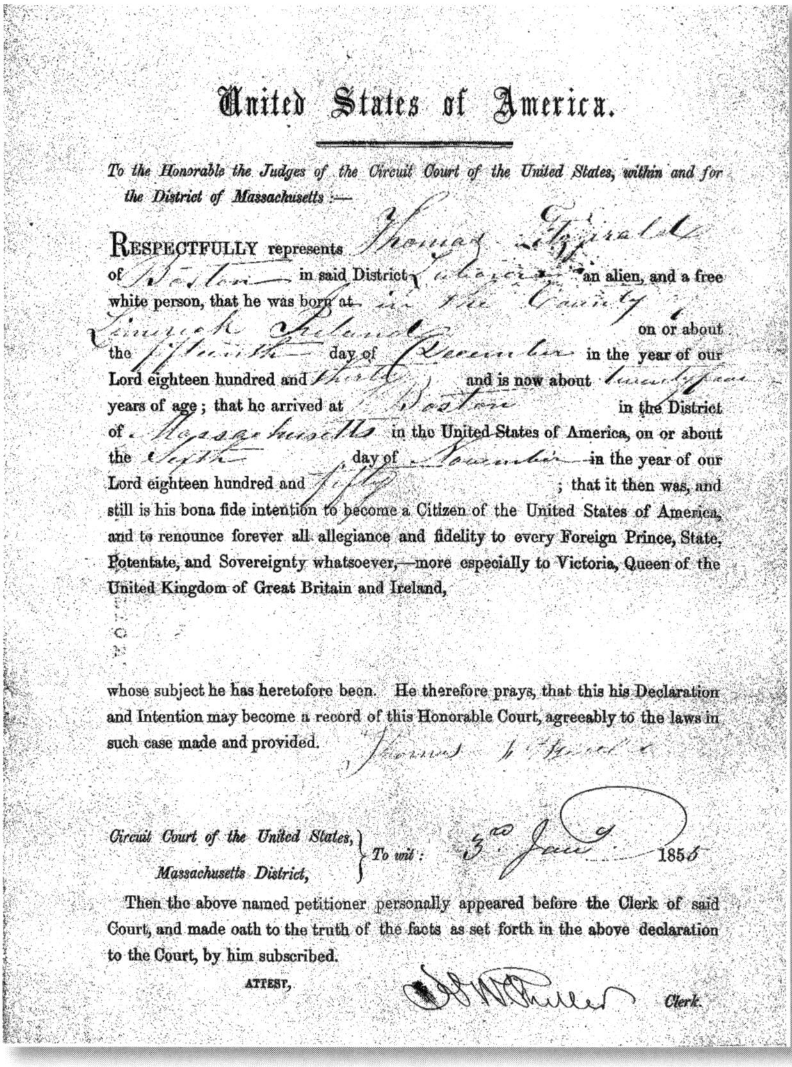

Figure 4.7. Declaration of Intent, Thomas Fitzgerald
U.S. Circuit Court, Boston, January 3, 1855.

---

[3] Immigration and Ships Passenger Lists Research Guide, Genealogical Society of Bergen County, New Jersey, njgsbc.org/files/immigration/shipguide.html.

Keep in mind that the first provision, of arriving when less than 18 years old, led many immigrants to claim later dates of birth or earlier arrival dates. Sometimes, the declaration will have more information, including a more detailed birthplace, than the petition. You can determine the court and date of the declaration from the petition. In the case of Thomas Fitzgerald, he stated on his petition that he had made his initial declaration of intent in the U.S. Circuit Court on 3 January 1855 (see Figure 4.7). For Thomas Fitzgerald, the declaration did not show additional information about his birthplace. But the small percentage of instances in which more information was recorded make declarations always worth pursuing. Sometimes, the immigrant never reached the step of petitioning for citizenship after having made a declaration of intent. The omission could have been due to death, imprisonment, avoidance, or just plain laxity. Therefore, searching for declarations of intent is always worthwhile.

The National Archives Northeast Region has the U.S. court declarations for New England; other regional National Archives have declarations for their respective regions. The Family History Library in Salt Lake City has many state and county court declarations on microfilm. In some cases they have been digitized and are available for searching or browsing on FamilySearch.org.

Post-1906 naturalization records

The Bureau of Immigration and Naturalization was created in 1906 to standardize the process of applying for citizenship. After this date, immigrants went to federal courts to apply for citizenship. Many of these federal records have been microfilmed and digitized and are now available on websites such as Ancestry.com and Fold3. The post-1906 records provide much more detail, including not only the date and port of arrival, but also the name of the ship the immigrant sailed on, which can lead to useful passenger arrival lists. Later records list the spouse and children and their dates of birth. Many later records that have not been filmed or digitized—such as those from the 1930s and 1940s—are located at regional National Archives. These records frequently include photographs of the immigrant.

In Figure 4.8, Patrick McCarthy applied for U.S. citizenship in New York in 1931. He stated that he had been born on 14 March 1900 in County Kerry and had lived in Ontario, Canada. He had entered the United States at Sault Ste. Marie on 3 August 1925. He also stated that he had married his wife, Mary, in New York City on 10 November 1931, and that she had been born in Listowell [Kerry], Ireland in May 1908.

With the information provided in the naturalization petition, you can search marriage indexes at Ancestry.com and FamilySearch.org. At FamilySearch, the information on the marriage records has been extracted to include the names of the parents of the bride and groom. Thus a search for the marriage of Patrick McCarthy, with a spouse named Mary, who married in New York City in 1931, yields an extracted record showing that Mary's surname was Donoghue; that the names of their parents were John McCarthy and Mary Ryan, and Daniel

Donoghue and Mary O'Brien; and that the date of the marriage was 10 November 1931 (which matches the date reported on the naturalization petition.)[4] See Figure 4.8.

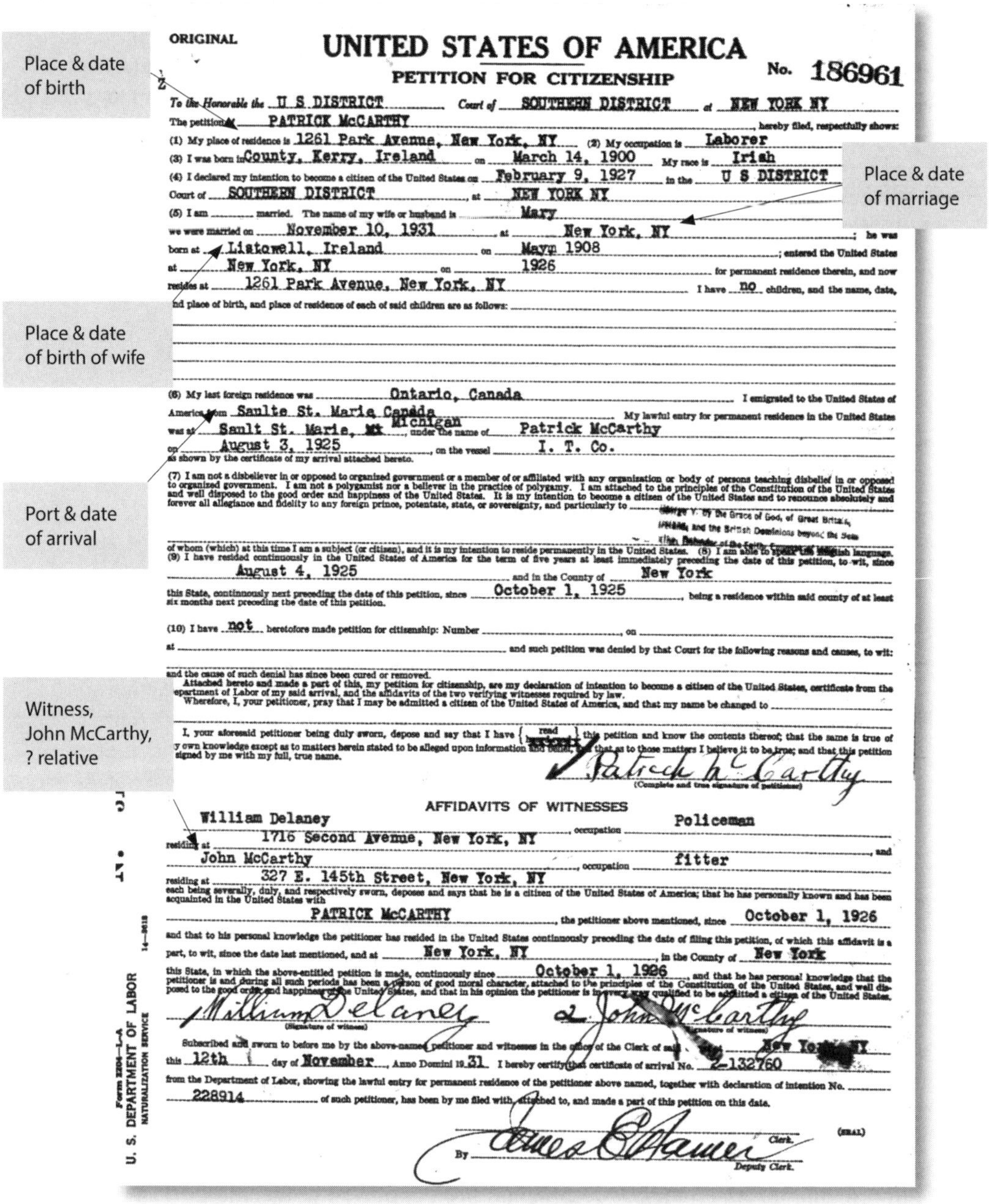

UNITED STATES OF AMERICA
PETITION FOR CITIZENSHIP
No. 186961

- Place & date of birth: County, Kerry, Ireland, March 14, 1900
- Place & date of marriage: New York, NY, November 10, 1931
- Place & date of birth of wife: Listowell, Ireland, May 1908
- Port & date of arrival: Sault St. Marie, Michigan, August 3, 1925
- Witness, John McCarthy, ? relative

Petitioner: PATRICK McCARTHY
Residence: 1261 Park Avenue, New York, NY
Occupation: Laborer
Wife: Mary
Vessel: I. T. Co.
Witnesses: William Delaney (Policeman), 1716 Second Avenue, New York, NY; John McCarthy (fitter), 327 E. 145th Street, New York, NY

Figure 4.8. November 12, 1931 Naturalization Petition, Patrick McCarthy, U.S. District Court for the Southern District of New York.

---

[4] *New York, New York City Marriage Records, 1829–1940* database at FamilySearch.org, Marriage, Manhattan, New York, New York, United States, New York City Municipal Archives, New York; FHL microfilm 1,684,396.

Check Travel and Passport Records

The millions of Irish people who left their country and moved to the United States clearly did so for a range of powerful economic, religious, and family reasons. Whether pushed or pulled by circumstances, they had a determination to pursue better long-term opportunities, no matter the risks and costs. Often motivated by some combination of hope and desperation, they each arrived at a juncture when they gathered their resources, arranged for passage (either through direct payment, loan, government transport grant, indenture, or some other means), embarked on what could be a dangerous and uncomfortable journey—and thus entered a system of travel-related paperwork. Both the country and port being left and the destination generated lists, forms, and receipts, particularly as the nineteenth century advanced to the twentieth. Though that system of recordkeeping was minimalistic by present-day standards, and rife with gaps and inaccuracies, it still leaves a paper trail that can be useful to genealogists, particularly in combination with records of immigration and citizenship.

Border-crossing records

From 1895 through 1954, the United States Immigration Service kept records of persons crossing the United States border from Canada. Before that, many immigrants chose to travel to Canada first, since the fares were less expensive and they could evade inspection by immigration officials. In 1894, the Immigration Service established an agreement with Canadian railroad and shipping companies to collect information on United States–bound immigrants, and later, long-time Canadians of foreign birth and Canadian natives who intended to immigrate to the United States.

Patrick McCarthy (shown in Figure 4.8) stated on his naturalization petition that he entered the United States at Sault Ste. Marie on August 3, 1925, at the age of 25 years. Found on Ancestry.com, the Canadian border-crossing record (Figure 4.9) shows a 25-year-old Patrick McCarthy crossing the United States–Canadian border at Sault St. Marie, Michigan, on that date. The record shows that his place of birth was Bunglashan, Ireland, where his mother, Mary, lived. His sister, Nora, resided at the State Hospital at East 116th Street, New York, New York. He was five feet nine inches in height, with light brown hair and blue eyes. He had arrived at Quebec on the SS *Megantic* on June 7, 1924.

With this information, the link to the Irish place of origin comes into focus. The 1911 census of Ireland shows a 13-year-old Patrick McCarthy living with his parents, John and Mary McCarthy, in the townland of Bunglasha, parish of Duagh, Union of Listowel, County Kerry. A sister Nora also lived in the same household.

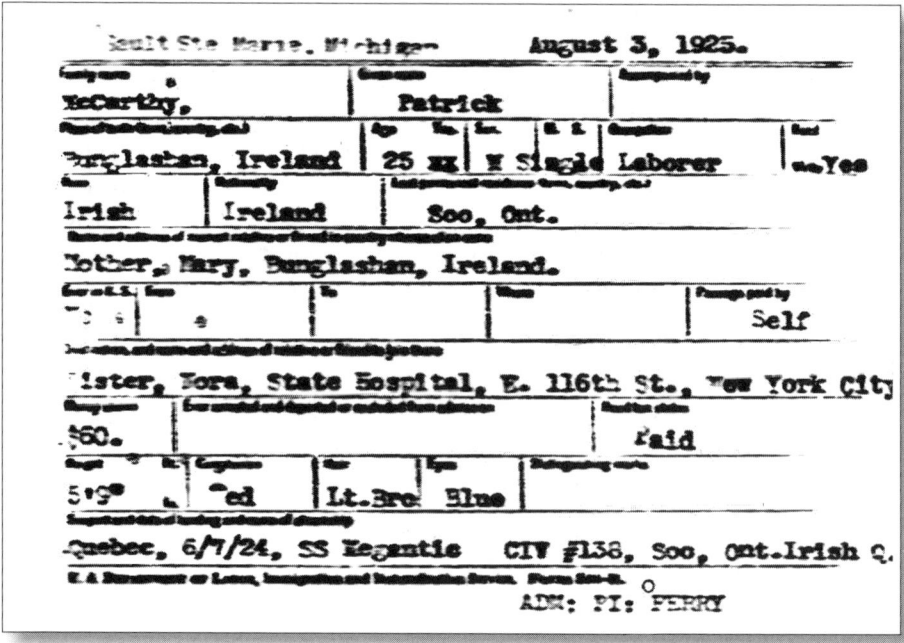

Figure 4.9. Canadian Border-Crossing Record, August 3, 1925, Patrick McCarthy.[5]

Passenger arrival lists

Many beginning genealogists start their search by looking for the ship their ancestor came on. While this information, if findable, can add dramatic stories to the saga of our ancestor's lives, nineteenth-century passenger lists generally do not provide information on an ancestor's birthplace in Ireland. Furthermore, locating ancestors who had common Irish names is difficult on these lists, if not impossible. For instance, if you are looking for a Patrick Murphy who arrived in New York in 1850, you will find that in that year, twenty-eight Patrick Murphys arrived in New York, and among these twenty-eight passengers, twenty-three had sailed from Liverpool, Glasgow, or London. In the nineteenth century, Irish immigrants commonly traveled to ports, primarily Liverpool and Glasgow, before sailing for America. So, in all likelihood, neither the passenger lists nor the port of embarkation will provide you with a hint of your ancestor's place of origin in Ireland.

As in this example, if a family immigrated together, they can be readily identified on passenger lists. In the next chapter, we will see the McClements family of Brighton, Michigan, with several children born in Ireland. Because they left Ireland when the children were young, the family traveled together. Even then, they left from Liverpool, and their origin cannot be determined from the passenger arrival list (Figure 4.10). But generally and more often, family members would travel to the new country separately, then reunite upon arrival, or reunite

---

[5] Although a Patrick McCarthy arrived on the SS *Megantic* later in June 1925, this immigrant came from Dingle, County Kerry, which was not near Duagh, and his father was named Daniel.

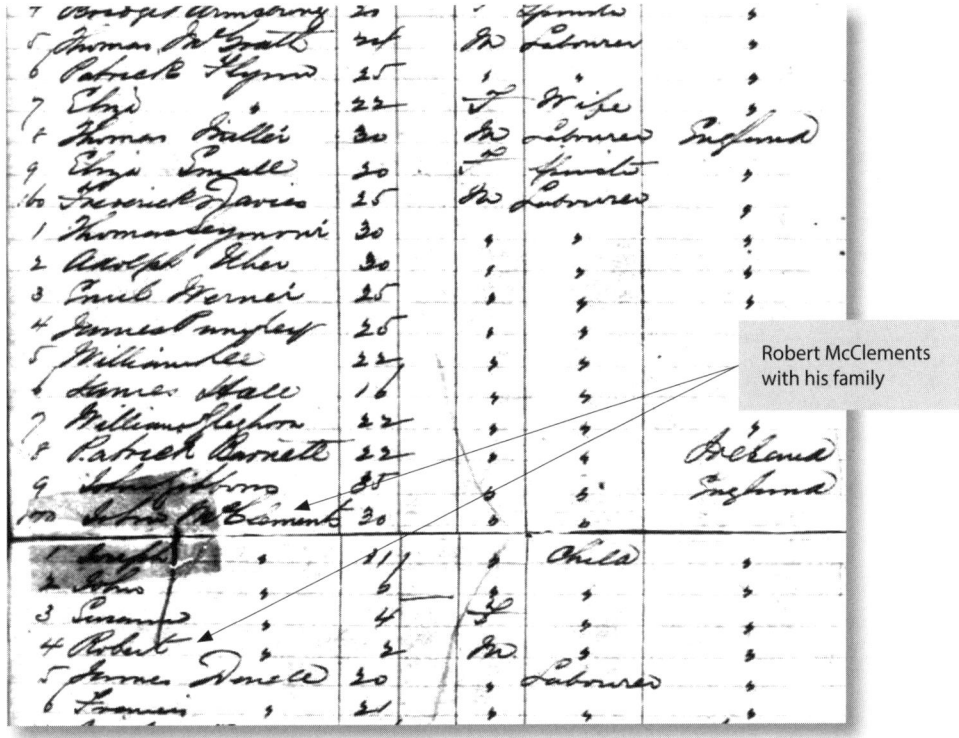

Figure 4.10. Passenger arrival list for Robert McClements of County Down, *SS Virginia*, March 16, 1870, arrival in New York from Liverpool.

even years later. Young adult sons or daughters often left home first and then sent money back to their families to fund the passages of other siblings and perhaps eventually parents. So you may not find your family traveling together as a unit. The immigration stories of our ancestors are replete with urban legends and old wives' tales. Common stories are "five brothers came over together," or, in reference to a married couple, "they met on the ship coming over." If your family oral tradition includes these stories, be prepared to consider other possibilities.

You can glean approximate dates of arrival from United States naturalization records and the 1900, 1910, 1920, and 1930 census records. But the dates can be years off. The census taker may have interviewed the spouse or someone else, rather than the immigrant. Frequently, our ancestors did not remember the exact date they arrived, and in some cases, outright lied about their arrival. Be sure to select at least "±2 years," or even "±5 years," for the arrival date.

To-Do List

- Use census to determine citizenship status and immigration date
- Look for naturalization petition and declaration of intent
- Note date and port of arrival
- Look for passenger list and border crossing records

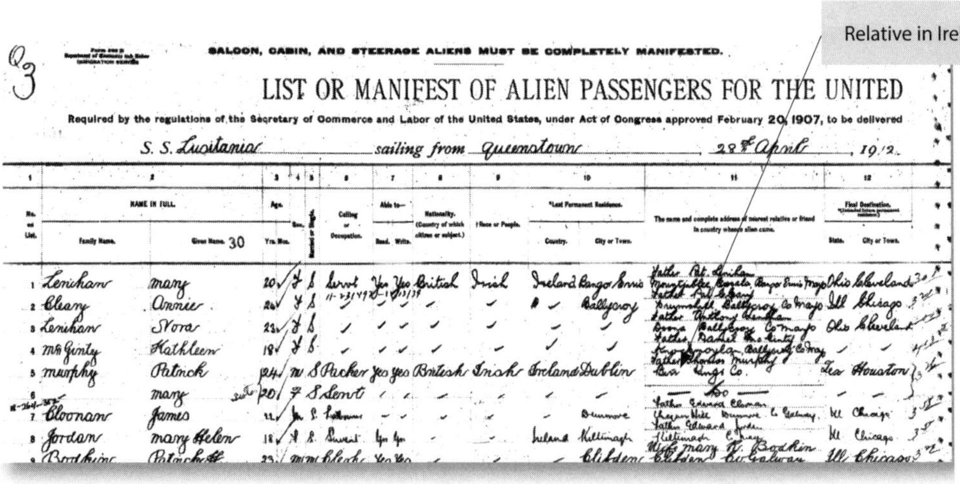

Figure 4.11a. New York passenger arrival list,
Patrick Murphy, SS *Lusitania*.

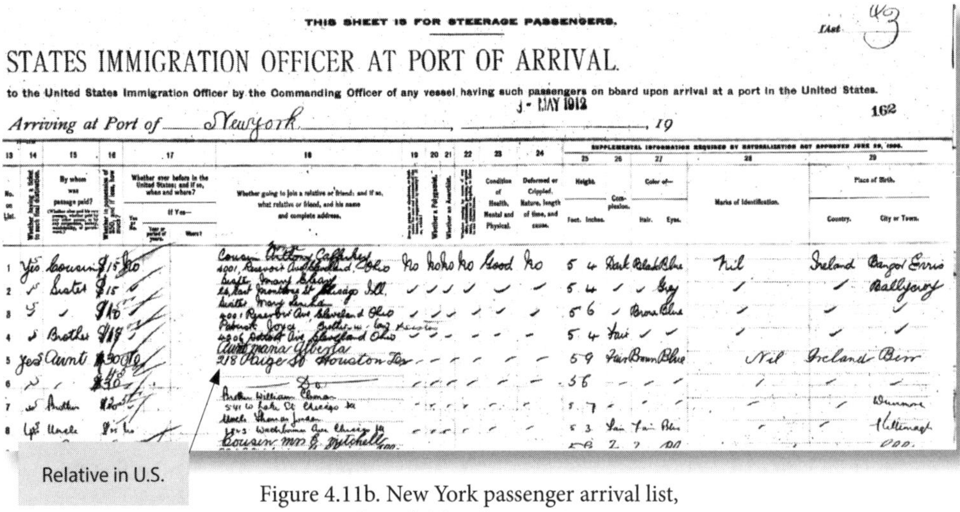

Figure 4.11b. New York passenger arrival list,
Patrick Murphy, page 2..

Although nineteenth-century passenger arrival manifests may prove disappointing, twentieth-century passenger arrival lists can prove useful in determining the origin of your ancestor. Frequently the passenger lists detail the name and address of a relative back in Ireland, the birthplace of the immigrant, and the name and address of their American contact. In the example shown in Figure 4.11a and b, a 24-year-old Patrick Murphy and his sister, Mary, sailed on the SS *Lusitania* from Queenstown on April 28, 1912. They arrived in New York on May 2, 1912. The passenger manifest listed Patrick's occupation as packer and Mary's as servant, their last permanent address as Dublin, and their destination as Houston, Texas. It listed the name of their father, Thomas Murphy, and his address in Birr, King's

County, Ireland. On the next page, the manifest recorded the name and address of their aunt, Maria Alberta, of Houston, Texas; the fact that Patrick was five feet nine inches tall and had a fair complexion, brown hair, and blue eyes; and the information that he had been born in Birr, King's County. Note that the last residence is not always the birthplace.

With this information, it is possible then to find Patrick and Mary Murphy, living with their father, Thomas Murphy, in Birr, King's County, in the 1901 and 1911 census records for Ireland.

Passenger lists supply information not only about the passengers themselves, but also their relatives in Ireland, as well as their United States contacts. We see on the passenger list that Patrick and Mary Murphy referred to an aunt, Maria Alberta, at 218 Paige Street, Houston, Texas. In the 1920 census, we see a Maria Alberti living at 218 Paige Street in Houston with her married daughter, Martha. The passenger list not only shows information on the passengers, but also sheds light on the origins of their contacts, who may have immigrated years earlier for when records were much less informative. In this way, researching the later arrivals in the same family may identify the origins of earlier immigrants.

In some cases, an ancestor may have returned to Ireland to visit relatives. So even though the earlier passenger arrival list provided little information, the later twentieth-century century passenger arrival lists may give more information, including birthplace and address of Irish relatives. Furthermore, ancestors returning from visits back to Ireland may appear in outward-bound passenger lists for the United Kingdom.

United States passport applications

Passport applications from October 1795 to March 1925 are available at the National Archives. They have been digitized and are searchable online at Ancestry.com and browsable online at FamilySearch.org. These records can be very useful for determining birthplace in Ireland, even when you are researching the second generation. The passports sometimes listed the birthplaces of the parents, and information about their immigration and citizenship. Therefore, you should search for passports of the children of immigrants, as well as the immigrants themselves. The Reverend Joseph W. Murphy, an Episcopal minister from Hillsboro, North Carolina, applied for a passport in 1891. On the application, he stated that he had been born on November 10, 1828 in Newmarket (County Cork), Ireland, that he had immigrated to the United States in 1832, after having been in Canada several years. He stated that his father, Jeremiah W. Murphy, had naturalized in Superior Court of North Carolina in Lincolnton in August 1839.

To review, the passport application identified the father of Reverend Murphy, the arrival date and process through Canada, the exact birthplace in Ireland—Newmarket—and the date and court of naturalization. Even though Reverend Joseph Murphy had been born in Ireland, his father was naturalized when Joseph was 11 years old. Joseph automatically gained citizenship at that time.

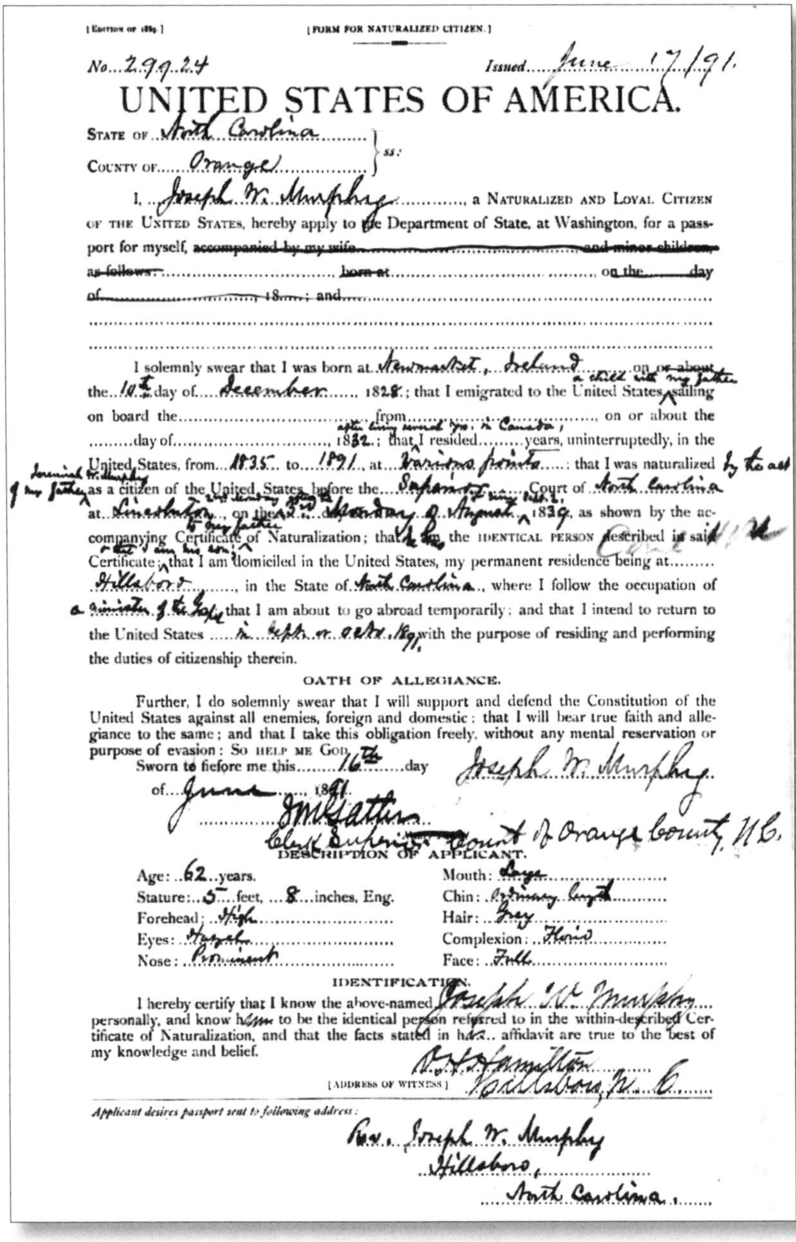
[Edition of 1889.] [FORM FOR NATURALIZED CITIZEN.]

No. 29924 Issued June 17/91.

UNITED STATES OF AMERICA.

State of North Carolina } ss:
County of Orange }

I, Joseph W. Murphy, a Naturalized and Loyal Citizen of the United States, hereby apply to the Department of State, at Washington, for a passport for myself, ~~accompanied by my wife, and minor children, as follows:~~ ~~born at~~ ~~on the day of~~ ~~18 ; and~~

I solemnly swear that I was born at Newmarket, Ireland on or about the 10th day of December, 1828; that I emigrated to the United States, a child with my father, sailing on board the ..., from ..., on or about the ... day of ..., 1832; that, after living several yrs. in Canada, I resided ... years, uninterruptedly, in the United States, from 1835 to 1891, at various points; that I was naturalized by the act of my father, Jeremiah Murphy, as a citizen of the United States before the Superior Court of North Carolina at Lincolnton, on the ... Monday of August, 1839, as shown by the accompanying Certificate of Naturalization to my father; that I am the IDENTICAL PERSON described in said Certificate, that I am his son; that I am domiciled in the United States, my permanent residence being at Hillsboro, in the State of North Carolina, where I follow the occupation of a minister of the Gospel; that I am about to go abroad temporarily; and that I intend to return to the United States in Sept. or Octr. 1891 with the purpose of residing and performing the duties of citizenship therein.

OATH OF ALLEGIANCE.

Further, I do solemnly swear that I will support and defend the Constitution of the United States against all enemies, foreign and domestic; that I will bear true faith and allegiance to the same; and that I take this obligation freely, without any mental reservation or purpose of evasion: So help me God.

Sworn to before me this 16th day of June 1891. Joseph W. Murphy

J. M. Latta
Clerk Superior Court of Orange County, N.C.

DESCRIPTION OF APPLICANT.

Age: 62 years.	Mouth: large
Stature: 5 feet, 8 inches, Eng.	Chin: ordinary length
Forehead: High	Hair: Gray
Eyes: Hazel	Complexion: Florid
Nose: Prominent	Face: Full

IDENTIFICATION.

I hereby certify that I know the above-named Joseph W. Murphy personally, and know him to be the identical person referred to in the within-described Certificate of Naturalization, and that the facts stated in his affidavit are true to the best of my knowledge and belief.

D. H. Hamilton
[Address of Witness.] Hillsboro, N. C.

Applicant desires passport sent to following address:

Rev. Joseph W. Murphy
Hillsboro,
North Carolina.

Figure 4.12. 1891 Passport Application, Rev. Joseph W. Murphy, Hillsboro, North Carolina.

Summary

In conclusion, records of immigration, citizenship, and travel are many times the most fruitful sources for determining an immigrant's exact origin in Ireland. Use census records to establish the date of arrival and possible naturalization date, and then look for the citizenship documents and passenger arrival lists. The information on these documents can identify relatives in the United States and Ireland and can lead to other useful sources, such as birth, baptism and marriage records, and Irish census records.

Further Reading

Naturalization Records

- McClure, Rhonda. *Portable Genealogist: U.S. Naturalization.* Boston: NEHGS, 2013.
- National Archives, Naturalization Records, www.archives.gov/research/naturalization/naturalization.html.
- Schaefer, Christina K. *Guide to Naturalization Records of the United States.* Baltimore: Genealogical Pub. Co., 1997.
- United States Naturalization and Citizenship wiki, FamilySearch.org/learn/wiki/en/United_States_Naturalization_and_Citizenship.

Passenger Arrival Records

- Coleman, Terry. *Going to America.* New York: Pantheon Books, 1972; rept. Baltimore: Genealogical Publishing Co., 1998.
- Colletta, John Philip. *They Came in Ships: A Guide to Finding Your Immigrant Ancestor's Arrival Record.* Orem, Utah: Ancestry, 2002.
- Dobson, David. *Ships from Ireland to Early America, 1623–1850.* Baltimore: Printed for Clearfield Company by Genealogical Publishing Co., 1999–2004.
- Mitchell, Brian. *Irish Passenger Lists, 1803–1806: Lists of Passengers Sailing from Ireland to America: Extracted from the Hardwicke Papers.* Baltimore: Genealogical Publishing Co, 1995.
- Mitchell, Brian. *Irish Passenger Lists, 1847–1871: Lists of Passengers Sailing from Londonderry to America on Ships of the J. & J. Cooke Line and the McCorkell Line.* Baltimore: Genealogical Publishing Co., 1988.
- Tepper, Michael. *American Passenger Arrival Records: A Guide to the Records of Immigrants Arriving at American Ports by Sail and Steam.* Baltimore: Genealogical Publishing Co., 1993.
- Tepper, Michael, and Ira A. Glazier. *The Famine Immigrants: Lists of Irish immigrants Arriving at the Port of New York, 1846–1851.* Baltimore: Genealogical Publishing Co., 1983–1986.
- Schlegel, Donald M. *Passengers from Ireland: Lists of Passengers Arriving at American Ports between 1811 and 1817.* Baltimore: Genealogical Publishing Co., 1980.
- Immigration Records (Ship Passenger Arrival Records), National Archives, www.archives.gov/research/immigration.
- US Immigration Passenger Arrival Records, FamilySearch.org wiki, FamilySearch.org/learn/wiki/en/US_Immigration_Passenger_Arrival_Records.

Chapter 5
Researching Your Ancestors through Gravestones, Newspapers, and Business Records

Although records of citizenship and travel often indicate the origins of immigrants, sometimes you need to consult other sources, such as gravestone inscriptions, newspapers, business records, and the archives of fraternal organizations. These other records can help you to determine where in Ireland your ancestors originated.

Find Relevant Gravestone Inscriptions

In the eighteenth and nineteenth centuries, many Irish immigrants in North America included their places of origins on family gravestones. Not all Irish immigrants had gravestones, or if they did, the gravestones did not survive or are now so worn as to be illegible. But gravestones with useful information occur often enough to make them worth locating.

In small communities, there may be only one graveyard in town, making the task of locating the cemetery easy. In large cities, however, locating a gravestone can be daunting, especially since many cemetery records are either missing or deficient. Check the death record, which may indicate the place of burial and the undertaker. Other helpful clues might come from the fact that, in larger cities, many graveyards can be categorized by religion and time period. Until the twentieth century, most Catholics were buried in Catholic graveyards. In many cities, Catholic graveyards are located outside the city center in surrounding "streetcar" suburbs, since the density of land development in the city center precluded acquiring enough open land for a cemetery. The development of many cemeteries was frequently chronological rather than geographic. That is, since grave lots were sold when the burial ground was established, a person who died in the mid-nineteenth century is not likely to be buried in a seventeenth-century graveyard.

For example, a resident of Charlestown, Massachusetts, who died in 1875 may not have been buried in the Charlestown Catholic Cemetery on Bunker Hill, which was established in 1830, since most of the lots in that cemetery were sold by 1850. Nineteenth-century Irish graveyards tended to fill up quickly since mortality rates were high. Look for graveyards established closest to the year of your ancestor's death. Checking sources such as *A Guide to Massachusetts Cemeteries* by David Allan Lambert (Boston: NEHGS, 2009) will reveal that Holy Cross Cemetery in Malden would be a more likely location for an 1875 burial of a Charlestown Catholic.

But families may have purchased a grave lot in a much earlier time period for the burial of a child. Therefore, a 75-year-old parent who died in 1875 could be buried in a lot that was purchased in 1830 for a deceased child. Looking at the history of the family over time, especially at the lives and deaths of the children, may help determine where an immigrant ancestor is buried.

Newspaper obituaries—full articles summarizing the life of the deceased—may also name the graveyard of the deceased's burial, but ordinary one- or two-line death notices of the nineteenth and early twentieth century do not usually list the burial place. Look for local newspapers or a regional newspaper published in a nearby city, which would include news of many surrounding towns. Many newspapers are now being digitized and are searchable on the web: see the website of New England Historic Genealogical Society (NEHGS), AmericanAncestors.org, as well as newspapers.com and genealogybank.com. The latter has several Irish newspapers based in New York City. Local libraries may have subscriptions to online newspaper archives and offer remote access to town residents. For a comprehensive list of online newspaper archives, consult www.cyndislist.com.

> **To-Do List**
> - Determine the cemetery and its location.
> - Find the gravestone within the burial ground.
> - Make note of other gravestones in the cemetery.
> - Consult online and printed sources.
> - Be wary of the information gleaned.

Once you determine the location of the cemetery, you need to find the specific grave. Burial records may refer to a row and a grave number, and rectangular graveyards may be laid out in a grid. In those cases, locating the grave is relatively easy and straightforward. Without this sort of information, the search can be more challenging. It can be helpful to recall that the grave lots were sold consecutively over time. So graveyards will often be laid out from the oldest to the newest sections. Look at the dates of death inscribed on the other gravestones to get a sense of the layout.

Don't focus solely on your ancestor. Make note of the other gravestones in the burial ground. The information inscribed on them may reveal a cluster of immigrants from specific areas in Ireland. Write down the inscriptions of others with the same surname. Perhaps your ancestor did not have a gravestone but his or her cousin did. Keeping a wide focus will lead to more success.

Consult websites and printed sources of gravestone inscriptions, such as www.findagrave.com or *Tombstones of the Irish Born: Cemetery of the Holy Cross, Flatbush, Brooklyn* by Joseph M. Silinonte (Bowie, Md.: Heritage Books, 1994). When viewing online sources, look at the inscriptions on the other gravestones in the cemetery. Even if you strike out with your own ancestor, the other gravestones in the cemetery may help reveal the origins of other Irish immigrants in the area.

Figure 5.1 below, from Chapel Hill Cemetery in Trescott, Maine, the gravestone of John McQuaig shows he was a native of Rathlin Island, County Antrim. A number of other gravestones near his indicate a Rathlin Island birthplace. Although the burial ground is located in Trescott, the Rathlin Island immigrants lived primarily in Lubec and Pembroke. At the time of the Great Famine, hundreds of Rathlin Islanders settled in Washington County, Maine.[1]

The information on gravestones isn't foolproof and should be viewed with some skepticism, since the data could have been transcribed incorrectly by the stonecutter. In addition, some monuments are erected years after the person died, with the information obtained from oral history rather than primary sources such as death records. Even death records can be erroneous, since the informant is often the undertaker, who obtains the information from the bereaved family. The age upon death in particular should be viewed with circumspection.

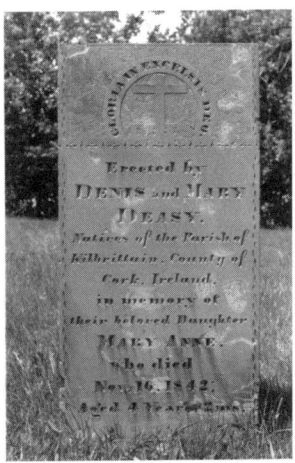

Figure 5.1. Gravestones showing Irish places of origin.

The place name in Ireland is often misspelled on gravestones, since the families were often illiterate, and the stone carvers were unfamiliar with Irish names and places. So it may take some imagination and patience to decipher the place of birth on a gravestone. King Sale, County Cork, is probably Kinsale. County Mede is probably County Meath, and so on. One good source for determining place names is *General Alphabetical Index to the Townlands and Towns, Parishes and Baronies of Ireland: Based on the Census of Ireland for the Year 1851* (Baltimore: Genealogical Publishing Co., 1984), otherwise known as the "Townland Index." The book contains alphabetical listings of townlands, parishes, and baronies. Another online source is the place name search function at John Grenham's website, www.JohnGrenham.com. The site allows you to perform wildcard searches for parts of place names, which is especially useful in discerning corrupted or hard-to-read places on

---

[1] Marie E. Daly, "Rathlin Islanders Down East," *Nexus*, 6: 6 (1989).

gravestones. For gravestone inscriptions, see Find A Grave, findagrave.com, a site that relies on volunteer efforts to transcribe and photograph graveyards not only in the United States, but in other countries as well. But keep in mind that negative results on a search do not mean that no gravestone exists, but rather that no one has transcribed the gravestone.

Include Newspaper Records in Your Search

Newspapers can provide a wealth of information about the origins of Irish immigrants, in obituaries, biographical notices, and "missing friends advertisements." In the nineteenth century, the cities of the East Coast supported numerous newspapers, often associated with political points of view or ethnic groups. Not necessarily focused on only one location, these newspapers reported on news from across the country and beyond. The example below was taken from a New York City newspaper, the *Irish American Weekly,* but it reported on deaths from San Francisco, Baltimore, and Chicago. This newspaper is searchable online at GenealogyBank, www.genealogybank.com.

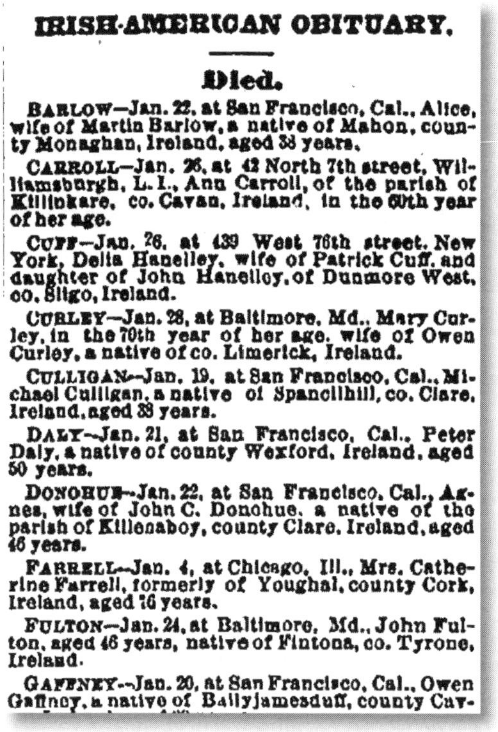

IRISH-AMERICAN OBITUARY.

Died.

BARLOW—Jan. 22, at San Francisco, Cal., Alice, wife of Martin Barlow, a native of Mahon, county Monaghan, Ireland, aged 38 years.

CARROLL—Jan. 26, at 42 North 7th street, Williamsburgh, L. I., Ann Carroll, of the parish of Killinkare, co. Cavan, Ireland, in the 60th year of her age.

CUFF—Jan. 26, at 139 West 76th street, New York, Delia Hanelley, wife of Patrick Cuff, and daughter of John Hanelley, of Dunmore West, co. Sligo, Ireland.

CURLEY—Jan. 28, at Baltimore, Md., Mary Curley, in the 70th year of her age, wife of Owen Curley, a native of co. Limerick, Ireland.

CULLIGAN—Jan. 19, at San Francisco, Cal., Michael Culligan, a native of Spancilhill, co. Clare, Ireland, aged 38 years.

DALY—Jan. 21, at San Francisco, Cal., Peter Daly, a native of county Wexford, Ireland, aged 50 years.

DONOHUE—Jan. 22, at San Francisco, Cal., Agnes, wife of John C. Donohue, a native of the parish of Killenaboy, county Clare, Ireland, aged 46 years.

FARRELL—Jan. 4, at Chicago, Ill., Mrs. Catherine Farrell, formerly of Youghal, county Cork, Ireland, aged 76 years.

FULTON—Jan. 24, at Baltimore, Md., John Fulton, aged 46 years, native of Fintona, co. Tyrone, Ireland.

GAFFNEY—Jan. 20, at San Francisco, Cal., Owen Gaffney, a native of Ballyjamesduff, county Cav-

Figure 5.2. Death notices in the *Irish American Weekly* newspaper, New York, February 2, 1877.

The *Boston Pilot* newspaper published death notices and obituaries from various locations in the United States and Canada. In 1864, the *Boston Pilot* charged 25 cents for a death notice and $1 for an obituary. The following is an example: "Died in Albany, NY, December 28th, 1863—BRIDGET, wife of James BURKE, aged 53 years. She was a native of Nanagh, Co. Tipperary, Ireland. . . ."

In the nineteenth century, a family's immigration was often accomplished in stages: one person left first, established himself or herself, and sent money back to Ireland to fund the passages of other family members. In the chaos of the Great Famine, the Irish fled in whatever ship they could find, sailing to whatever port they could afford. Communication lines were poor, and families often lost track of each other. Family members frequently placed advertisements in Irish American newspapers, such as the *Boston Pilot,* seeking lost siblings, parents, or children. Because the ads frequently mentioned the place of origin in Ireland, they are extremely useful for genealogists. Some 35,000 ads were placed between 1831 and 1916 in the *Boston Pilot* alone.[2]

Here's an example of how newspaper records such as immigrant advertisements can help you in your genealogical search. Say you were to research President John F. Kennedy's Fitzgerald ancestors in the North End of Boston. You would see that his great-great-grandfather, Thomas Fitzgerald, was naturalized in the United States District Court in Boston on April 29, 1857.[3] The birthplace was recorded as County Limerick—which doesn't give enough information to find the family in Ireland. Note, however, that one of the witnesses to the naturalization petition was an Edmond Fitzgerald. (See Chapter 3, Using North American Church Records to Widen Your Search, for a discussion of Edmond Fitzgerald as a sponsor at the baptism of Michael Fitzgerald, a child of Thomas Fitzgerald.)

Your next step would be to search the NEHGS database *Irish Immigrant Advertisements, 1831–1920 (Search for Missing Friends)* at AmericanAncestors.org. You would enter Fitzgerald in the surname field and Boston in the field for place of last residence. See Figure 5.3.

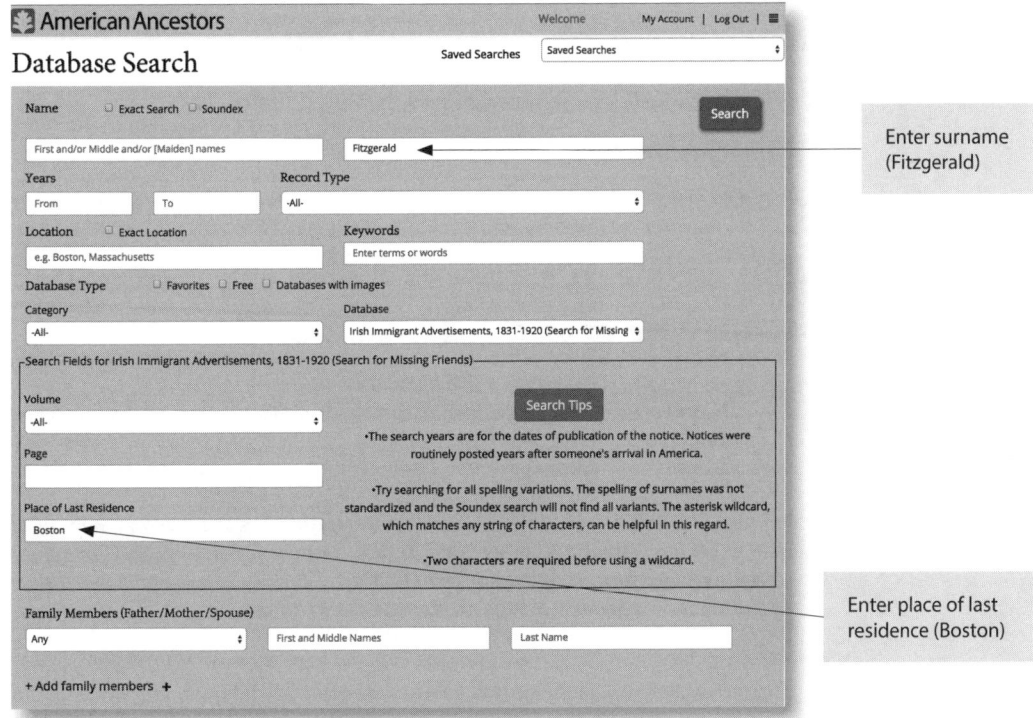

Figure 5.3. *Missing Friends* database search page, AmericanAncestors.org.

---

[2] The *Boston Pilot* is available on microfilm at the New England Historic Genealogical Society; at libraries in Boston, New York City, and Chicago: and at numerous university libraries. NEHGS has transcribed the ads from the *Pilot* and placed them in a searchable database, *Irish Immigrant Advertisements, 1831–1920 (Search for Missing Friends)* at its website, AmericanAncestors.org.

[3] United States District Court, Boston, Massachusetts, Naturalization Petition, vol. 26, p. 64.

Twenty-nine results come back. You have to scan through all of them, but it is better to be more inclusive than too exact. If you had typed "Thomas Fitzgerald" in the name fields, you would have missed this important information: an 1857 advertisement placed by Edmond Fitzgerald of 192 North Street (a North End address), Boston. He was looking for his son, James Fitzgerald, a native of the parish of Bruff, County Limerick. (See Figure 5.4.) Edmond Fitzgerald was the godfather of one of Thomas Fitzgerald's children and a witness to Thomas Fitzgerald's naturalization petition. So here is a good clue that the Fitzgerald family came from Bruff, County Limerick.[4]

You can manipulate the database to show other information. For instance, you can leave the name fields blank and type Bruff in the keyword field to see where other people from Bruff, County Limerick, settled. You can also leave the name fields blank and enter the town of last residence to see where people in an American town came from. This technique works only for smaller towns, since you will have too many results for large cities such as Boston, Philadelphia, or Montreal.

Missing Friends   11

24 January 1857   *INFORMATION WANTED*

OF THOMAS REILLY, Antwerp, N Y, at the PILOT Office.

OF JAMES FLAVEN, formerly of Chicago, Ill, at the PILOT Office.

OF WILLIAM ROBINSON, from the north of Ireland, who left Oswego 6 years ago. Information received by Rev Mr Kelly, Oswego, N Y.

OF JAMES COSTELLO, who formely [sic] resided at 187 Washington street, New York. He will hear of something much to his advantage by addressing Thomas Leo, Care of Geo F Hooper Esq, Colorado River, Cal.

$10 Reward.
OF JOHN and PATRICK MALONEY, from Gibbonstown, parish Bulligiddon [co. Limerick]; when last heard of were in Cambridge county 2 years ago. Please address their afflicted mother, Catherine Maloney, Manayunk P O, Pa.

OF JAMES FITZGERALD, wheelwright by trade, aged 21 years, native of parish Bruff [co. Limerick], who came to this country 7 years ago; left Boston 1 year ago last October, and has not been heard from since. Please address his father, Edmond Fitzgerald, 192 North street, Boston, Mass.

Figure 5.4. Advertisement for James Fitzgerald placed by Edmond Fitzgerald in the *Boston Pilot*, transcribed in *Irish Immigrant Advertisements, 1831–1920 (Search for Missing Friends)* database, AmericanAncestors.org.

---

[4] *Irish Immigrant Advertisements, 1831–1920 (Search for Missing Friends),* online database, AmericanAncestors.org.

> **Sources for newspaper "missing friends" ads, biographical notices, obituaries, and vital statistics**
>
> - *Irish Immigrant Advertisements, 1831–1920 (Search for Missing Friends)*, online database, AmericanAncestors.org. Originally published as *The Search for Missing Friends: Irish Immigrant Advertisements Placed in The Boston Pilot 1831–1920, Vols. 1–8,* edited by Ruth-Ann M. Harris and B. Emer O'Keeffe (Boston: NEHGS, 1989).
> - *Boston Pilot* [newspaper on microfilm] (Boston: Graphic Service Corporation [for the Archdiocese of Boston], 1937).
> - *Voices of the Irish Immigrant: Information Wanted Ads in "The Truth Teller" New York City, 1825–1844,* compiled by Diane Fitzpatrick Haberstroh and Laura Murphy DeGrazia (New York: New York Genealogical and Biographical Society, 2005).
> - GenealogyBank newspapers:
>   *Irish American Weekly (New York, New York) Newspaper Archives* (1849–1914)
>   *Irish World (New York, New York) Newspaper Archives* (1890–1905)
>   *Shamrock (New York, New York) Newspaper Archives* (1810–1817)
>   *Western Star (New York, New York) Newspaper Archives* (1812–1813)
>   *Exile (New York, New York) Newspaper Archives* (1817–1817)
>   *Irish Citizen (New York, New York) Newspaper Archives* (1867–1868)
>   *Irish Nation (New York, New York) Newspaper Archives* (1881–1883)

From 1842 through 1844, numerous "repeal societies" formed in support of Daniel O'Connell's quest to repeal the Act of Union between Great Britain and Ireland. Meetings were held throughout Irish communities in the United States and Canada, and some newspapers reported the names and origins of the attendees. The reports typically listed the attendees, their Irish county of origin, and their donation amount. The *Boston Pilot,* in particular, reported on meetings not only in large communities such as Boston, Portland, Providence, and Springfield, but also in small villages such as Dalton and Stockbridge, Massachusetts. The *Albany Evening Journal* reported on meetings in West Troy and Albany, and those reports have been made available online on the Old Fulton NY Post Cards website, www.fultonhistory.com. The Family History Library has a wiki about using the Old Fulton NY Post Card website, listing all the newspapers in its database: FamilySearch.org/learn/wiki/en/Old_Fulton_NY_Post_Cards.

Access Historic Business Records

With the large influx of Irish immigrants to America, many businesses sprang up to provide financial services and to meet the needs of a transplanted community. For instance, business agents assisted with the widespread practice of transferring money back home. And some savings and loan institutions catered specifically to immigrant markets, providing bank services to groups working hard

> Rev. John O'Brien, co Clare 5; G B Wager, Esq, Harper's Ferry, Va., 5; John Jamison Esq, Martinsburg, Va, 5; Wm H Moore, Harper's Ferry Va, 1; Dr Jas Garry, T'uam 5; P Cunningham, co Donegal 5; R D Doran, King's co 4.25, James Larkin do 1; John McCormick do 1; Wm Lover co Cork 1; Saml Lover do 1; Mary Lover do 1; Martin Grace co Kilkenny 1; Wm Megran co Down 1; Edw Fitzpatrick Queen's co 1; Thos Burly co Roscommon 1; Edw'd Savan, King's co 1; Pat McGuire co Fermanagh 1; Mich McGuire do 1; Martin Broderick co Longford 1; Laughlin Sloan co Down 1; John Payne Jefferson co Va 1; John G Stephens do 1; Tim Cahill co Kilkenny 1; Pat Farrell King's co 1; John Savan do 1; Pat Wynne do 1; Mat Sinnett co Kilkenny 1; Thos Hannegan co Donegal 1; Wm Hannegan do 1; Tim Sullivan co Cork 1; Dan Sweeney do 1; John Crowley do 1; Jas Conlan co Louth 1; Ed McGuigan do 1; Mich McKenny King's co 1; Philip Burkhart, Jefferson co, Va 1; Ed Tierney do 1; Jas Tierney do 2; Arnold S Stephens do 1; Geo Berkeley, Germany 1; Jas Sheridan co Monaghan 1; John Little Pennsylvania 1; Rich McCabe co Meath 1; Peter Little do 1; Chris Montague do 1; John Murray do 1; Rob Lewis co Wexford 1; Alex'r Kelly co Kilkenny 1; Pat Shea do 2; Benjamin Cooke co Derry 1; Geo Caldwell, Emmitsburg, Md 1; Jas Mulligan,

Figure 5.5. Subscribers to Harpers Ferry (West Virginia) repeal association, published in the *Boston Pilot,* August 5, 1843.

to get established. These business activities created information-rich records of transactions and accounts, with details about customers and their families and backgrounds. If the documents have survived and are findable, they can aid you in learning about your ancestor's place of origin in Ireland.

Business agents

Many Irish immigrants to America sent money back to Ireland to help support their families and to pay for the passages of their relatives. In both large cities and small towns, business agents worked in Irish American communities to provide financial services to transfer money and tickets to Ireland. Their records often contain the name and address of the sender and the name and address of the recipient, therefore potentially providing you with crucial information about your ancestor's link back to Ireland. See, for example, Figure 5.6, an excerpt from a business agent's records published by the Central New York Genealogical Society in its journal, *Tree Talks*. Business agent records may be hidden in local archives around the country, unrecognized by Irish American genealogists. Since business agents sometimes placed advertisements in local newspapers, researching newspapers may be one way to identify a business agent operating in the area where your ancestor lived. Once identified, you will then have to search for his records—if they were preserved. They can be in any number of archives or libraries of local municipalities, states, universities, or private organizations.

1852, Oct. 22	George Verian Sends to Mrs. George Verian, Rooska West, Bantry, Cork Co., Ireland $30.00
1852, Dec. 29	Michael Ryan sends to John Ryan – Limerick City. Care of John Fitz Gerald of Rosboyan [Rosbrien], Ireland. Wishes his brothers passage paid & the bal paid to him. $21.00

Figure 5.6. Business agent entries from Broome and Delaware Counties, New York.

Bank records

Records of bank depositors can also be another source for documenting an ancestor's Irish origins. The most well-known collection of banking records is the *New York Emigrant Savings Bank, 1850–1883*, available on microfilm, and also as a database at Ancestry.com. In the days before photo identifications, banks kept detailed information about the depositors, such as name, address, birthplace, next of kin, and passenger ships.

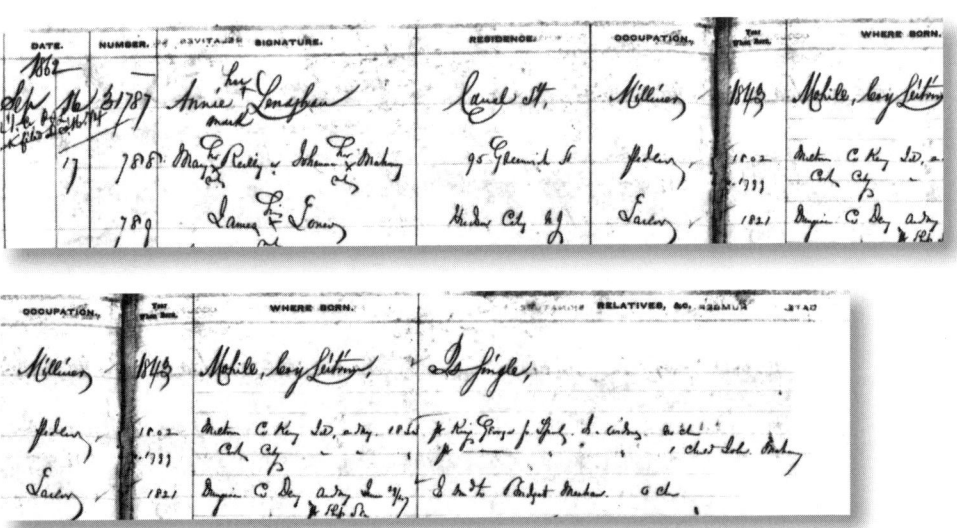

Figure 5.7. Records for Annie Lenaghan, Mary Reilly, Johanna Mahoney, and James Toner indicating address, occupation, birth year, birthplace, and relatives, New York Emigrant Savings Bank, September 16, 1862.

Other banking institutions can be equally useful in supplying information about Irish immigrants. Some of the records have been collected by various archives. In the case of the Old Stone Bank of Providence, Rhode Island (formerly the Providence Institution for Savings, founded in 1819 as a mutual savings bank), its records are preserved at the Rhode Island Historical Society. The incoming correspondence of depositors from 1885 to 1897 has been partially abstracted and are available on the website of the Rhode Island Historical Society, www.rihs.org. After 1882, signature books in this collection routinely gave a depositor's birthplace. Other bank records are located in archives such as the Boston Athenaeum, Boston College, the Massachusetts Historical Society, and the Historical Society of Pennsylvania.

Although bank records can be useful, finding them can take some patient research. In large cities, Irish immigrants tended to favor certain banks, perhaps as a result of a more welcoming attitude on the bank's part. Inventories in probate records of wills and administrations often detailed the name of the bank and the amount in the account of the deceased. Even if your own ancestor did not leave a probate record with a detailed inventory, researching other Irish immigrants in the same neighborhood will give you a starting point. City directories frequently listed the banks, with accompanying addresses and lists of officers.

Small towns or small cities may have had only one bank. Researching the history of the town, local directories, newspapers, and probate records will help identify the banks. Many banks in the nineteenth century were established through an act of the state legislature, and the acts and resolves of the legislature can be searched online or in print at state archives. (See Figure 5.8.)

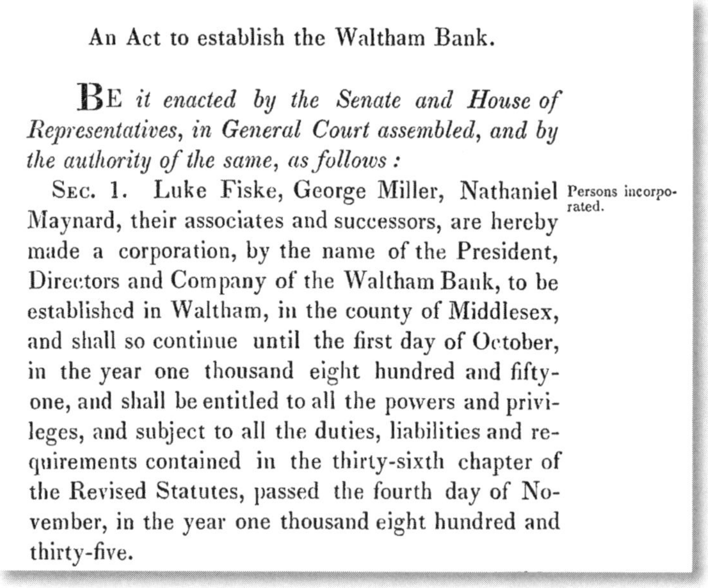

An Act to establish the Waltham Bank.

BE *it enacted by the Senate and House of Representatives, in General Court assembled, and by the authority of the same, as follows:*

SEC. 1. Luke Fiske, George Miller, Nathaniel Maynard, their associates and successors, are hereby made a corporation, by the name of the President, Directors and Company of the Waltham Bank, to be established in Waltham, in the county of Middlesex, and shall so continue until the first day of October, in the year one thousand eight hundred and fifty-one, and shall be entitled to all the powers and privileges, and subject to all the duties, liabilities and requirements contained in the thirty-sixth chapter of the Revised Statutes, passed the fourth day of November, in the year one thousand eight hundred and thirty-five. — Persons incorporated.

Figure 5.8. 1836 Chap. 0253 Act to Establish the Waltham Bank, Acts and Resolves Passed by the General Court, Massachusetts.

Once you have identified a likely bank, the next step is to determine the bank's status. Many banks are no longer operating under their original names, having merged with, or been taken over by, other banks. The U.S. Federal Reserve System operates a useful website, National Information Center (ffiec.gov), which allows researchers to track the history and status of a financial institution. If the acquiring bank is still in business, you can contact the current bank to determine the status of historical records. Many national banks have archives where historical records of the institution are stored. For instance, Wells Fargo Bank, founded in 1852, maintains corporate archives in San Francisco, as well as several corporate history museums.[5] But if the records have not been preserved nor made available, you might be out of luck in pursuing this avenue.

In the example shown in Figure 5.9, a researcher wanted to find what happened to the Waltham Savings Bank, which was founded in 1853. The bank went through several mergers over its nearly 150-year history. It was renamed Sterling Bank in 1990, and then acquired by Fleet Bank in 1994. If you search on the Online Computer Library Center (OCLC) website ArchiveGrid, you will find the records were deposited in the Massachusetts Historical Society. (As explained in Chapter 3, ArchiveGrid is an online catalog that searches records of archival collections held by thousands of libraries, museums, historical societies, and archives. It is a good resource for locating local and state collections that may include business records.)

Event Date	Historical Event
1853-03-19	WALTHAM SAVINGS BANK located at WALTHAM, MA was established as a State Savings Bank.
1987-10-01	WALTHAM SAVINGS BANK **moved** to 1 MOODY ST WALTHAM, MA.
1990-11-02	WALTHAM SAVINGS BANK was **renamed** to STERLING BANK and **moved** to 1 MOODY STREET WALTHAM, MA.
1994-08-16	STERLING BANK was **acquired** by FLEET BANK OF MASSACHUSETTS, NATIONAL ASSOCIATION.
1994-08-16	STERLING BANK was **renamed** to STERLING MAIN BR and **became** a branch of FLEET BANK OF MASSACHUSETTS, NATIONAL ASSOCIATION.
2000-06-17	Institution is **closed**.

Figure 5.9. Institutional History of the Waltham Savings Bank
National Information Center, United States Federal Reserve System.

Examine the Records of Fraternal Organizations

In the nineteenth century, fraternal organizations provided outlets for social and civic life in cities and towns throughout America. Many were organized around the provision of benefits, particularly life insurance. Their records, when preserved, can document birthplaces in Ireland, as well as other important data.

---

[5] www.wellsfargohistory.com/archives.

Masonic lodges

Freemasonry is the oldest and largest fraternal organization in the world. Each lodge belonged to a Grand Lodge, and there is a Grand Lodge in every state. Each Grand Lodge is sovereign, so there is no master database of records covering the entire country. To find the name and address of Masonic Grand Lodges around the world and in the United States, you can access the Masons' website: masonicinfo.com/grandlodges.htm.

Membership applications to Freemasonry lodges occasionally document detailed birthplaces in Ireland. Although many Grand Lodges will provide information for free, others, such as New York, charge a fee to search their records. Some state records, such as those of California and Arkansas, burned.[6] The membership cards of the Grand Lodge of Massachusetts are available online at AmericanAncestors.org: Massachusetts, Grand Lodge of Masons Membership Cards, 1733–1990. Figure 5.10 shows an example.

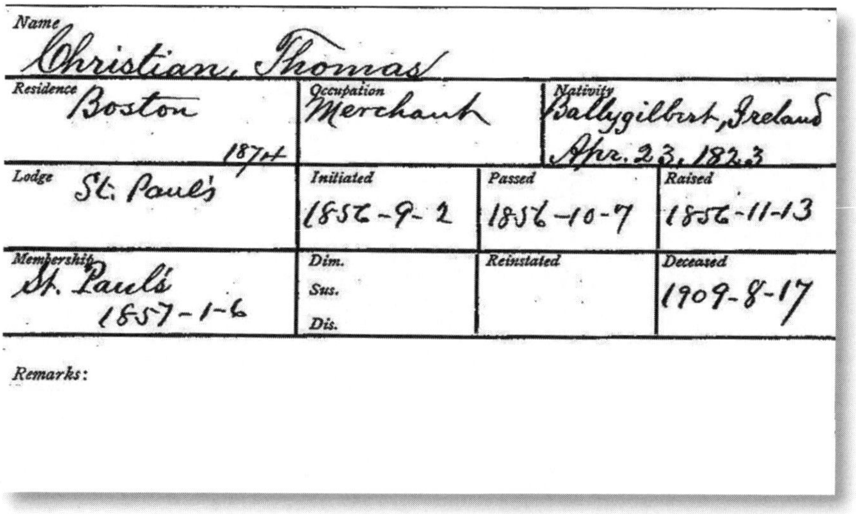

Name Christian, Thomas
Residence Boston 1874
Occupation Merchant
Nativity Ballygilbert, Ireland Apr. 23, 1823
Lodge St. Paul's
Initiated 1856-9-2
Passed 1856-10-7
Raised 1856-11-13
Membership St. Pauls 1857-1-6
Dim.
Sus.
Dis.
Reinstated
Deceased 1909-8-17
Remarks:

Figure 5.10. Membership card of Thomas Christian,
St. Paul's Masonic Lodge, Boston, Massachusetts.

Catholic Order of Foresters

In 1879, members of the St. Vincent de Paul Society in Boston organized the Massachusetts Catholic Order of Foresters to provide insurance benefits to its mainly Irish immigrant members. By 1930, there were sixty thousand members in Massachusetts. The organization changed its name to the Catholic Association of Foresters in 1958. A similar but separate organization established in Chicago in 1884 was named the Catholic Order of Foresters of Illinois.

The Irish Ancestral Research Association (TIARA) was granted ownership of the records of the Massachusetts Catholic Order of Foresters and then deeded owner-

6 "Now What? Online: Researching Ancestors Who Were Freemasons," *Family Tree Magazine*, posted 12/12/2011, familytreemagazine.com/article/Now-What-Freemason-Records.

ship to the University of Massachusetts Boston. The records from 1880 to 1935 have been digitized and will eventually be available on the Family History Library website, FamilySearch.org. The records (see Figure 5.11) include applications, beneficiary records, correspondence, and death disbursements. The records are preserved and maintained in the Joseph P. Healey Library of the University of Massachusetts Boston. New index records are being added monthly; records more than 72 years old may be requested by researchers. An index to the records—and information about how to cobtain a copy of a record—is available on the TIARA website, tiara.ie. Start by selecting Foresters Project under the Projects dropdown and search the index on the TIARA website.

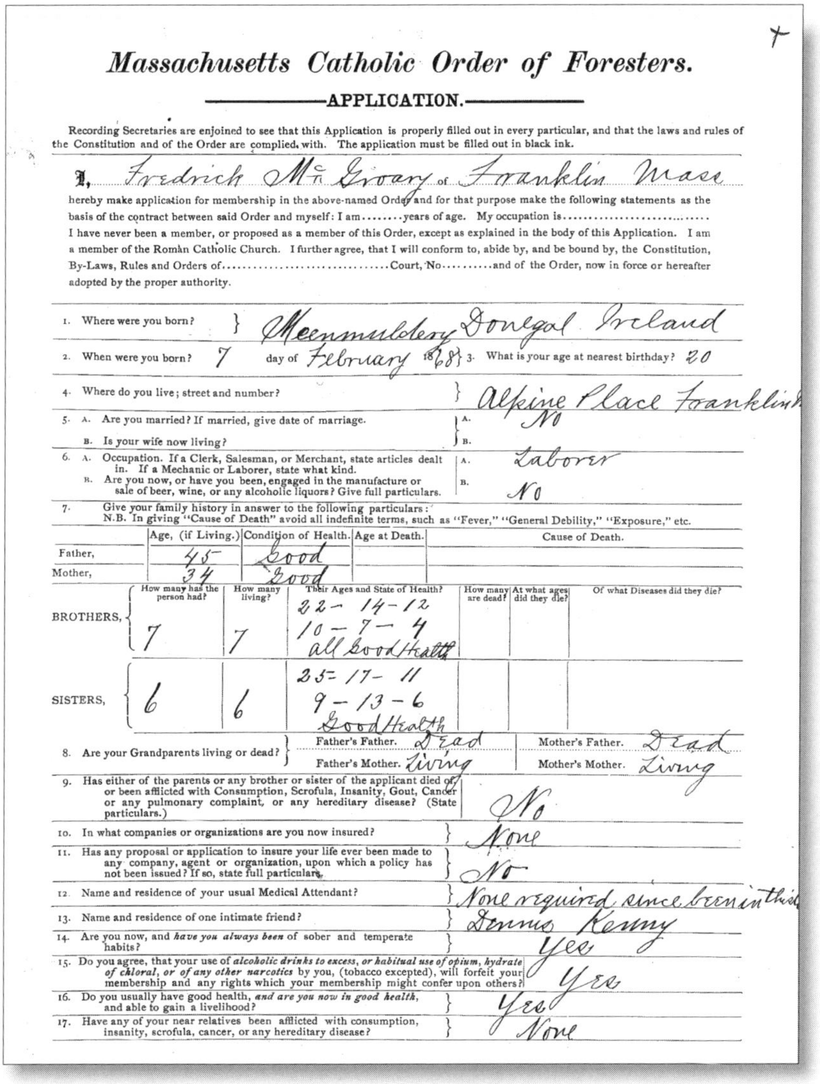

Massachusetts Catholic Order of Foresters.

—APPLICATION.—

Recording Secretaries are enjoined to see that this Application is properly filled out in every particular, and that the laws and rules of the Constitution and of the Order are complied with. The application must be filled out in black ink.

I, Fredrick Mc Groary of Franklin Mass hereby make application for membership in the above-named Order and for that purpose make the following statements as the basis of the contract between said Order and myself: I am........years of age. My occupation is.......................... I have never been a member, or proposed as a member of this Order, except as explained in the body of this Application. I am a member of the Roman Catholic Church. I further agree, that I will conform to, abide by, and be bound by, the Constitution, By-Laws, Rules and Orders of..............................Court, No..........and of the Order, now in force or hereafter adopted by the proper authority.

1. Where were you born? } Meenmuldery Donegal Ireland
2. When were you born? 7 day of February 1868 } 3. What is your age at nearest birthday? 20
4. Where do you live; street and number? } Alpine Place Franklin
5. A. Are you married? If married, give date of marriage. A. No
   B. Is your wife now living? B.
6. A. Occupation. If a Clerk, Salesman, or Merchant, state articles dealt in. If a Mechanic or Laborer, state what kind. A. Laborer
   B. Are you now, or have you been, engaged in the manufacture or sale of beer, wine, or any alcoholic liquors? Give full particulars. B. No
7. Give your family history in answer to the following particulars: N.B. In giving "Cause of Death" avoid all indefinite terms, such as "Fever," "General Debility," "Exposure," etc.

	Age, (if Living.)	Condition of Health.	Age at Death.	Cause of Death.
Father,	45	Good		
Mother,	34	Good		

	How many has the person had?	How many living?	Their Ages and State of Health?	How many are dead?	At what ages did they die?	Of what Diseases did they die?
BROTHERS,	7	7	22 – 14 – 12 10 – 7 – 4 all Good Health			
SISTERS,	6	6	25 – 17 – 11 9 – 13 – 6 Good Health			

8. Are your Grandparents living or dead? } Father's Father. Dead | Mother's Father. Dead | Father's Mother. Living | Mother's Mother. Living
9. Has either of the parents or any brother or sister of the applicant died of, or been afflicted with Consumption, Scrofula, Insanity, Gout, Cancer or any pulmonary complaint, or any hereditary disease? (State particulars.) No
10. In what companies or organizations are you now insured? } None
11. Has any proposal or application to insure your life ever been made to any company, agent or organization, upon which a policy has not been issued? If so, state full particulars. } No
12. Name and residence of your usual Medical Attendant? } None required since been in this
13. Name and residence of one intimate friend? } Dennis Kenny
14. Are you now, and *have you always been* of sober and temperate habits? } Yes
15. Do you agree, that your use of *alcoholic drinks to excess, or habitual use of opium, hydrate of chloral, or of any other narcotics* by you, (tobacco excepted), will forfeit your membership and any rights which your membership might confer upon others? Yes
16. Do you usually have good health, *and are you now in good health,* and able to gain a livelihood? } Yes
17. Have any of your near relatives been afflicted with consumption, insanity, scrofula, cancer, or any hereditary disease? } None

Figure 5.11. Membership application of Frederick McGroary of Franklin, Massachusetts, Massachusetts Catholic Order of Foresters.

Courtesy University Archives and Special Collections, University of Massachusetts Boston.

Summary

Records other than citizenship and travel documents can help you locate the origin of your family in Ireland. Because the records are not always digitized and searchable in databases, accessing the information may require visiting a graveyard or scanning through microfilm in a library. Nineteenth-century gravestone inscriptions might show at least county of origin, and sometimes even parish or townland, but the information can be inaccurate. Newspaper records, such as obituaries, "missing friends" advertisements, and repeal society reports, can shed a great deal of light on the lives of our ancestors. Business records are less frequently available and may require some in-depth investigation as to their existence and location. They may be still privately held, and accessing them will require diplomacy and cooperation. Records of fraternal and social organizations may document the birthplaces of immigrant; the status and availability of these records vary by locality. Although the sources mentioned in this chapter can be somewhat difficult to find and do not always provide easily accessible facts about an ancestor's links to Ireland, you will want to pursue these records for the valuable information they may contain and their inherent interest.

Further Reading

- Harris, Ruth-Ann M., and Donald M. Jacobs, editors; B. Emer O'Keeffe, associate editor; Dominique M. Pickett, assistant editor, *The Search for Missing Friends: Irish Immigrant Advertisements Placed in the* Boston Pilot. Boston: New England Historic Genealogical Society, 1989– .

- McVetty, Suzanne. "Using the Records of the Emigrant Savings Bank." *New York Genealogical and Biographical Society Newsletter,* Winter 1998.

- Murphy, Ronald Chase, and Janice Church Murphy. *Irish Famine Immigrants in the State of Vermont: Gravestone Inscriptions.* Baltimore: Clearfield, 2000.

- Rich, Kevin J. *Irish Immigrants of the Emigrant Industrial Savings Bank.* Massapequa, N.Y.: Broadway-Manhattan Co., 2001–2005.

 Chapter 6
Looking Further Back: Early Irish Immigration to North America

To trace an ancestor back to Ireland in the seventeenth and eighteenth centuries, you need to determine, if possible, the exact origin of the person in Ireland. In other words, what is true for immigrants who came later is true as well for those who came earlier. Irish records are organized by place, and Irish names, such as Sullivan, Montgomery, or Hamilton, are very common, so to sort out which John Sullivan or James Hamilton is an ancestor, you must narrow down the location of where your relative came from. And the best method for determining exact origin is to research in American records, not Irish records.

Trace the Outline of Seventeenth-Century Irish Immigration

Irish immigrants have been coming to North America since the seventeenth century, and perhaps even earlier. Historian Kerby A. Miller estimates that between fifty and a hundred thousand Irish men and women left for the colonies in the seventeenth century, many as indentured servants, convicts, and slaves.[1] On the other hand, other scholars have different estimates, stating that the number of Irish indentured servants arriving in the seventeenth century was approximately five thousand.[2] Additional immigrants were likely Anglo-Irish who had connections to English settlers of New England or Virginia. The origins and destinations of these early immigrants frequently reflected the trade routes among England, southern Ireland, the Caribbean, and North America. New England Puritans,

---

[1] Kerby A. Miller, *Emigrants and Exiles: Ireland and the Irish Exodus to North America* (New York: Oxford University Press, 1985), p. 137.

[2] Aaron S. Fogleman, "From Slaves, Convicts, and Servants to Free Passengers: The Transformation of Immigration in the Era of the American Revolution," *The Journal of American History* 85, no. 1 (June 1998): 46, 68. Fogleman estimated the breakdown of Irish immigrants from 1607 to 1699 as follows: indentured servants, 3,000; convicts and prisoners, 300; free, 1,700.

including leader John Winthrop, had connections to other Puritan settlements in Ireland, such as Bandon, a town with many Puritans in County Cork.[3] And in 1676, Rev. Increase Mather's brother in Dublin may have helped organize a ship delivering aid from Ireland to distressed colonists in New England, following King Philip's War.[4]

Irish Quakers who came to Pennsylvania beginning in 1682 are documented in an online source book, *Immigration of the Irish Quakers into Pennsylvania, 1682–1750: With Their Early History in Ireland* (available on www.archive.org, and Ancestry.com), which gives a good history and cites specific examples and sources.[5] Some historians have tried to determine the religion of the Irish colonists based upon their surnames, but this method is fraught with error. Unless the Irish settlers came as part of a group of religious refugees, the religion of these seventeenth-century immigrants is difficult to ascertain, since nearly all (except Quakers) joined the local Protestant churches upon arrival.

Research Seventeenth-Century Records with Resourcefulness

Researching these colonial arrivals is challenging at best, since records that detail their origins are rare. You will need to focus on American town vital records, records of the Virginia Company, records of early leaders, such as John Winthrop, John Smith, and Daniel Gookin,[6] church records, civil and criminal court records, probate records, and deeds. While the chances of success are poor with any one set of records, specific references occur with enough frequency to warrant thorough investigation of these records. For instance, Irish indentured servants who came to Ipswich, Massachusetts, on the ship *Goodfellow* in 1653 appear in early Essex County court records, where they claimed they had been kidnapped and sold against their wills.[7] Others may show up in early land records, such as John Moore of Ballehonicke (near Ladysbridge), County Cork, and Joseph Moore of Wexford town, sons of "the late Ann Hibbins" of Boston, who was hanged as a

---

[3] Francis J. Bremer, *John Winthrop: America's Forgotten Founding Father* (New York: Oxford University Press, 2003), p. 139.

[4] Charles Deane, "The Irish Donation in 1676," *The New England Historical and Genealogical Register 2*, no. 3 (July 1848): 245, 398.

[5] Albert Cook Myers, *Immigration of the Irish Quakers into Pennsylvania, 1682–1750: With Their Early History in Ireland* (Swarthmore, Pa.: the author, 1902)

[6] John Smith, *Generall Historie of Virginia, New England & the Summer Isles* (New York: Macmillan Company, 1907). "1621. The 22. of November arrived Master Gookin out of Ireland, with fifty men of his owne, and thirty passengers, exceedingly well furnished with all sorts of provision and cattle, and planted himself at Nurpors-newes."

[7] *Records and Files of the Quarterly Courts of Essex County, Massachusetts, Vol. II, 1656–1662* (Salem, Mass.: Essex Institute, 1912), pp. 294–295. "Defence of William Downing and Philip Welch: 'We were brought out of or owne Country, contrary to our Owne wills & minds, & sold here unto Mr Symonds, by ye master of the Ship, Mr Dill, but what Agreement was made between Mr Symonds & ye Said master, was neuer Acted by our Consent or knowledge." . . . Bill of sale, dated May 10, 1654, from George Dell, Master of the ship Goodfellow, who 'sould unto Mr Samuel Symonds two of the Irish youths I brought over by order of the State of England: the name of one of them is william Dalton: the other Edward welch, to serue him," 17th May 1654.

witch in 1656.[8] In fact, Suffolk County, Massachusetts, deeds show a number of seventeenth-century references to Ireland. These deeds help link early colonists with specific places in Ireland. One general source for seventeenth-century Irish immigrants in New England is Michael J. O'Brien's *Pioneer Irish in New England* (Baltimore: Genealogical Publishing Co., 1998).

However, for the descendant of the average indentured Irish servant in the seventeenth century, tracing the origins and ancestors will be impossible, due to the lack of records in America and Ireland. At best, you can determine the general area of origin in Ireland by the ship, if known, or by the general trade routes from Ireland to the American port.

Trace the Outline of Eighteenth-Century Irish Immigration

By the early eighteenth century, the number of Irish immigrants to North America increased significantly, and between 1700 and 1775, an estimated 108,000 arrived. Within this group, approximately 36 percent were indentured servants, 16 percent were convicts and prisoners, and 48 percent were free persons.[9] Although most immigrants were Presbyterian in this time period, the wave included Catholics, Anglicans, and Quakers as well.[10] Immigrants were both from southern Ireland and from Ulster province in the north. Many Scots Irish Presbyterians had earlier migrated to Ulster in "plantation" settlement programs backed by the British government, and at this time they were moving again, in search of better economic conditions and greater religious tolerance. In the 1710s, a series of harvest failures, a credit crisis, and falling demand for linen increased the number of people throughout all of Ireland who were looking elsewhere for opportunity.[11] Implementation of Penal Laws, affecting not only Catholics but also Presbyterians, generated additional grievances against the Church of Ireland hierarchy. Furthermore, many below-market leases of the 1690s were expiring, and landlords were raising rents exponentially. In Ulster province, tenants were able to sell improvements to property (called tenant right), which enabled 80 percent to fund passage to America as freely paying passengers.[12] So not only did Ulster Presbyterians have financial and religious incentives to emigrate, they also had the financial ability to do so.

---

[8] Suffolk County Deeds, Volume III, p. 82, in *Suffolk Deeds, Liber III* (Boston: Rockwell and Churchill, 1885); D. Brenton Simons, *Witches, Rakes, and Rogues: True Stories of Scam, Scandal, Murder, and Mayhem in Boston, 1630–1775* (Beverly, Mass.: Commonwealth Editions, 2005).

[9] "From Slaves, Convicts and Servants to Free Passengers: The Transformation of Immigration in the Era of the American Revolution," *The Journal of American History* 85, no. 2 (June 1998): 71, at jstor.org/stable/2568431.

[10] Fogleman, "Migrations to the Thirteen British North American Colonies, 1700–1775: New Estimates," *The Journal of Interdisciplinary History* 22, no. 4 (Spring 1992): 691–709, at jstor.org/stable/205241.

[11] Patrick Griffin, "The People with No Name: Ulster's Migrants and Identity Formation in Eighteenth Century Pennsylvania," *The William and Mary Quarterly*, 3rd ser., 58, no. 3 (July 2001): 591, at jstor.org/stable/2674296.

[12] Ibid., pp. 591–592.

The first mass migrations occurred between 1717 and 1719, when hundreds of Ulster Presbyterians sailed for New England and Delaware River ports.[13] In New England, a good portion of the migration resulted from correspondence and a possible meeting among Rev. Cotton Mather, William Homes (a sea captain engaged trade between Great Britain and America), his son, Robert Homes, and some land speculators who wanted settlers for the Kennebec River area in Maine. Elsewhere, in 1718 Reverend William Boyd petitioned Massachusetts Governor Samuel Shute, on behalf of the Presbyterians of the area of the River Bann in Ulster, inquiring about the possibility of their sailing for Massachusetts.[14] In the decade between 1720 and 1730, the wave of early eighteenth-century Irish immigration averaged about a thousand passengers per year arriving in New Castle, Delaware, with the number of new arrivals cresting between 1727 and 1730.[15] Other areas also saw a welcome influx. In the 1730s, South Carolina officials wanted to attract European settlers to their colony and offered assistance in the form of provisions and tools. In 1736, James Patton lured many settlers from northwest Ulster to his land grant in Virginia.[16] And in North Carolina, Ulster immigrant Henry McCulloh, an agent for Lord Granville, enticed Scots-Irish settlers to that state. Other families were brought to Fort Hamilton and Warrenbush, New York, in 1740 and 1741.

Figure 6.1. Uwchlan Meeting House, Chester, Pennsylvania, built in 1756.

The immigrants' transition to America was not always a smooth one. The early Ulster immigrants who settled in Pennsylvania initially experienced what historian Patrick Griffin calls "isolation and disorder on the frontier," in Chester County and Lancaster County, in a region called Conestogoe. Settlers in communities along the Susquehanna River, such as Donegal, Paxton, Derry, Colrain, and Londonderry, engaged in struggles over land distribution and valuation and related issues of law, deeds, titles, taxes, fees, and surveys.[17] Underlying many of the conflicts was a central question of whether an orderly community is best achieved by wealthy elites, making paternalistic land grants and imposing a system of governing rules, or by individualistic, hardscrabble settlers, motivated more by self-interest than public concerns. The wealthy landholders tended

---

[13] Ibid., p. 592.

[14] R. J. Dickson, *Ulster Emigration to Colonial America, 1718–1775* (London: Routledge and Kegan Paul, 1966), pp. 21–22; Charles Knowles Bolton, *Scotch Irish Pioneers in Ulster and America* (Boston: Bacon and Brown, 1910; rept. Boston: NEHGS, 2013), p. 17; also at archive.org/stream/scotchirish00boltrich/scotchirish00boltrich_djvu.txt.

[15] Dickson, *Ulster Emigration to Colonial America 1718–1775*, p. 592.

[16] Ibid., pp. 49–54.

[17] Griffin, "The People with No Name."

to populate towns with protective (yet restrictive or controlling) ministers, landlords, sheriffs, and others who enforced fees and regulations. Settlers, on the other hand, tended to see their own freedom and self-determination as their best path to prosperity. They worked on their own behalf to tame the wilderness, build buildings, clear land, protect their interests, raise their families, develop businesses, and establish stable trade conditions. In area after area in America, some compromise was reached between these "top-down" and "bottom-up" routes to a lawful society, ensuring order would win over anarchy and allowing the immigration and settlement processes to advance productively, as almost all parties wanted.[18]

In this period, most immigrants from southern Ireland arrived between 1730 and 1769. Existing trade routes, particularly from Cork, influenced the movement of these Irish immigrants. Cork was involved in the export of provisions, particularly butter and beef, to the West Indies and America. While the merchant ships carried provisions, they usually included some passengers in addition to the freight. Most immigrants from the northern counties arrived in the 1760s.[19] They made up 61 percent of the total number of Irish immigrants.

Think "Community" When Researching Eighteenth-Century Records

As mentioned earlier, your starting point in tracing an ancestor back to Ireland in the eighteenth century will be to determine the exact origin of the person in Ireland, where he or she started out from. Irish records are organized by place.

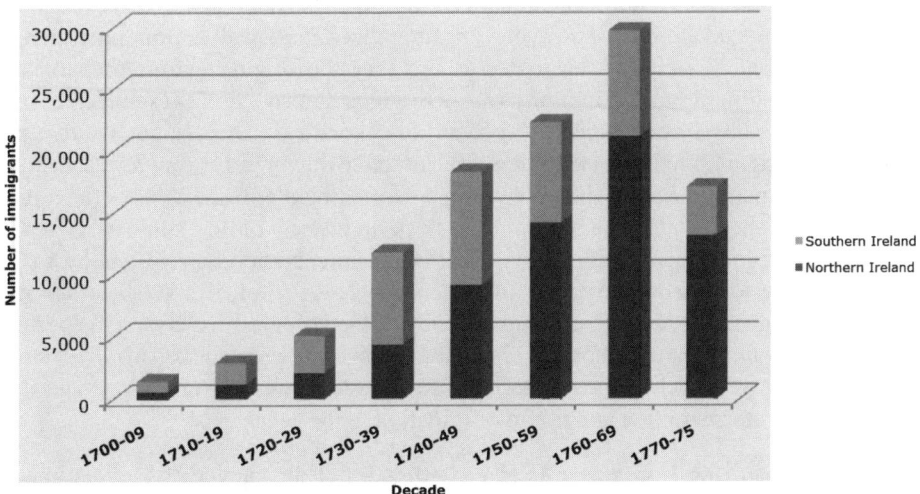

Figure 6.2. Estimated Irish immigration to the thirteen colonies, 1700–1775.

---

[18] Richard K. MacMaster, "Searching for Order: Donegal Springs, Pennsylvania 1720-1730s," in Warren R. Hofstra, ed., *Ulster to America: The Scots-Irish Migration Experience, 1680–1830* (Knoxville: University of Tennessee Press, 2011), p. 54.

[19] "Provisions Trade" at Cork: Merchant City website, corkarchives.ie/merchantcity/home/provisionstrade; Thomas M. Truxes, *Irish–American Trade 1660–1783* (New York: Cambridge University Press, 1988), p. 159; Fogleman, "Migrations to the Thirteen British North American Colonies, 1700–1775: New Estimates," p. 707.

The process can be difficult, since common Irish names, both first and last names, recur with great frequency. To determine whether the Margaret O'Toole mentioned in a particular record is your ancestor, you must narrow down the location. And again, to emphasize a key point, the place to determine exact origin is in *American* records, not Irish records.

When researching ancestors from the eighteenth century, you need to consider the American community in which your ancestors lived. Understanding the group or community will provide clues about individuals, specifically in light of group and chain migrations that occurred from specific areas in Ireland to frontier towns in America. Group migrations occur when an extended family or a cluster of relations, friends, neighbors, or fellow members of congregation decide to pool their resources and emigrate together to the same place in the new country. Chain migrations occur when already settled immigrants—often young men who have moved long distances to find work or women eager to reconnect with those left behind—assist their family and friends in joining them in the new country. Sending encouragement, information, and money, they help the newcomers with room, board, transportation, social contacts, employment referrals, and whatever else is needed. Both types of migration patterns underscore the importance of an ancestor's network of family and friends.

Although you may not find much documentation about your specific ancestors, you may glean more clues by connecting immigrant ancestors to others within the community for which there are more details known. For instance, some of the settlers of Rutland, Massachusetts, brought letters of dismissal permitting them to leave the congregation, from "Rev. Mr. Halliday at Ardstraw in County Tyrone." Our ancestors tended to maintain relationships in America that had been formed in the Old Country. So if your ancestors lived in a small community, such as a Rutland, you may be able to deduce that they, too, originated from the same place as another in the community whose origin is known—in this example, Ardstraw in County Tyrone. Similarly, you can sometimes learn about your ancestor's place of origin from the fact that the Scots Irish often migrated as a congregation, following their minister to the New World. Researching the Irish origins of the minister may shed light on the roots of their flock. In the case of Rev. James MacGregor of Aghadowey and Londonderry, New Hampshire, session books (kept by a ruling body comprising the pastor and elders), such as that of Irish Presbyterian parish of Aghadowey at the New England Historic Genealogical Society, can help identify early immigrants to Boston.[20] In addition, presbytery records and histories, such as for the Pennsylvania presbyteries of New Castle upon Delaware and Donegal, can provide interesting and useful information to the genealogist.[21]

Researching Irish ancestors in early decades of the eighteenth century can also be challenging, as it can be when working with seventeenth-century records.

---

[20] Presbyterian Church in Ireland, Session Book [Aghadowey, Co. Londonderry, Ireland], 1702–1725.

[21] Presbyterian Historical Society, *The records of the Presbytery of New Castle upon Delaware* (Philadelphia: Presbyterian Historical Society, 1931); Presbytery of Donegal, Minutes of Donegal Presbytery: 1732–1750, 1759–1765, 1766–1786 (Philadelphia: Presbyterian Historical Society, n.d.). Also, Donegal Presbyterian Church, The Donegal Presbyterian Church, Founded Prior to 1721 . . . *The Donegal People, Their History, and Other Historical Documents* (Harrisburg, Pa.: The Evangelical Press, 1935).

You will find, however, that there are gradually more sources to consult, as the eighteenth century advances. For instance, early American newspapers often document the arrival of passenger ships and even provide the port of embarkation, but they do not usually list the names of the passengers. Still, you can use newspaper shipping records that show the port of embarkation, to determine the general area of origin in Ireland. Furthermore, our immigrant ancestors may have lived far enough into the eighteenth and even into the nineteenth century, when there is a better chance of appearing in newspaper obituaries, local histories, and biographical dictionaries. Early American newspapers are now searchable in online databases provided by companies such as Readex, Proquest, and GenealogyBank. An index to the *Belfast Newsletter,* 1737 to 1800, is available online at the University of Louisiana at Lafayette website, www.ucs.louisiana.edu/bnl/.

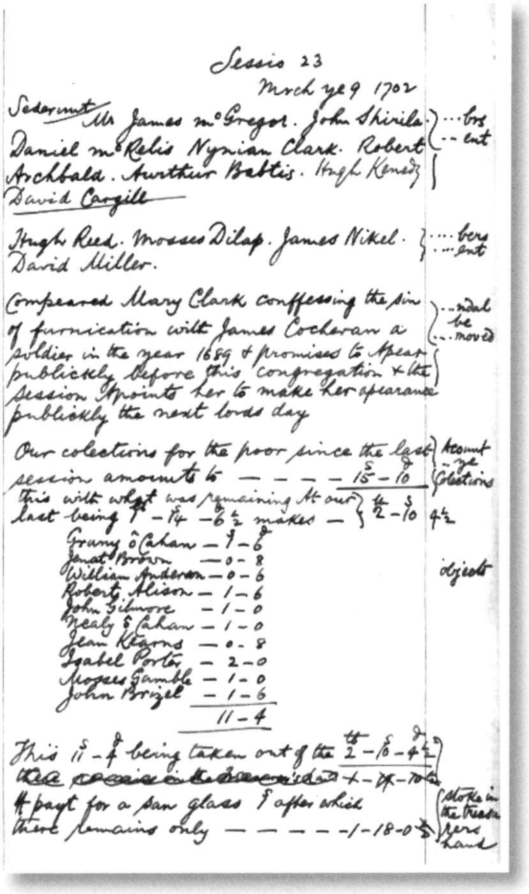
Sessio 23
Mrch ye 9 1702
Sedarunt Mr James mcGregor. John Shirila
Daniel mcRalis Nynian Clark. Robert
Archbald. Aurthur Babtis. Hugh Kenedy
David Cargill
Hugh Reed. Mosses Dilap. James Nikel.
David Miller.
Compeared Mary Clark conffessing the sin
of furnication with James Cocharan a
soldier in the year 1689 & promises to Apear
publickly before this congregation & the
Session Apoints her to make her apearance
publickly the next lords day
Our colections for the poor since the last
session amounts to — — — — 15 – 10
this with what was remaining At our
last being 1 – 14 – 6½ makes — 2 – 10 4½
Granny ô Cahan — 1 – 6
Janat Brown — 0 – 8
William Anderson — 0 – 6
Robert Alison — 1 – 6
John Gilmore — 1 – 0
Nealy ô Cahan — 1 – 0
Jean Kearns — 0 – 8
Isabel Porter — 2 – 0
Mosses Gamble — 1 – 0
John Brizel — 1 – 6
11 – 4
This 11 – 4 being taken out of the 2 – 16 – 4½
payt for a san glass after which
there remains only — — — — – 1 – 18 – 0½

Figure 6.3. Excerpt from the session book, Aghadowey, County Londonderry. Presbyterian Church in Ireland, Session Book [Aghadowey, Co. Londonderry, Ireland].

Correspondence among the immigrants themselves, their leaders, or even other individuals in the same communities can provide some helpful detail. Researchers have analyzed historic manuscript collections in many archives and reproduced them in published volumes, such as Kerby Miller and colleagues did in *Irish Immigrants in the Land of Canaan: Letters and Memoirs from Colonial and Revolutionary America, 1675–1815.*[22] One of the largest repositories of emigrant letters (letters from people who had emigrated and wrote back home to Ireland) is the Public Record Office of Northern Ireland.[23]

Local histories and associated biographical dictionaries can be useful, especially since many were compiled in the nineteenth century when the authors were much closer to the era of the immigrant generation. A few local histories have published the genealogies of the early or founding families, for example. For the Londonderry, New Hampshire, migrants, the local history of Windham mentions the origins of

[22] Kerby A. Miller, Arnold Schrier, Bruce D. Boling, and David N. Doyle, *Irish Immigrants in the Land of Canaan: Letters and Memoirs from Colonial and Revolutionary America 1675–1815* (New York: Oxford University Press, 2003).

[23] Public Record Office of Northern Ireland, 2 Titanic Boulevard, Belfast, BT3 9HQ, Northern Ireland, nidirect.gov.uk/proni.

some of the Londonderry pioneers.[24] The origins and family histories of many Pennsylvania Scots-Irish families are documented in *Pennsylvania Genealogies: Chiefly Scotch-Irish and German.*[25] For South Carolina, Jean Revill compiled a list of four thousand Protestant Irish settlers in South Carolina, which is available at many libraries, including the New England Historic Genealogical Society.[26] But many local history books do not cite their sources and often rely on oral history for their authentication, so their assertions should be used with caution. Indeed, some descendants identify their ancestors as "Scotch-Irish" when in fact their ancestors came from the south of Ireland. Claiming they were Scots Irish when in fact they had southern Irish roots, many descendants of colonial Irish immigrants sought to differentiate themselves from the nineteenth-century Famine immigrants.

Collections of manuscript materials that contain family papers and records of organizations may also prove useful. For example, if you are doing Pennsylvania research, the collection of the Scotch-Irish Foundation Library and Archives has membership files, genealogies, letters, organizational files, and other materials. You may access its finding aid online.[27] *(Note:* In 2002, the Balch Institute for Ethnic Studies, which had formerly housed this collection, merged into the Historical Society of Pennsylvania, the organization which now houses it.) A good source for locating Irish manuscript materials in America is *The Irish in America: A Guide to the Literature and the Manuscript Collections* by Patrick J. Blessing (Washington, D.C.: Catholic University Press, 1992).

Records of probate, civil, and criminal courts, as well as land records can furnish an abundance of information regarding our ancestors. Many of these records have been microfilmed by the Family History Library (FHL) in Salt Lake City and are available to borrow through local FHL centers. Genealogists have abstracted court records and deeds over the years and published them in books or on the Web. For Virginia, *Chronicles of the Scotch-Irish Settlement in Virginia: Extracted from the Original Court Records of Augusta County, 1745–1800* affords easy access to thousands of entries, since the book is online at Archive.org and Ancestry.com.[28] Other Pennsylvania published print sources for Chester County and Lancaster County include abstracts of wills, records of the courts of quarter sessions, tax lists, and published birth records. The Family History Library has microfilmed original probate records and deeds for most counties in the United States, and these films can be borrowed through local FHL centers. The FHL is currently digitizing its

---

[24] Leonard A. Morrison, *The History of Windham in New Hampshire (Rockingham country), 1719–1883: A Scotch Settlement (commonly called Scotch-Irish), Embracing Nearly One Third of the Ancient Settlement and Historic Township of Londonderry, N.H. . . .* (Boston, Mass.: Cupples, Upham & Co., 1883).

[25] William Henry Egle, *Pennsylvania Genealogies: Chiefly Scotch-Irish and German* (Harrisburg, Pa.: Harrisburg Publishing Company, 1896).

[26] Janie Revill, *A Compilation of the Original Lists of Protestant Immigrants to South Carolina, 1763–1773* (Baltimore: Genealogical Publishing Co., 1981), reprinted from original of 1939.

[27] The Historical Society of Pennsylvania, Collection 3093, Scotch-Irish Foundation Library and Archives, Finding Aid: http://hsp.org/sites/default/files/legacy_files/migrated/findingaid3093scotchirish.pdf.

[28] Lyman Chalkley, *Chronicles of the Scotch-Irish Settlement in Virginia: Extracted from the Original Court Records of Augusta County 1745–1800* (Rosslyn, Va.: Mary Lockwood, 1912), also available at archive.org/details/chroniclesscotc00lockgoog.

microfilm collections, and many of the early vital records are already available online at FamilySearch.org.

Once a place of origin in Ireland is known, you can consult a variety of online Irish sources, such as the 1740 Protestant Householders Census, seventeenth-century Hearth Money Tax rolls, forty-shilling freeholders lists, church records, and estate records. A good general guide to researching in Ulster is William J. Roulston, *Researching Scots-Irish Ancestors: the Essential Genealogical Guide to Early Modern Ulster, 1600–1800* (Belfast: Ulster Historical Foundation, 2005). In addition, the Public Record Office of Northern Ireland has a number of searchable eighteenth-century databases on its website, www.nidirect.gov.uk/proni. This topic, using Irish records, is the subject of Part 3.

Sources of Information:
Researching an Eighteenth-Century Irish Immigrant

American Sources	Irish Sources
• Archival collections of letters, family papers, and the records of organizations	• 1740 Protestant Householders Census
• Session books	• Seventeenth-century Hearth Money Tax rolls
• Presbytery records and histories	• Forty-shilling freeholders lists
• Early American newspapers, for notices on arrival of passenger ships and ports of embarkation and (in nineteenth-century) obituaries	• Church records
	• 1766 Religious Census
	• Estate records
• Local histories	• Newspapers
• Biographical dictionaries	• Will abstracts
• Family histories, lists of settlers, and cemetery records compiled by genealogists	• 1796 Flax Growers List
	• Deeds and leases
• Records of probate, civil, and criminal courts, land records, and deeds (in books or online)	• Londonderry Companies' records
• Military records, such as pensions, muster rolls, and enlistment lists—which may identify possible place of birth in Ireland	
• Vital records, abstracts of wills, quarter session books, tax lists, and published birth records	

Summary

The paucity of comprehensive record keeping in the seventeenth- and eighteenth-century frontier communities presents major obstacles to you in researching your ancestors. Many Irish immigrants came to America in some state of un-freedom as indentured servants, convicts, and slaves, and they left few traces of their lives. You will need to examine your ancestors in the context of the community in which they lived, so that you can maximize your chances of finding the elusive links back to Ireland.

Further Reading

- Bolton, Charles Knowles. *Scotch Irish Pioneers in Ulster and America*. Boston: Bacon and Brown, 1910; rept. Boston, NEHGS, 2013.
- Dickson, R. J. *Ulster Emigration to Colonial America, 1718–1775*. London: Routledge and Kegan Paul, 1966.
- Griffin, Patrick. *The People with No Name: Ireland's Ulster Scots, America's Scots Irish, and the Creation of a British Atlantic World, 1689–1764*. Princeton, N.J.: Princeton University Press, 2001.
- Miller, Kerby A. *Emigrants and Exiles: Ireland and the Irish Exodus to North America*. New York: Oxford University Press, 1985.
- Miller, Kerby A., Arnold Schrier, Bruce D. Boling, and David N. Doyle. *Irish Immigrants in the Land of Canaan: Letters and Memoirs from Colonial and Revolutionary America 1675–1815*. New York: Oxford University Press, 2003.

Chapter 7
Identifying Irish Place Names and Administrative Divisions

Congratulations! You have uncovered your ancestor's place of origin in Ireland. You are now ready to make that leap into online Irish records. *Or are you?* In our online environment today, researchers face a strong temptation to jump right onto the computer and begin trawling through digitized archives. Before continuing the quest for your elusive ancestor, however, you will do well to stop at this critical stage and ask, "What exactly is this place name I have discovered?" Our Irish ancestors may have given a variety of responses to the question, "Where are you from?" in the records of their adopted country. The place name you have found may simply be the county. It could be a parish name or another of many land divisions. There could be other snags, relating to changing spelling practices. This chapter is designed to help you navigate the potentially confusing topic of Irish place names and administrative divisions.

First, a few basics. The most important land division that you, as a researcher, need to find is usually the *townland*. For many of our Irish ancestors, the name of the townland would be what indicated their exact home place or "address." Once you know the townland, you will ordinarily be able to identify all of the administrative divisions associated with this place. Why is it important to be able to do so? Because genealogical and historical records in Ireland are organized by the various administrative divisions such as baronies, civil parish, county, and so on. Therefore, the key to successful archival research is to first unravel the mystery of what type of place name you have uncovered and where it is located.

Many townlands in Ireland have their origins in the Irish language. The origins of place names can come from local topographical features, such as mountains, rivers, and lakes, or from manmade structures, such as bridges or castles (Castletown, County Laois). Common elements in location names are, for example, Bally or Baile (place), Carriag/Carrig/Carrick (rock), Loch (lake), and Tullagh (hill). However, it is not uncommon for a researcher to discover a place name and then be unable to locate it in any indexed listing of townlands or parishes for that county. Spelling variations are often behind this type of snag. The people who were making the records often wrote down place names phonetically. And over time, many place names have been anglicized. If your ancestor emigrated before standardized spelling took hold, as is likely, a place name you have in your records may not resemble the current official name used today. Further discussion of the topic of standardized spelling of place names continues on page 97, in our coverage of the Ordnance Survey maps.

Taken as a whole, mastering the subject of Irish place names and administrative divisions can be time consuming. However, learning this important background information will pay off in the end. The more context you have about the place names of your ancestors, the more success you will have in identifying the records needed for research.

Become Familiar with Ireland's Administrative Divisions

Ireland is divided into four provinces and further divided into thirty-two counties. Since 1922, Ireland has consisted of the twenty-six counties of the Republic of Ireland and the six counties of Northern Ireland. The primary administrative divisions, in descending order by size, are province, county, barony, parish, and the smallest division, the townland. There are other administrative division names that Irish family historians will need to know, particularly if your research focuses on records created in the nineteenth and early twentieth centuries. As you will discover, many of these division names come from the historic Gaelic and Norman influences of Ireland. Some are obsolete today, but all are extremely important in Irish genealogical research.

Province

Ireland is divided into four provinces: Connaught, Leinster, Munster, and Ulster. These divisions in the Irish language are called *cúigí*, meaning the "fifth parts," and are based on the original divisions of five provinces prior to the Norman invasion of Ireland in the late twelfth century. The origins of these provinces are from the Irish dynastic families of O'Brien (Munster), MacMurrough-Kavanagh (Leinster), O'Neill (Ulster and Meath), and O'Conor (Connacht).[29] The province of Meath was later merged with Leinster.

The nine counties in the Province of Ulster, Ireland's northernmost province, present Irish family historians with additional complexity due to the partition of Ireland in 1922. The struggle, and resulting conflicts, for home rule (the movement to re-establish an Irish parliament while remaining within the British Empire) in the nineteenth and early twentieth centuries escalated into the Irish War of Independence, 1919–1922. The passage of the Government of Ireland Act of 1920 established two separate regions each still remaining under British rule. The counties of Antrim, Armagh, Down, Fermanagh, Londonderry, and Tyrone, with its Protestant majorities, formed Northern Ireland. The other three counties of the province—Donegal, Cavan, and Monaghan—remained with Southern

---

[29] Dr. William Nolan, "Historical and Administrative Divisions of Ireland," Chap. 2 in *Irish Genealogy: A Record Finder*, ed. Donal F. Begley (Dublin: Heraldic Artists Ltd., 1981).

Ireland. The Anglo-Irish Treaty of 1922 ended the conflict and established an Irish Free State. Northern Ireland, given the option under the 1920 ruling to remain under British home-rule, chose to do so.

Genealogists planning to research their Donegal, Cavan, and Monaghan ancestors in Ireland should take special care to identify the location in Dublin and Belfast of needed records. Don't assume that because Donegal is "in the north" that you will be able to use, for example, a record set such as Griffith's Revised Valuation books at the Public Record Office (PRONI) in Belfast. You will be disappointed to find that these records for Donegal are located at the Valuation Office in Dublin.

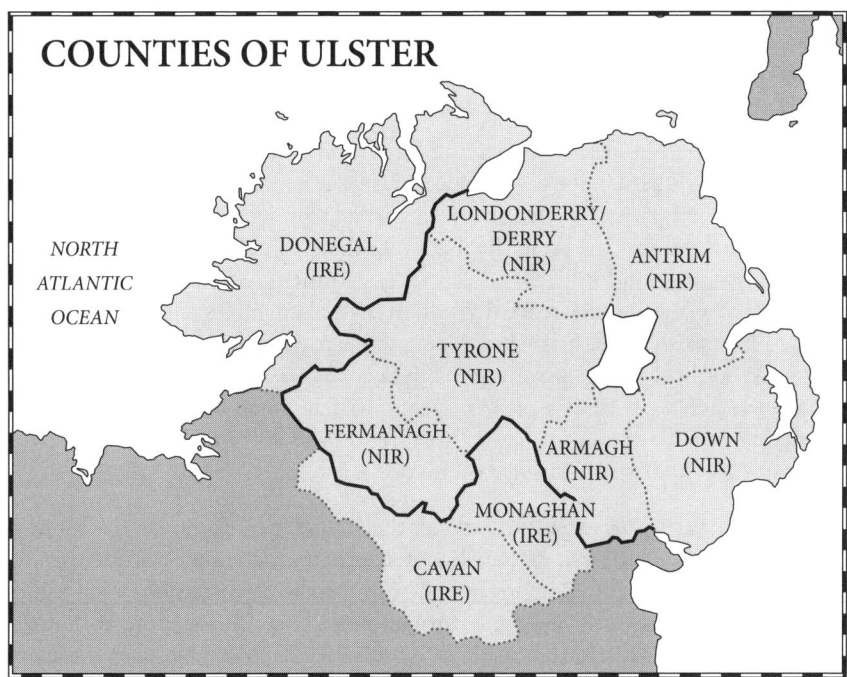

Figure 7.1. The counties of Ulster.

County

The counties of Ireland were created by the English and established between the time of the Norman invasion (1170) and 1606, when the last county (County Wicklow) was formed. Each county consists of several civil parishes. The county is frequently the place name that researchers discover first in their research. Over time, some county names have changed, and researchers should make note of the following:

- Queen's County is now County Offaly.
- King's County is now County Laois (sometimes spelled Leix).
- County Londonderry and County Derry are used interchangeably and formerly known as County Coleraine.

Baronies

The origin of baronies in Irish history is vague. These entities appear to have been established sometime after the Norman Conquest and most certainly by the seventeenth century, when the first land surveys were being conducted. Although use of the term is obsolete today, baronies play an important role in Irish genealogical research. Some genealogical records organized by barony are the pre-published Griffith's valuation manuscript material, such as the house and field books. You will need the barony name not only when using the originals in Ireland but also for searching for the microfilm copies in the Family History Library catalog. It is also needed when working with records in the Registry of Deeds as well as seventeenth-century records such as the Civil Survey of 1654–1656, the Books of Survey and Distribution, and Petty's Down Survey Barony maps, 1656–1658.

Parishes

The parish system in Ireland is made up of civil and ecclesiastical parishes. The term *civil parish* is used in the organization of government records as well as church records. The civil parish has its roots in medieval Christian Ireland. Because the Church of Ireland was the established church, the civil parish name was used as an administrative unit for local and central government records. The civil parish is considered a key administrative division in Irish research. It's not uncommon to discover the parish name first when trying to determine your ancestor's place of origin. As you will see in upcoming chapters, many Irish records of genealogical value use the civil parish as a primary geographic unit and can help lead you to identifying your ancestor's townland. Researchers should be aware that civil parishes can cross county and barony boundaries.

The two major religious groups in Ireland, the Church of Ireland and the Roman Catholic Church, have separate parish systems. This separation occurred during the Reformation when the Roman Catholic Church had its monasteries, land, and other assets confiscated. While the Reformation saw the Church of Ireland move into the role of the "Established Church," it left the Catholic Church in disarray. The Penal Laws of the early eighteenth century further weakened the Church and its people by restricting them from exercising their political rights, such as holding public office or entering a profession and denying them their right to practice their faith. The extreme poverty of the Catholic population and the restrictions placed on the Church and its clergy resulted in much larger parishes spread out over larger areas than civil parish boundaries. Thus Roman Catholic parishes can include several civil parishes. Most Catholic parish names are different from the civil parish names, although some retain the same name.

Family historians may come across a Catholic place name in North American records such as gravestones in Catholic cemeteries and parish records.[30] Researchers should note that the Church of Ireland parishes tend to have similar boundaries to the civil parish and share the same name. Both religious parish systems can cross county and barony boundaries. For more information concerning the growing collection of online church records and how to use them, consult Chapter 8, Finding Your Ancestors in Irish Church Records and Civil Registration.

---

[30] John Grenham, "Irish Place Names," askaboutireland.ie/reading-room/history-heritage/irish-genealogy/irish-genealogy/irish-place-names.

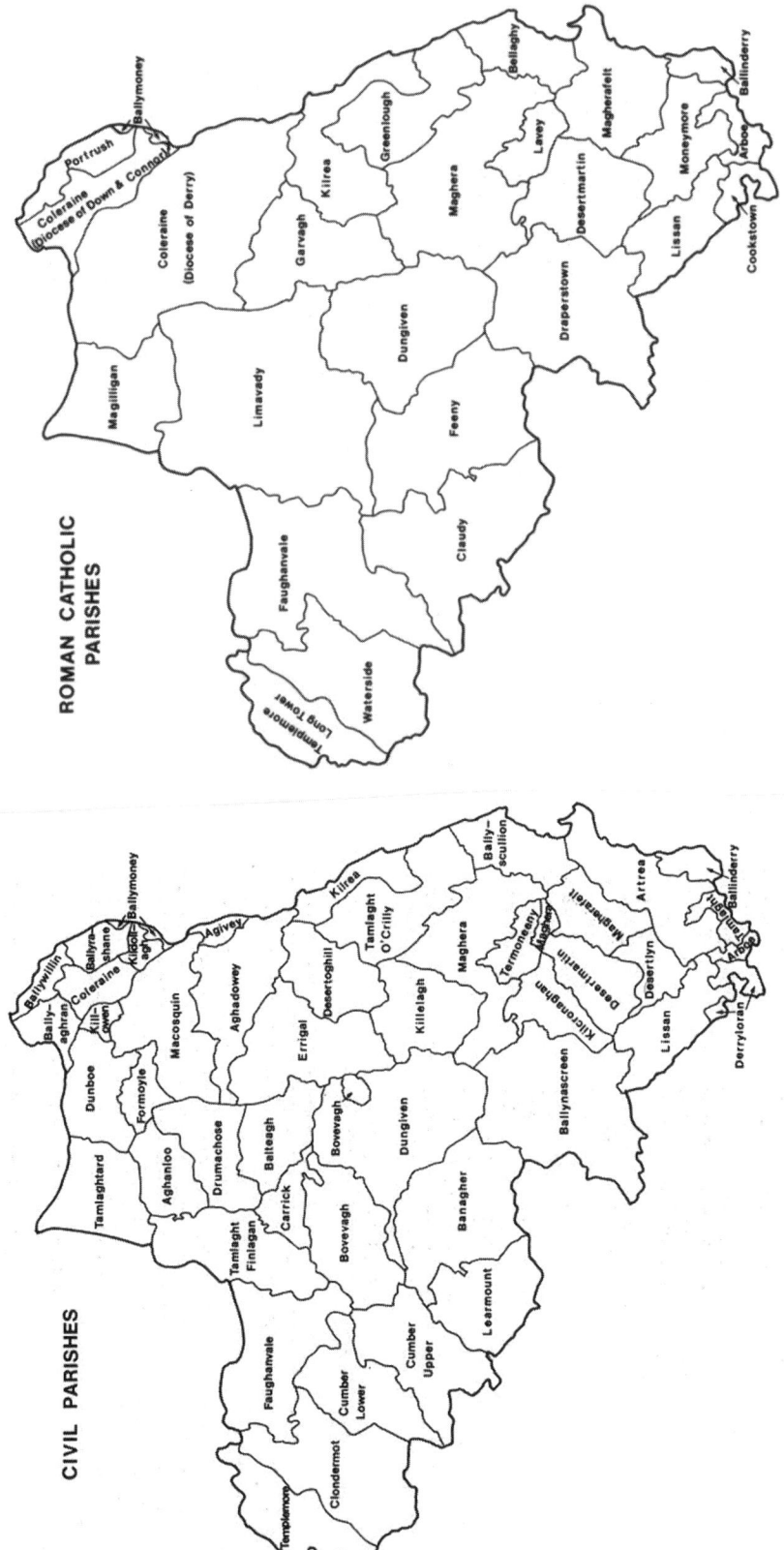

Figure 7.2. Example showing civil parishes and Roman Catholic parishes of the same county—here, County Londonderry.

Diocese

Parishes fall within dioceses, a larger ecclesiastical unit. In its early history, each Church (Anglican and Roman Catholic) had twenty-two dioceses. Today, there are twelve dioceses for the Church of Ireland in two ecclesiastical provinces, Armagh and Dublin. The Roman Catholic Church retains the same number of dioceses (twenty-two) in four diocesan provinces, Armagh, Cashel and Emly, Tuam, and Dublin.

Presbyterian Church parishes

Although no formal administrative division defines Presbyterian churches, Presbyterian congregations deserve a mention since they are the third largest religious group in Ireland.[31] The religion was introduced to Ireland during the seventeenth century, when Scottish planters migrated to the Plantation of Ulster. Researchers of the Scots Irish will quickly discover that the Presbyterian congregations do not follow a parish structure similar to the Anglican or Roman Catholic parishes. In the Presbyterian denomination, no strict parish boundaries exist and parishes were often formed as needed.[32] Brian Mitchell's *New Genealogical Atlas of Ireland* (2002) contains Presbyterian maps that can assist researchers in identifying where congregations are located.

Poor law unions

The Poor Law Act of 1838 established a system of relief for the poor based on the workhouse, and it resulted in the creation of unions of townlands. Each *poor law union* was named after a local large market town where the workhouses were located. The poor law unions were later divided into electoral divisions. You will find them used in several record groups of the nineteenth century, including Griffith's Primary Valuation, 1847–1864; civil birth, marriage, and death records; and twentieth-century census records. Like civil parishes, poor law unions can cross county boundaries.

Electoral divisions

District electoral divisions (often abbreviated as D.E.D. in records) consist of a number of townlands. They were created from the poor law unions for the purpose of electing a Board of Guardians for each union. They become important to researchers who will want to use Griffith's Valuation Cancellation Books, since these books are arranged by D.E.D. In addition, census returns of 1901 and 1911 use this administrative division.

Superintendent registrar's district

With the onset of Civil Registration in the mid-nineteenth century (1845 for non-Catholic marriages; 1864 for Catholic marriages and all births and deaths), an

---

[31] James Ryan, ed., *Irish Church Records: Their History, Availability and Use in Family and Local History Research* (Glenageary, Co. Dublin: Flyleaf Press, 2001), p. 10.

[32] Christine Kinealy, "Presbyterian Church Records," in Ryan, *Irish Church Records*, p. 76.

administrative unit known as the *superintendent registrar's district* was established to compile civil births, marriages, and deaths. Remembering this administrative division name is relatively simple, as it is the same as the poor law union. The superintendent registrar's district name is used in the all-Ireland indexes produced by the General Register Office in Dublin. Be aware that Ireland produced two sets of civil registration records: one set was kept locally, and the other was sent to the General Register Office in Dublin, where a master index was made. For further discussion of this topic, consult Chapter 8, Finding Your Ancestors in Church Records and Civil Registrations.

Probate district

Until 1857 the Church of Ireland was responsible for testamentary records (wills, letters of administration, and administration bonds). In 1858 eleven district registries, as well as a principal probate registry, were created for handling the filing of wills and letters of administration. In 1858 eleven probate district registries, as well as a principal probate registry in Dublin, were created for the process of proving the validity of wills and granting letters of administration. Probate district boundaries follow county or barony divisions.

Townlands

Last, but certainly not least in our list, is the *townland*. Simply put, townlands are rural areas. There are more than sixty thousand townlands in Ireland. The size ranges from a few to several thousand acres, with most averaging several hundred acres. A common misconception is that a townland is a town. Townlands are not towns, *but* a town could be part of one or more townlands. As mentioned earlier, this smallest of the administrative divisions is by far the most important to the genealogical researcher. Knowing your ancestor's townland can help you distinguish your Patrick Ryan of the Parish of Clogher, County Tipperary, from another Patrick Ryan of the same parish.

Townland sub-denominations

Do you have an ancestral place name found among family papers or in a record of their adopted country, but you cannot locate it in any standard index to townlands? Have you exhausted all alternate spellings and come up empty handed? If so, it may be a *townland sub-division,* an unofficial, local place name. Often the name comes from a farm or a place in the area that the residents of the area knew well. These sub-townlands are not in official townland indices so you must use other sources to locate the exact place. In many published and online guides covering this topic, researchers are frequently directed to a manuscript index titled "Manuscript Index to the Original 6" to the Mile Ordnance Survey Maps." This excellent index of all place names compiled by the Ordnance Survey includes sub-townland names. The problem is access to the index, which is found on microfilm at the National Library of Ireland (film numbers p. 4621–4625) and at the Irish Cultural and Heritage Center of Wisconsin in Milwaukee. Frustrated by the inability to readily access such records, researchers will frequently ask us

"Isn't there anything online I can use?" Perhaps the Irish Townlands website at townlands.ie may be what you are looking for. This website is currently mapping all townland, civil parish, and barony boundaries in Ireland using out-of-copyright maps from Trinity College. All known townland sub-denominations are listed for each county. As this is an ongoing project, the information may not be as complete as the Manuscript Index, but it is a place to start.

Map 7.3. Map of Ireland showing the province and county divisions.

Identify Key Resources for Learning Place History

The next step in your research is to link your ancestor's place of origin to the administrative divisions of that locality. You have a variety of tools, both online and in print format, that are helpful in identifying the administrative divisions associated with your place name.

Place-name reference works

For Irish genealogists who are working with place-name identification, the "go to" reference source is the *General Alphabetical Index to Townlands and Towns, Parishes and Baronies of Ireland*. Published in 1861, this index of townlands, parishes, and baronies is based on the 1851 Census of Ireland. The index to townlands is organized alphabetically and lists the barony, civil parish, and poor law union for each townland along with its Ordnance Survey map number.

Subsequent editions based on the censuses of 1871 and 1901 have also been published and include alphabetical index lists for additional jurisdictions such as the poor law union, local registrar district, and the district electoral division. Don't overlook these other land division lists in the Townlands Index. Not only can you can use them to confirm a spelling of a place name but—if a townland is unknown to you but you have identified a parish name—you can consult the parish index to make sure there is not more than one parish by the same name in the same county.

Several online versions of the Index to Townlands make research from home quick and easy. An online version of the 1851 Index to Townlands, and a popular one for Irish genealogists, is the *IreAtlas Townland Database,* at thecore.com/seanruad (also found within the Leitrim-Roscommon genealogy website, leitrim-roscommon.com). A revised and updated version of the database can be found at SWilson.info/townlands.php. This free database, run by Shane Wilson, a family historian from Dublin, has a large collection of historic maps, directories, and other interesting genealogical information. This version of the *Townland Database* has a much more robust search capability with Soundex and wildcard options for searching part of a place name. The Irish Genealogical Research Society has a searchable database for the 1901 Index to Townlands at irishancestors.ie. Simply click on the tab "Resources—Unique Resources" from the Society's home page for access.

Those with Northern Ireland roots will also want to be aware of two websites that may be helpful when trying to identify place names. The Northern Ireland Placename Project (placenamesni.org) was created by the School of Modern Languages at Queens University, Belfast. The purpose of this project is to study the origin and meaning of more than thirty thousand place names in the six counties of the North. Among the townland names of Ulster, some show their Irish origins, while others show the English and Scottish influences. This site's searchable place-name database, launched in 2013, allows researchers to enter a place name and get back results listing the administrative divisions associated with the townland. It also provides an historical name form, or the place name as it appears in records and maps from its earliest usage to present day. A link to a map displays each townland and its boundaries. This site also gives you the ability to enter an historical form

ALPHABETICAL INDEX TO THE TOWNLANDS AND TOWNS OF IRELAND.

No. of Sheet of the Ordnance Survey Maps.	Townlands and Towns.	Area in Statute Acres. A. R. P.	County.	Barony.	Parish.	Poor Law Union in 1857.	Townland Census of 1851, Part I. Vol.	Page
21	Acres	11 2 29	Fermanagh	Clanawley	Boho	Enniskillen	III.	189
27, 28	Acres	44 3 13d	Fermanagh	Magherastephana	Aghalurcher	Lisnaskea	III.	214
17, 30	Acres	8 3 36	Galway	Dunmore	Tuam	Tuam	IV.	35
94	Acres	4 3 27	Galway	Galway	Rahoon	Galway	IV.	37
125	Acres	23 3 34	Galway	Leitrim	Ballynakill	Loughrea	IV.	50
31	Acres	191 3 6	Galway	Tiaquin	Kilkerrin	Glennamaddy	IV.	76
44, 54	Acres	818 1 5	Kerry	Corkaguiny	Ballinvoher	Dingle	II.	173
1, 2	Acres	467 3 36	Kerry	Iraghticonnor	Kilconly	Listowel	II.	191
48, 58	Acres	77 2 37	Kerry	Magunihy	Aglish	Killarney	II.	199
29	Acres	56 1 20	Leitrim	Carrigallen	Cloone	Mohill	IV.	90
18	Acres	58 3 32	Leitrim	Drumahaire	Inishmagrath	Manorhamilton	IV.	95
23	Acres	37 1 4b	Leitrim	Leitrim	Kiltoghert	Car^k. on Shannon	IV.	100
35, 37	Acres	85 2 36	Leitrim	Mohill	Mohill	Mohill	IV.	107
52	Acres	162 3 10	Limerick	Glenquin	Killeedy	Kanturk	II.	245
9	Acres	38 0 11c	Longford	Granard	Clonbroney	Granard	I.	154
91	Acres	89 1 4	Mayo	Clanmorris	Mayo	Claremorris	IV.	135
19, 24	Acres	77 2 3	Monaghan	Cremorne	Ballybay	Castleblayney	III.	259
5	Acres	46 0 2	Monaghan	Monaghan	Tedavnet	Monaghan	III.	278
40	Acres	133 3 34	Roscommon	Ballintober South	Roscommon	Roscommon	IV.	190
10	Acres	125 2 39	Roscommon	Frenchpark	Kilmacumsy	Boyle	IV.	203
31	Acres	7 1 9	Waterford	Decies without Drum	Dungarvan	Dungarvan	II.	354
61	Acre West	11 1 13	Galway	Killian	Ahascragh	Mountbellew	IV.	42
18	Acton	22 0 31	Armagh	Orior Lower	Ballymore	Newry	III.	55
18	ACTON T.	—	Armagh	Orior Lower	Ballymore	Newry	III.	56
142, 143	Adam's Island	1 3 31	Cork, W.R.	East Carbery,(W.D.)	Kilfaughnabeg	Skibbereen	II.	183
86	Adamstown	436 1 6	Cork, E.R.	Kerrycurrihy	Ballinaboy	Cork	II.	91
3, 4, 6, 7	Adamstown	565 3 11	Dublin	Balrothery West	Garristown	Dunshaughlin	I.	22
17	Adamstown	111 1 11	Dublin	Newcastle	Aderrig	Celbridge	I.	32
40	Adamstown	219 3 16	Limerick	Smallcounty	Athneasy	Kilmallock	II.	258
15, 18	Adamstown	311 3 33	Louth	Ardee	Drumcar	Ardee	I.	172
37	Adamstown	277 0 14	Meath	Lower Moyfenrath	Laracor	Trim	I.	210
29	Adamstown	289 3 14	Tipperary, N.R.	Eliogarty	Templemore	Thurles	II.	272
16, 17	Adamstown	247 3 20	Waterford	Middlethird	Kilmeadan	Waterford	II.	368
17	Adamstown	69 2 10	Waterford	Middlethird	Lisnakill	Waterford	II.	368
25, 32	Adamstown	551 3 14	Westmeath	Moycashel	Castletownkindalen	Mullingar	I.	277
25	Adamstown	35 0 3	Westmeath	Rathconrath	Conry	Mullingar	I.	282
30, 31	Adamstown	1,076 2 15	Wexford	Bantry	Adamstown	New Ross	I.	299
13	Adamstown Lower	189 1 25	Kilkenny	Crannagh	Tullaroan	Kilkenny	I.	87
13	Adamstown Upper	284 2 18	Kilkenny	Crannagh	Tullaroan	Kilkenny	I.	87
20, 29	Adamswood	302 1 18	Limerick	Connello Lower	Croagh	Rathkeale	II.	227
21	Adare	856 1 21	Limerick	Coshma	Adare	Croom	II.	241
21	ADARE T.	—	Limerick	Coshma	Adare	Croom	II.	241
27	Addane	85 0 6	Tipperary, N.R.	Upper Ormond	Dolla	Nenagh	II.	290
30	Addanstown	155 0 12	Meath	Upper Navan	Trim	Trim	I.	216
18	Addergoole	114 1 23	Clare	Inchiquin	Kilkeedy	Corrofin	II.	25
23	Addergoole	2,658 3 25d	Galway	Ballynahinch	Ballynakill	Clifden	IV.	11
69	Addergoole	493 0 36	Galway	Clare	Annaghdown	Galway	IV.	16
44	Addergoole	151 1 39	Galway	Clare	Killererin	Tuam	IV.	20
99, 107	Addergoole	606 1 10	Galway	Longford	Abbeygormacan	Ballinasloe	IV.	56
81	Addergoole	942 0 16	Mayo	Costello	Aghamore	Claremorris	IV.	136
34	Addergoole	103 1 18	Queen's Co.	Clarmallagh	Aghmacart	Abbeyleix	I.	236
5	Addergoole Beg	161 1 7	Galway	Dunmore	Dunmore	Tuam	IV.	33
47	Addergoole or Knockmaria	227 0 22	Mayo	Tirawley	Addergoole	Castlebar	IV.	163
17	Addergoole More	278 3 37	Galway	Dunmore	Dunmore	Tuam	IV.	33
61, 74	Addergoole North	1,068 1 3e	Galway	Killian	Ahascragh	Ballinasloe	IV.	42
74	Addergoole South	54 3 8f	Galway	Clonmacnowen	Ahascragh	Ballinasloe	IV.	23
74	Addergoole West	53 2 23	Galway	Clonmacnowen	Ahascragh	Ballinasloe	IV.	23
9	Addergown	454 2 17	Kerry	Clanmaurice	Rattoo	Listowel	II.	173
10, 19	Adderville	752 3 18	Donegal	Inishowen East	Clonmany	Inishowen	III.	117
58	Adderwal	722 0 14g	Donegal	Boylagh	Inishkeel	Glenties	III.	112
9, 14	Addinstown	968 0 16	Westmeath	Delvin	Castletowndelvin	Castletowndelvin	I.	264
81	Addragool	149 1 2h	Galway	Moycullen	Moycullen	Galway	IV.	70
38	Addrigoole	102 3 31	Waterford	Decies within Drum	Lisgenan or Grange	Youghal	II.	352
17, 18	Addroon	148 1 12i	Clare	Inchiquin	Ruan	Corrofin	II.	28
11	Aderavoher	34 0 14	Sligo	Tireragh	Easky	Dromore, West	IV.	233
31	Adereen	56 0 9	Leitrim	Leitrim	Kiltoghert	Car^k. on Shannon	IV.	100
108	Aderg	129 1 25	Mayo	Costello	Annagh	Claremorris	IV.	137
17	Aderrig	259 1 29	Dublin	Newcastle	Aderrig	Celbridge	I.	32
78	Admiran	135 2 30j	Donegal	Raphoe	Stranorlar	Stranorlar	III.	142
28, 29, 33	Adoon	699 3 37k	Leitrim	Mohill	Cloone	Mohill	IV.	105
26, 27	Adragool	231 1 13	Roscommon	Castlereagh	Kilkeevin	Castlereagh	IV.	200
24	Adramone Beg	92 2 36	Waterford	Decies without Drum	Kilrossanty	Kilmacthomas	II.	357

(a) Including 4A. 2R. 7P. water.
(b) Including 2A. 1R. 19P. water.
(c) Including 10A. 0R. 35P. water.
(d) Including 4A. 1R. 9P. water.
(e) Including 25A. 0R. 16P. water.
(f) Including 1A. 1R. 24P. water.
(g) Including 10A. 3R. 10P. water.
(h) Including 42A. 3R. 3P. water.
(i) Including 3A. 3R. 6P. water.
(j) Including 8A. 3R. 17P. water.
(k) Including 57A. 3R. 30P. water.

Figure 7.4. Page from *General Alphabetical Index to the Townlands*.

of a place name and to find, in the search results, the current name it has been assigned in the database.

Another important reference work is George Handran's *Townlands in Poor Law Unions*. This work is sometimes overlooked, but its importance is undeniable. Originally published in 1885 as a series of pamphlets, it was created as a reference tool for Civil Registration officials to use to identify electoral divisions in registrar districts. It is organized alphabetically by poor law union, and it includes those poor law unions dissolved between 1864 and 1923. Within each poor law union section, administrative divisions are organized by registrar districts. Under each district all townlands are listed along with the respective district electoral division, barony, and civil parish for that area. The list of all townlands for each parish is what genealogists will find to be the most valuable feature in this work, as it can help identify neighboring townlands.

> **To-Do List**
> - Learn the administrative divisions associated with ancestor's place name.
> - Use maps to locate ancestral home and neighboring townlands and parishes.
> - Consult gazetteers and local histories to learn about the area where your ancestor lived.

Maps

Genealogists researching their Irish ancestry will quickly learn the vital importance of maps. Maps not only provide us with a visual representation of where an ancestral home is located but they play a valuable role in identifying boundaries, such as to neighboring townlands, parishes, and counties. Knowing what borders the area of where your ancestor lived is essential in Irish research. Your ancestors may have lived in a townland and parish very close to a county border, and it would not be unusual for them to baptize or marry in the parish in the neighboring county. An excellent published source to consult is *A New Genealogical Atlas of Ireland* by Brian Mitchell (Baltimore, Genealogical Publishing Co., 2002). Mitchell's atlas not only provides county maps but maps of all the main administrative divisions including civil parishes, Roman Catholic, and Presbyterian congregations in each county.

In addition to Mitchell's work, several other online websites are helpful to the Irish genealogist. Beginning in the late 1820s, the government of Ireland commissioned geographical surveys of the whole country. Completed by 1842, these surveys resulted in Ordnance Survey maps on a scale of 6 inches to a mile, with details of townlands. This work for the first time standardized the spelling of townland names. You can view these maps at irishhistoricmaps.ie. The work to carry out the task of creating one standardized name for a place was done by several individuals with knowledge of the Irish language, the most prominent and well known of the group being John O'Donovan. His subsequent work of taking the Irish versions of names along with recording the English spelling used for the maps resulted in the Ordnance Survey Name Books. A free and online version of the Name Books can be found at askaboutireland.ie in the section on Griffith's Valuation. Consult

Figure 7.5. Poor law unions of Ireland.

Chapter 10, Making the Most of Online Census and Land Valuation Records, for an example of how to incorporate this important work in your research.

John Grenham's website Irish Ancestors, www.JohnGrenham.com, offers online civil parish and Roman Catholic parish maps, as well as a townland index. The civil parish feature allows you to click on a specific parish on the map. This click brings you to the parish page with a list of all townlands in the parish, the top ten surnames of that area, its bordering parishes, and corresponding map numbers with a link to a contemporary Google map of the area. Additional features include links to the Ordnance Survey maps and the 1901 and 1911 census.

Gazetteers

What was life like in Ireland back in the time of an ancestor? Where did he or she worship? Were there schools nearby? These are not unusual questions one hears at the genealogical library's reference desk. The most relevant resource to consult depends upon the time period and place you are interested in. For the history of a place in Ireland, the following is excellent: Samuel Lewis's *Topographical Dictionary* (full title *A Topographical Dictionary of Ireland: Comprising the Several Counties, Cities, Boroughs, Corporate, Market, and Post Towns, Parishes, and Villages, with Historical and Statistical Descriptions . . .*). This dictionary provides a description of each civil parish, city, town, and barony. Each sketch includes places of worship, schools, and total acreage. Published in 1837, it gives genealogists many details about an area prior to the period of the Great Famine. An easy to use online version of Lewis's work can be found at libraryireland.com/topog.

For those who are researching ancestors in the Ulster provinces, the *Ordnance Survey Memoirs* are truly a rare and valuable source. Compiled in the 1830s with the purpose of accompanying the Ordnance Survey maps, the *Memoirs* are detailed descriptions of the parishes in the Province of Ulster. The published volumes describe the parish's socioeconomic conditions, topographical features, emigration, and social customs, among other types of information. Out of the six counties of Northern Ireland, Counties Antrim and Londonderry receive the most comprehensive coverage. Due to the ultimately unmanageable size and scope of the project, work was stopped on the project in 1840. Some parishes in Counties Cavan, Donegal, and Monaghan have been published as well as some in Counties Sligo, Leitrim, and Louth. They are not available online but can be accessed at major libraries in the United States and Ireland. NEHGS has all published volumes. Consult WorldCat.org for where you can find the volumes in the library closest to you.

Summary

The importance of place in Irish research cannot be underestimated. Ireland is organized by various administrative divisions, and genealogists will need to identify and learn these geographic units associated with their ancestor's place of origin. Uncovering the place name, identifying the administrative divisions, and studying the history of the area are critical steps that the Irish family historian must undertake for successful research in Irish records.

Further Reading

- Andrews, J. H. *A Paper Landscape: The Ordnance Survey in Nineteenth Century Ireland.* Dublin: Four Courts Press, 1993.

- *General Alphabetical Index to the Townlands and Towns, Parishes and Baronies of Ireland: Based on the Census of Ireland for the Year 1851.* 1861; rept. Baltimore: Genealogical Publishing Co., 1984.

- Grenham, John. "Irish Place Names." Online at askaboutireland.ie/reading-room/history-heritage/irish-genealogy/irish-genealogy/irish-place-names.

- Handran, George B. *Townlands in Poor Law Unions: A Reprint of Poor Law Union Pamphlets of the General Register Office.* Salem, Mass.: Higginson Book Company, 1997.

- Joyce, P. W. *The Origin and History of Names of Places.* Dublin: Educational Co., 1920.

- Lewis, Samuel. *A Topographical Dictionary of Ireland: Comprising the Several Counties, Cities, Boroughs, Corporate, Market and Post Towns, Parishes and Villages with Historical and Statistical Descriptions.* London: S. Lewis, 1837.

- Mitchell, Brian. *A New Genealogical Atlas of Ireland.* Baltimore: Genealogical Publishing Co., 2002.

- Nolan, William. "Historical and Administrative Divisions of Ireland." In *Irish Genealogy: A Record Finder,* ed. Donal F. Begley. Dublin: Heraldic Artists Ltd., 1981, pp. 35–50.

- Prunty, Jacinta. *Maps and Map-Making in Local History.* Maynooth Research Guides for Irish Local History No. 7. Dublin: Four Courts Press, 2004.

- Ryan, James, ed. *Irish Church Records: Their History, Availability and Use in Family and Local History Research.* Glenageary, Co. Dublin: Flyleaf Press, 2001.

- Stockman, Gerard, et al. *Place-names Northern Ireland.* Belfast: Institute of Irish Studies, 1992– .

- *The Parliamentary Gazetteer of Ireland.* 10 vols. Dublin: A. Fullarton and Co., 1846.

PART III
Using Irish Records

Now that you have identified the name of your immigrant ancestors, the names of his or her parents and the place of origin in Ireland, you are ready to begin researching in Ireland. Many people start planning a trip to Ireland at this point But more and more genealogical information is being digitized and made available online, making researching Irish ancestors from your computer more productive and rewarding. By investigating your Irish ancestors in the available records online, you can concentrate your research in Ireland on records still in manuscript or print form. Even better, you can avoid trips to records repositories altogether and spend your time visiting the old homestead and meeting your Irish relatives. This part of the book will highlight the civil registration, church, and land records that are available online, and—more important—how to use these websites.

CHAPTER 8
Finding Your Ancestors in Irish Church Records and Civil Registrations

Many genealogists have searched unsuccessfully for documents in North America that detail the exact origins of their Irish immigrant ancestors. In numerous states, naturalizations recorded only Ireland as the place of origin, occasionally with, if you are lucky, the county of origin. Many immigrants from Ireland did not have gravestone markers or obituaries, nor do other burial records tend to mention the exact origin in Ireland. However, even if you encounter such brick walls, there are still strategies you can employ to locate your ancestors in Ireland. You can look for the births of your immigrant ancestors or their siblings by accessing online databases of church records and civil registrations. Since Irish surnames are frequently common, searching in these databases for people such as Thomas Fitzgerald or Mary Murphy will yield too many results. To narrow your search parameters, you must identify the names of the parents, including the maiden name of the mother.

The goal of your American research, then, is to determine either the names of the parents in Ireland or the exact place of origin in Ireland. Reviewing the case study of Thomas Fitzgerald of Boston, for example, we have established that his uncle, Edmond Fitzgerald of Boston, placed a "missing friends" advertisement in the *Boston Pilot* stating that his son was a native of Bruff, County Limerick.[1] The naturalization petition for Thomas Fitzgerald shows that he had been born in County Limerick.[2] His marriage and death records establish that Thomas Fitzgerald was the son of Michael and Ellen Fitzgerald. Church records reveal godparents named Bridget Fitzgerald and Andrew Williams. The 1901 death record of Bridget Williams, maiden name Fitzgerald, documents the names of her parents

---

[1] *Irish Immigrant Advertisements, 1831–1920 (Search for Missing Friends)*, online database, AmericanAncestors.org; originally published as *The Search for Missing Friends: Irish Immigrant Advertisements Placed in the Boston Pilot 1831–1920*, edited by Ruth-Ann M. Harris and B. Emer O'Keeffe (Boston: NEHGS, 1989).

[2] Naturalization petition of Thomas Fitzgerald, U.S. District Court, Boston, Vol. 26, p. 64.

as Michael Fitzgerald and Ellen Wilmot.[3] Next, by searching on FamilySearch.org for all deaths in Boston, Massachusetts, for children of Michael Fitzgerald and Ellen Wilmot, we found two more siblings: Ellen (Fitzgerald) Olson and Hannah (Fitzgerald) Miller. So we have established that Thomas Fitzgerald was a native of County Limerick, very likely from the parish of Bruff. We have also identified the probable parents of Thomas Fitzgerald as Michael Fitzgerald and Ellen Wilmot. We are now ready to tackle Irish records.

Catholic parishes often had different boundaries than civil parishes in Ireland. If you locate a family in Catholic parish registers, you need to determine what civil parishes fall within the Catholic parish. You can check the Catholic parish maps at John Grenham's Irish Ancestors website, www.JohnGrenham.com. The Catholic parish of Bruff included the civil parishes of Bruff, Dromin, Glenogra, Monasternenagh, Tullabracky, and Uregare.

Search in Irish Church Records Databases

Irish civil registration for births and deaths began in 1864, for Protestant marriages in 1845, and for other marriages in 1864. For records of births, marriages, and deaths before these dates, church records can compensate for the lack of civil records. Recent developments in the online availability of church records have increased the choices genealogists have for searching for their ancestors. Several websites now offer church records in online databases: IrishGenealogy, RootsIreland, Ancestry, Findmypast, and the Catholic Parish Registers at the National Library of Ireland (registers.nli.ie). The first four sites allow you to search databases of church records; the National Library of Ireland website is browsable only—meaning you need to scan through the records yourself because there is no search function. Each of these websites searches on different criteria and handles variant spelling of given and last names, so that the number and quality of the results will vary from one site to another.

Let's return to our example of Thomas Fitzgerald. Since Thomas was born before 1864, when civil registration began, we must turn to church records to find evidence of his birth. We have enough information to look for the baptism of Thomas Fitzgerald, son of Michael and Ellen Fitzgerald in the parish of Bruff, County Limerick. But we should also search for surrounding parishes and for baptisms of his relatives as well. Perhaps an ancestor was born before the records began, or there is a gap in the register. By looking not only for the direct immigrant ancestors, but also for his siblings and associates, you increase your chances of success.

IrishGenealogy

Let's look first at IrishGenealogy, at irishgenealogy.ie, a free web portal run by the Irish government's Department of Art, Heritage, and the Gaeltacht. You can perform a general search on the home page, and you will get results for a number of

---

[3] *Massachusetts, Deaths, 1841–1915,* database at FamilySearch.org (https://familysearch.org/pal:/MM9.1.1/N7NW-SM8: accessed 19 Jul 2014), Bridget Fitzgerald Williams, 22 Sept. 1901; FHL microfilm 2057735.

Irish online records, such as census records, census substitutes, and wills. The site also has the index to civil registrations.

To search church records, you need to select the tab Church Records on the home page. Not only can you search for a baptism of a child, but you can also enter the names of the parents. Some handy features are the abilities to cross-reference names and to perform advanced searches with the names of the children and the names of their parents. For the Cork diocese, the site allows you to see scans of the actual parish registers. However, in the case of Catholic entries, once you have identified a baptism or a marriage in other dioceses, such as Kerry, you can find the image of the event in the browsable registers on the National Library website, as explained on page 105.

Only certain counties and records are currently included in the church records database: the Catholic and Church of Ireland dioceses of Kerry and Cork and Ross, and Dublin City and the Church of Ireland parish registers for County Carlow. Those in charge of the site say they are currently working on the Catholic records for County Monaghan. It remains to be seen if the impetus to add more records to the site will continue with the Catholic registers now on the other sites. Keep in mind that many northern and eastern County Cork parishes are in the diocese of Cloyne, and a few West Cork parishes are in the diocese of Kerry. (The diocese of Cloyne records are on RootsIreland.) On the Church Records homepage, you can access a current list of available parishes.

Irish Family History Foundation (RootsIreland)

Another major search engine for church registers is the RootsIreland website at rootsireland.ie, a subscription site that provides transcribed records. The site is run by the Irish Family History Foundation, which describes itself as a "coordinating body of county genealogy and family history centres." It includes most, but not all, Irish counties and dioceses. It does not include the Catholic or Church of Ireland dioceses of Kerry, Cork and Ross and Dublin City, which are available at Irish Genealogy. Rootsireland does have some Church of Ireland and Presbyterian records in its databases, especially for Ulster counties. For Catholic parishes, RootsIreland has transcriptions of records beyond 1880, which is the cutoff point for the National Library of Ireland, Ancestry and Findmypast websites. Also, for some counties only a few parishes have been transcribed so far on RootsIreland. Before subscribing to this site, check to make sure the database will include the parish of interest to you. On the home page, scroll down to the map of Ireland that shows the counties currently online. Click on the county of interest, and you will be taken to the individual county heritage site. Look for a link to the resources covered. On some sites, the link is at the bottom of the page; on others it may be off to the side. This will give you a list of what parishes and dates you will find in the database. When you click on County Limerick, for instance, you get to the Limerick Genealogy website. On the right side of the page, select, under church records, Roman Catholic. This will give you a list of the Catholic parishes included in the database, including Bruff baptisms 1781–1793 and 1804–1899 and Bruff marriages 1781–1899.

At the Limerick Genealogy website, we enter a search for the baptism of Thomas Fitzgerald, baptized ca. 1825. The results show forty-three Thomas Fitzgeralds born in 1825, "± 5 years." If you click on New search/refine results at the bottom of the page, you are taken to a page where you can enter additional data to lessen the number of hits. Entering the name of the father, Michael, narrows the results to five hits. Entering the given name of his mother, Ellen, yields just one hit. You can clinch the search by going to the drop-down Parish/District field and selecting Bruff Roman Catholic. You still get one hit. The results are a transcription of the baptism of Thomas Fitzgerald, son of Michael Fitzgerald and Ellen Wilmot, on December 4, 1823. No date of birth was entered, but in that time period, children were usually baptized within a few days of birth. The sponsor was El Wilmot. In this case, the townland was not recorded, but in many records, you can obtain the townland of residence.

The results confirm our research in the Massachusetts vital records, where the likely parents were either Michael Fitzgerald and Ellen Wilmot, or Michael Fitzgerald and Ellen Noonan. Since we had already determined that Thomas was the likely nephew of Edmund Fitzgerald, whose son had been born in Bruff, the results in the parish register support the name of his mother as Ellen Wilmot. You can verify your research by looking for the baptisms of other members of the Fitzgerald family, such as Bridget, Ellen, and Hannah. Furthermore, you may find a reference to a townland in a sibling's baptism record. The database indicates that there are baptism records for Bridget Fitzgerald, daughter of Michael Fitzgerald and Ellen Wilmot, in 1828 and for Honora Fitzgerald with the same parents. These names also appeared as sponsors for children of Thomas Fitzgerald and Rose Cox in Boston church records.

Ancestry.com and Findmypast.com

With the release of the Catholic parish registers that are on microfilm at the National Library of Ireland, Ancestry.com and Findmypast.com (aka Findmypast.ie) have indexed the registers, and these are now searchable on their respective websites. As of this writing, a search for the baptism of Thomas Fitzgerald was less successful than a comparable search on RootsIreland.

A search on Ancestry for all Thomas Fitzgeralds baptized in 1825 in Limerick, ± 5 years, resulted in 34 hits (versus 43 hits on RootsIreland), and none were for the parish of Bruff. A search for all Fitzgeralds using the keyword of Bruff plus parents' given names showed only four baptisms, those of Helen, Bridget, and two Marys, but none for Thomas. You can browse in the parish register for Bruff—as you can on the website of the National Library of Ireland (NLI).

The same search on Findmypast for Thomas Fitzgerald resulted in the same number of hits: 34, none for Bruff. However, you can browse and search within the parish of Bruff on the Findmypast website by clicking on the A–Z Record Sets button in the upper right corner of the screen, and then choosing Ireland Roman Catholic Parish Baptisms. You can then type in Bruff in the "browse parish" field—which allows you to search within only the parish of Bruff. A search for all Fitzgeralds born in 1825 ± 5 years, with father's first name of Michael, yielded two hits—for Bridget and Mary—but none for Thomas. The Bruff parish registers had been recorded in Latin, so the search engine may have difficulty with variants of the given names. A search for all Fitzgeralds within the parish of Bruff with the mother's maiden name of Wilmot yielded only one hit: Bridget.

If you search these or other sites and do not find a record of your ancestor, don't give up—another site, indexed differently, may yield results for you.

National Library of Ireland (NLI)

Although databases and transcriptions of church records are useful for finding and identifying ancestors in Ireland, you should always check the actual images whenever feasible. As convenient and useful as these search engines can be, mistakes in transcription can occur, and information from the original record left out. Verifying information by examining primary source records is always advisable, if possible.

Many church registers are available on microfilm at the Family History Library in Salt Lake City, the National Library of Ireland, the National Archives of Ireland, and the Public Record Office of Northern Ireland. Some original parish registers are available at the Representative Church Body Library in Dublin and the Presbyterian Historical Society in Belfast. The National Library of Ireland has placed online digital images of its Catholic Parish Registers microfilm collection. Most of the registers cover only to 1880, although IrishGenealogy and RootsIreland have post-1880 records in their databases. The NLI website allows you to lighten, darken, and improve the contrast of the images, as well as to download the image. The site is browsable only, so you cannot search for a record. But if you have a transcription from RootsIreland, Ancestry, or Findmypast, you can click a hyperlink

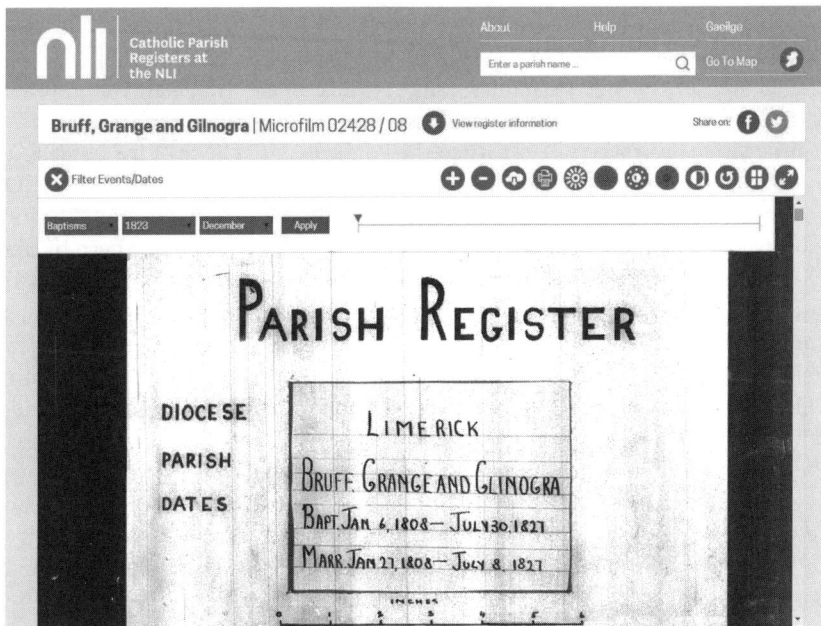

Figure 8.1. First page of parish register for Bruff, Grange, and Glinogra, County Limerick, National Library of Ireland website, registers.nli.ie.

that takes you to the NLI site for the parish—in the case of the Fitzgerald searches, the parish of Bruff, County Limerick. If you are using Ancestry, you will be taken to the page where the entry occurs. The other sites take you to the beginning of the register.

Figure 8.2. Baptism record of Thomas Fitzgerald, son of Michael Fitzgerald and Ellen Wilmoth, 4 December 1823, parish of Bruff, Grange and Glinogra, County Limerick, National Library of Ireland website, registers.nli.ie

Whenever you search in a parish register, browse not only for the baptisms and marriages of your ancestors and their siblings, but also for entries in which your ancestors appeared as godparents or witnesses. The names of the godparents and witnesses reveal networks of friends and relatives, perhaps neighbors in the same townland. Sometimes the parish registers omitted the townland of residence. By identifying the names of the godparents, or the baptisms for which your ancestor served as a godparent, you can accumulate a list of associates. You can sometimes then deduce the townland by cross-referencing the names in census records or census substitutes, such as Griffith's Valuation, a mid-nineteenth century record of land occupiers. (For more on Griffith's Valuation, see Chapter 9, Using Records of Property and Valuation in Ireland.)

Church of Ireland online registers

The Church of Ireland, an autonomous province of the Anglican Communion, was the established church in Ireland until 1871. Many Church of Ireland parish registers were destroyed in 1922 when the Public Record Office of Ireland (PROI) was burned. But other registers or copies of registers were never sent to the PROI, and many have been collected and archived by the Representative Church Body Library in Dublin or microfilmed by the Public Record Office of Northern Ireland. The Dublin library has embarked on a program to digitize and make available online baptism, marriage, and burial registers in its collection. A few registers are already available, and researchers can access the records free of charge at ireland.anglican.org. The website also features a comprehensive list of all Church of Ireland parish registers in the Irish Republic and Northern Ireland and includes notes on status (whether or not the registers survived) and location. For instance, the list shows that the Church of Ireland baptisms for Aghaderg, County Down, begin in 1814 and are available at the Public Record Office of Northern Ireland (PRONI). Furthermore, PRONI has an online guide to the parish registers in its collection at www.nidirect.gov.uk/proni. The Representative Church Body Library has recently added information from the PRONI guide to its list.

Other church records

Church records of some other denominations are included in the RootsIreland database, and many others have been microfilmed and are available in various Irish repositories. Many Presbyterian parish registers and session books have been microfilmed and are available at the Public Record Office of Northern Ireland in Belfast.

Many of the original Presbyterian records are available at the Presbyterian Historical Society in Belfast. Quaker records are available at the Quaker Libraries in Dublin and Lisburn (see box, next page), and the Family History Library has microfilms of many Quaker records. Most Methodist records date from the nineteenth century, and researchers should check Church of Ireland records for earlier baptisms and marriages. No matter what church your ancestors attended, you should always check the Church of Ireland records (if they are not among those that were destroyed), particularly for marriages. For more on Irish church records, see John Grenham's *Tracing Your Irish Ancestors: The Complete Guide*.

Search in Civil Registration Records

Many Irish people immigrated to the United States in the second half of the nineteenth century and early twentieth century. Sometimes married couples came with their children. Others came as single young men and women seeking work as laborers and domestic servants. With the wages they earned, the immigrants brought over their siblings and friends and sometimes their parents. The American marriage records of the children who had been born in Ireland or single young immigrants can be useful for identifying the names of their parents, and this information can also help locate their birth records in Ireland. Once the names of the parents are known, you can search not only for the immigrant's birth record but also the birth records of their brothers and sisters. Civil birth records and baptism records can help locate the immigrant's exact origin in Ireland.

Irish civil registration began in 1864 for births, marriages, and deaths, although Protestant marriages were recorded as early as 1845. Birth records typically documented the name of the child, the date of birth, the townland or town of birth, and the names of the parents. Marriage records provided the names of the bride and groom, their residences, the date of marriage, and the names of their fathers. So civil marriage records can be very useful in working your way back another generation. Death records listed the date of death, place of death, and cause of death. They did not list the names of the parents. As explained in the previous chapter, civil birth, marriage, and death records were documented in *civil registration districts*, districts originally created to administer Poor Laws, organized around market towns and hinterlands rather than parishes and townlands.

Even if your ancestor was born a few years before 1864 or after 1881, you can still look for the birth records of younger or older siblings. Irish civil registration records from 1864 to 1881 were abstracted and indexed in a database called *Ireland Births and Baptisms, 1620–1881* (previously published in the International Genealogical Index [IGI]), available at FamilySearch.org. The database has some extracted church records as well as the civil registrations. Be aware that these records are not comprehensive. Nevertheless, they are always worth checking.

Researching Irish Quakers
by Morrison deS. Webb

While most research into Irish families involves Catholics or the Ulster Protestants, a third religious group has played an important part in Irish history. Since the seventeenth century, Ireland has had a small, but influential, community of Quakers. Their records are a unique additional resource for genealogists.

The first meeting in Ireland of the Religious Society of Friends, or "Quakers," was held in Lurgan in 1654. George Fox, the founder of the Society, had been preaching in England for several years, and his followers there were frequently persecuted for their beliefs. These persecutions were extensively documented when efforts were made to secure religious tolerance from the English government.

The Quaker faith is practiced in local monthly meetings. George Fox was careful to instruct that each meeting keep the same vital records as were required of parishes in the Church of England. For most Quaker meetings in Ireland, those records still exist. Transcripts of the early Irish Quaker meeting registers are available on microfilm at the Family History Library under the title "Society of Friends, Ireland, register transcripts of monthly meetings, 1605–1872," Family History British Film Nos. 571395–571398. Indexed images of the registers are at Findmypast.com.

Where to find other Quaker materials:

For Southern Ireland: Friends Historical Library, Quaker House, Stocking Lane, Rathfarnham, Dublin 16; www.quakers-in-ireland.ie/historical-library. Officially the Historical Library of Ireland Yearly Meeting of the Religious Society of Friends, this library has a vast amount of original, non-microfilmed material in its archives: original meeting minutes and registers, family collections, manuscripts, school records, diaries, legal documents, Quaker marriage certificates (which are quite detailed), and the like.

As of this writing, the library catalogue is not online. Olive C. Goodbody's *Guide to Irish Quaker Records, 1654–1860* (1967; reprint, Baltimore: Genealogical Publishing Co., 1999) gives a very detailed description of the holdings.

For Northern Ireland: Society of Friends Library at the Meeting House, Railway Street, Lisburn, County Antrim. This library holds early records of monthly meetings in Ulster (Lisburn, Lurgan, Grange near Charlemont, Richhill, Ballyhagen, Antrim, and Cootehill) and accepts postal inquiries. More recent records are at the individual meetings. The Goodbody *Guide* notes which records have been microfilmed or photocopied and are available at the Public Record Office of Northern Ireland. PRONI's Card Index of Names is available on forty-four rolls of microfilm from the Family History Library, beginning with FHL British Film 1565676.

With vital records for the Irish Quaker community recorded at the monthly meeting level, a family researcher must identify the monthly meeting attended by a particular family in order to find relevant event entries. Other records may identify the meeting—but, if not, you can turn to the following:

"Jones Index to Quaker births, marriages and deaths in Ireland's Monthly Meetings, ca. 1606–1872," a manuscript index prepared by Isabel Jones, listing every surname occurring in the registers, along with the monthly meeting in which the name appears. The original index is in the Friends Historical Library in Dublin, but copies are available on FHL British Film 1559454, Item 10, and in print form (Dublin: Society of Friends [Ireland], 1998).

The "Webb Pedigrees," a massive collection of genealogical information about 232 Irish Quaker families prepared early in the twentieth century by genealogist Thomas Henry Webb. The manuscript lacks citations but identifies locations, making it easy to identify the monthly meeting source of the original data. The originals are at the Friends Historical Library in Dublin. Microfilm is available at the National Library of Ireland in Dublin, NLI microfilms 5382–85.

Recommended Readings

Besse, Joseph. *An Abstract of the Sufferings of the People Called Quakers.* London: J. Sowle, 1738. Available at the National Library of Ireland and in electronic form on Google Books.

Harrison, Richard S. *A Biographical Dictionary of Irish Quakers,* 2nd ed. Dublin: Four Courts Press, 2008.

Wigham, Maurice J. *The Irish Quakers; A Short History of the Religious Society of Friends in Ireland,* 2nd ed. Dublin: Historical Committee of the Religious Society of Friends in Ireland, 2003.

O'Sullivan, Michael O. *Memorial Inscriptions, Quaker Cemetery, Newtown, Waterford City.* Waterford, 1996. This book and other volumes of Quaker cemetery memorial transcriptions are held at the National Library of Ireland.

Identifying immigrants' parents' names

The first step is to identify the names of the immigrant's parents, preferably including the maiden name of the mother, in American or Canadian marriage or death records. Often the immigrants were married in the early twentieth century and may have lived to the 1940s or 1950s. While twentieth-century death records can be much more detailed than in previous time periods, death records can often contain errors regarding the names of the deceased's parents. Marriage records are more reliable because the information is originating from the bride and groom.

> **To-Do List**
> - Identify the immigrant's parents' names from the North American marriage or death record.
> - Search for the civil birth record in the FHL database *Ireland Births and Baptisms, 1620–1881*.
> - Send for the civil birth record from the FHL to determine the exact birthplace.

Searching for and obtaining the civil birth record

Once the names of the immigrant's parents have been determined from North American records, you can next search for the Irish birth record of the immigrant—or the birth records of his or her siblings. Using the database *Ireland Births and Baptisms, 1620–1881* at FamilySearch.org, type in the name of the immigrant, a birth date range of "±5 years," and the names of the parents. If you do not get any results, widen your search by looking for the births of siblings. Leave the given name field blank, but keep the names of the parents, and then widen the date range to 1864 to 1881—which will capture the first year of civil registration. (Many people confuse the civil registration district in this database for the place of birth.) Once you have located a birth record of your ancestor or his or her sibling in the database, borrow the film from the Family History Library to determine the exact birthplace in Ireland.

Build on Census Searches with Marriage and Death Records

Sometimes, in your attempt to identify immigrants' parents' names, you will need to correlate the results of census searches with marriage and death records. A look at the case of Robert McClements of Brighton, Michigan, illustrates the process of using marriage and death records in combination with census data. Robert William McClements immigrated as a child with his parents to the United States in 1870. The family settled in Brighton, Livingston County, Michigan, where they appear in the 1870 census (see Figure 8.3). The parents, Robert and Susan McClements, had several children born in Ireland: Joseph, born 1855; John, born 1863; Susanna, born 1865; and Robert, born 1867. Therefore, the older children were born before Irish civil registration, and only Susanna and Robert were born after 1864. In addition, we note in the census the family of Joseph and Agnes McClements next door. All of the children of Joseph and Agnes McClements were born in Michigan, beginning in 1858, so Joseph must have immigrated first. If you were researching your ancestor, Joseph, you would note the fact that John McClements, next door, had children born in Ireland after 1864. As a consequence, to research the origins of Joseph McClements, one strategy would be to look for the births of John's two children, Susanna and Robert, in the Irish civil registration records.

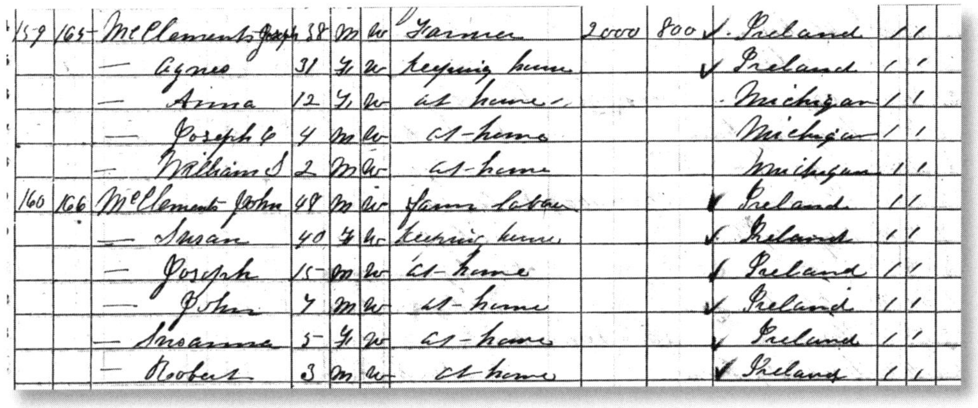

159	165	McClements Joseph	38	M	W	Farmer	2000	800	Ireland	1	1
		— Agnes	31	F	W	keeping house			Ireland	1	1
		— Anna	12	F	W	at home			Michigan	1	1
		— Joseph C	4	M	W	at home			Michigan	1	1
		— William S	2	M	W	at home			Michigan	1	1
160	166	McClements John	48	M	W	farm laborer			Ireland	1	1
		— Susan	40	F	W	keeping house			Ireland	1	1
		— Joseph	15	M	W	at home			Ireland	1	1
		— John	7	M	W	at home			Ireland	1	1
		— Susanna	5	F	W	at home			Ireland	1	1
		— Robert	3	M	W	at home			Ireland	1	1

Figure 8.3. Families of Joseph and John McClements, 1870 federal census, Brighton, Livingston County, Michigan.

By 1900, the youngest son, Robert, was living in a boarding house in Houghton County, Michigan, and working as a machinist. The census record (see Figure 8.4) indicates that he had immigrated to the United States in 1870. He was still single in 1900.

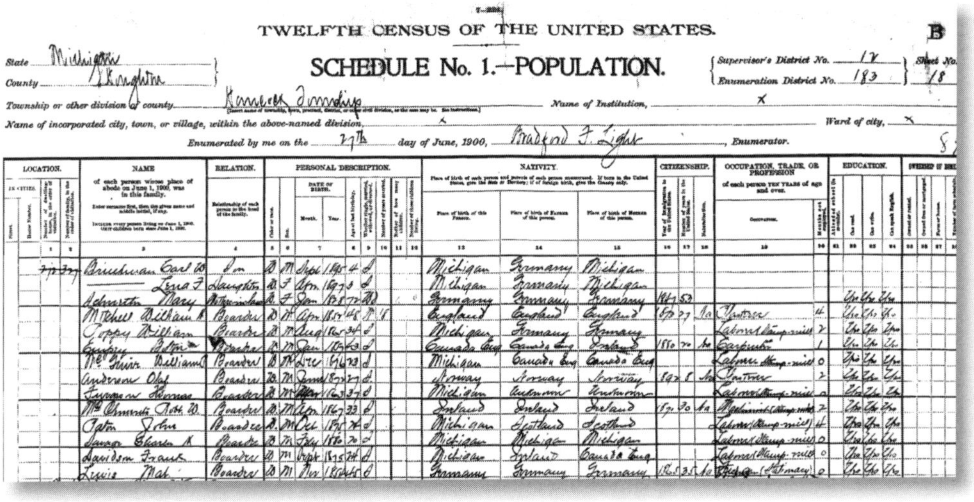

TWELFTH CENSUS OF THE UNITED STATES.

SCHEDULE No. 1.—POPULATION.

State Michigan
County Houghton
Township or other division of county Hancock Township
Supervisor's District No. 12
Enumeration District No. 183
Sheet No. 18
Enumerated by me on the 27th day of June, 1900, Bradford F. Light, Enumerator.

Figure 8.4. Robert W. McClements,1900 federal census, Hancock, Houghton County, Michigan.

Looking at marriage records

Robert W. McClements married H. May Jenks in South Lake Linden, Houghton County, Michigan, on January 22, 1901. The marriage record (Figure 8.5), found in the database *Michigan Marriages, 1868–1925* at FamilySearch.org, lists the names of his parents as John McClements and Susan Moorehead. Why does it help us to look for the marriage record of his parents? Even though the census records show the names of his parents, Robert's marriage record provides a vital piece of information: the maiden name of his mother. Knowing the maiden names of mothers is often essential to differentiate ancestors with common names. Note that the clergyman who married them was H. John McClements, who was probably Robert's brother, John.

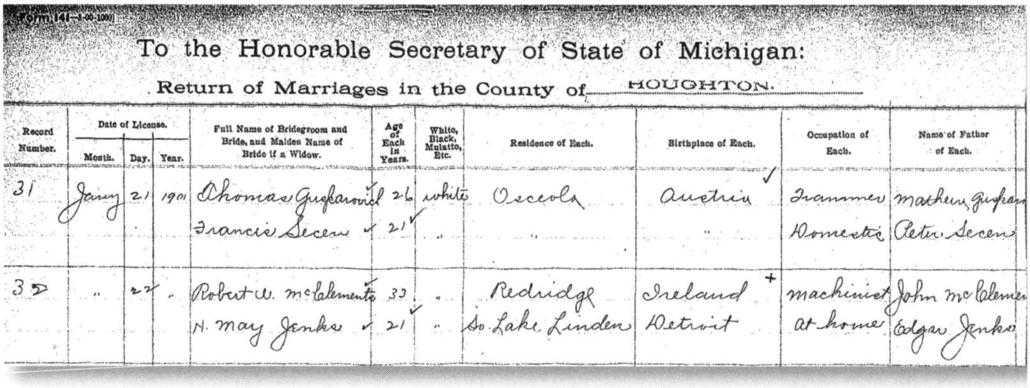

Form 141

To the Honorable Secretary of State of Michigan:

Return of Marriages in the County of HOUGHTON.

Record Number.	Date of License. Month.	Day.	Year.	Full Name of Bridegroom and Bride, and Maiden Name of Bride if a Widow.	Age of Each in Years.	White, Black, Mulatto, Etc.	Residence of Each.	Birthplace of Each.	Occupation of Each.	Name of Father of Each.
31	Jany	21	1901	Thomas Gasparovic	26	white	Osceola	Austria	Trammer	Mathew Gasparovic
				Francis Secew	21	"	"	"	Domestic	Peter Secew
32	"	22	"	Robert W. McClements	33	"	Redridge	Ireland	machinist	John McClements
				H. May Jenks	21	"	So. Lake Linden	Detroit	at home	Edgar Jenks

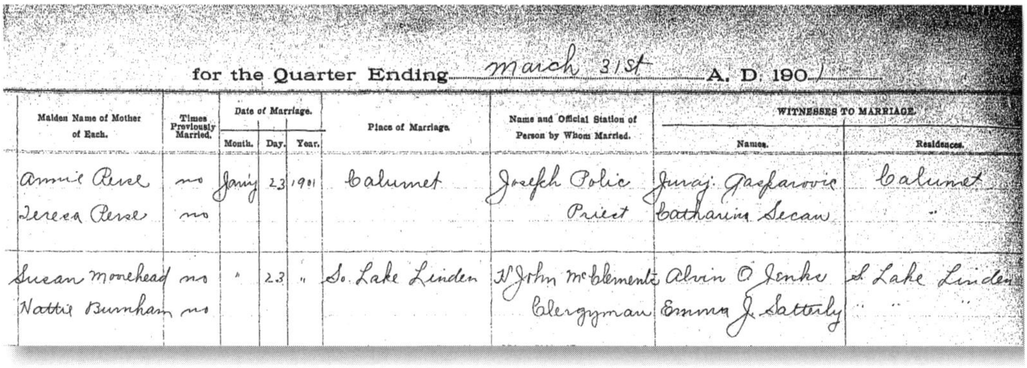

for the Quarter Ending March 31st A. D. 1901

Maiden Name of Mother of Each.	Times Previously Married.	Date of Marriage. Month.	Day.	Year.	Place of Marriage.	Name and Official Station of Person by Whom Married.	Witnesses to Marriage. Names.	Residences.
Annie Perse	no	Jany	23	1901	Calumet	Joseph Polic Priest	Juraj Gasparovic	Calumet
Tereza Perse	no						Catharina Secaw	"
Susan Moorehead	no	"	23	"	So. Lake Linden	H John McClements Clergyman	Alvin O Jenks	S Lake Linden
Nattie Burnham	no						Emma J. Satterly	"

Figure 8.5. Marriage record of Robert W. McClements and May Jenks, January 22, 1901, South Lake Linden, Houghton County, Michigan, page 1 *(above)* and page 2 *(below)*.

Looking at death records

We can ascertain more information about the McClements family by researching other members of the family, including the parents. John McClements, the father of Robert McClements, died in Brighton, Michigan, on September 7, 1901, at the age of 78 years, 6 months, and 16 days. Although most entries at Find A Grave do not include death records, we luck out with John's. It shows that he was born on February 19, 1823, in Ballygowan, Ireland, and was the son of John McClements and Mary B___ . Her surname is difficult to read but might be Brown.

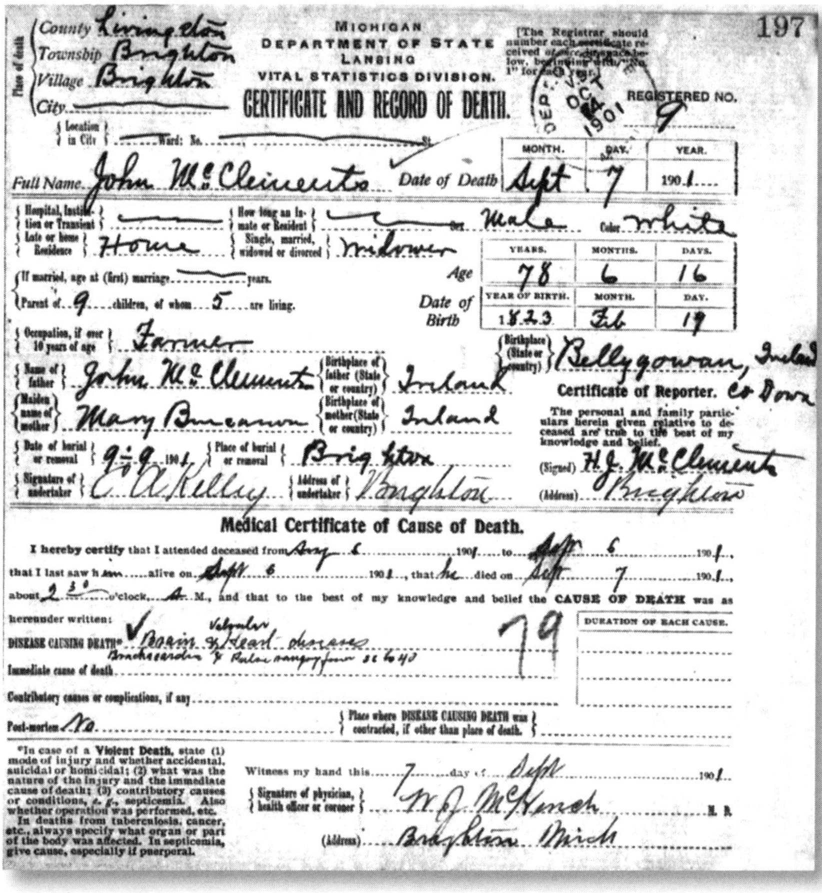
County Livingston
Township Brighton
Village Brighton
City

MICHIGAN
DEPARTMENT OF STATE
LANSING
VITAL STATISTICS DIVISION.
CERTIFICATE AND RECORD OF DEATH.

197

REGISTERED NO. 9

Location in City ... Ward: No. ... St.

Full Name John McClements

	MONTH.	DAY.	YEAR.
Date of Death	Sept	7	1901

Hospital, Institution or Transient —
How long an Inmate or Resident —
Sex Male
Color white
Late or home Residence Home
Single, married, widowed or divorced widower

	YEARS.	MONTHS.	DAYS.
Age	78	6	16

If married, age at (first) marriage ... years.
Parent of 9 children, of whom 5 are living.

	YEAR OF BIRTH.	MONTH.	DAY.
Date of Birth	1823	Feb	19

Occupation, if over 10 years of age Farmer
Birthplace (State or country) Bellygowan, Ireland Co Down
Name of father John McClements
Birthplace of father (State or country) Ireland
Maiden name of mother Mary Buchanan
Birthplace of mother (State or country) Ireland
Date of burial or removal 9-9 1901
Place of burial or removal Brighton
Signature of undertaker C. A. Kelley
Address of undertaker Brighton

Certificate of Reporter.
The personal and family particulars herein given relative to deceased are true to the best of my knowledge and belief.
(Signed) H. J. McClements
(Address) Brighton

Medical Certificate of Cause of Death.
I hereby certify that I attended deceased from Aug 6 1901 to Sept 6 1901, that I last saw him alive on Sept 6 1901, that he died on Sept 7 1901, about 2 30 o'clock A. M., and that to the best of my knowledge and belief the CAUSE OF DEATH was as hereunder written:

DISEASE CAUSING DEATH* Valvular Brain & Heart disease
Immediate cause of death. Bronchiectasis & Pulmonary ... 79

DURATION OF EACH CAUSE.

Contributory causes or complications, if any.
Post-mortem No
Place where DISEASE CAUSING DEATH was contracted, if other than place of death.

*In case of a Violent Death, state (1) mode of injury and whether accidental, suicidal or homicidal; (2) what was the nature of the injury and the immediate cause of death; (3) contributory causes or conditions, e.g., septicemia. Also whether operation was performed, etc. In deaths from tuberculosis, cancer, etc., always specify what organ or part of the body was affected. In septicemia, give cause, especially if puerperal.

Witness my hand this 7 day of Sept 1901
Signature of physician, health officer or coroner W. J. McHench M. D.
(Address) Brighton Mich

Figure 8.6. Death record of John McClements,
September 7, 1901, Brighton, Michigan.

Search for the Irish birth record

As mentioned previously, Ireland began civil registrations in 1864 for births, deaths, and Catholic marriages, and in 1845 for non-Catholic marriages. You can access many records at FamilySearch.org, either in databases or on microfilm. For records not available through the Family History Library, you can order photocopies or certified copies from the General Register Office of Ireland or Northern Ireland. (For most genealogical purposes, a photocopy is sufficient, and much less expensive.) You can order from the Republic of Ireland pre-1922 records pertaining to the six counties that are now in Northern Ireland. Data extracted from Irish civil records are available in the following databases at FamilySearch.org:

- *Ireland Births and Baptisms, 1620–1881* [*Note:* This database is the most comprehensive.]
- *Ireland Marriages, 1619–1898* [Only a few places are included in this database.]
- *Ireland, Deaths, 1864–1870* [Only a few places are included in this database.]

The indexes to Irish civil birth, marriage, and death records are available at FamilySearch, Ancestry, FindMyPast, and IrishGenealogy. The FamilySearch, Ancestry, and FindMyPast indexes cover years up to 1958. Owing to privacy restrictions, the IrishGenealogy online indexes go back only to births more than one hundred years ago, marriages more than seventy-five years ago, and deaths more than fifty years ago.

Now that we know the names of the parents of Robert W. McClements, John McClements and Susan Moorehead, we can look for Robert's birth record in the database *Ireland Births and Baptisms, 1620–1881*, at FamilySearch.org.[4] The results show a Robert William McClements, born on April 2, 1867, son of John McClements and Susan Moorhead, in Loughbrickland, County Down. (See Figure 8.7.) When you look at the record detail, you can see the film number in the lower right, 101145. You can order this film online and have it delivered to a local Family History Center.

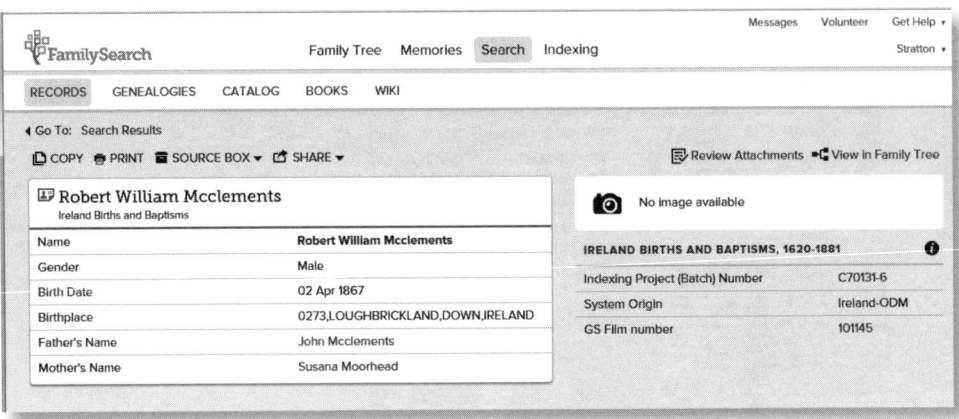

Figure 8.7. Results of search for the birth of Robert McClements, FamilySearch.org database, *Ireland, Births and Baptisms, 1620–1881*.

Although Loughbrickland was listed in the above as example as the birthplace, it is in fact the name of the registrar district, not necessarily the actual address where Robert was born. To determine the exact place of his birth, we have to order the film and look at the civil birth record. As noted in the box on page 109, we can order the film from the Family History Library. However, because the microfilm reel contains hundreds of pages of births, and it will be helpful first to determine the volume and page where the birth is recorded. We can find the volume and page number in the Family History Library database *Ireland, Civil Registration Indexes, 1845–1958*. When we search for Robert William McClements, born in 1867, the results (Figure 8.8) show an entry for a Robert William McClements born in 1867 in the "registration district" of Banbridge. Banbridge is the *superintendent* registrar's district, which is synonymous with the poor law union, and *not* the same as the registration district, which was Loughbrickland. The index shows that the birth record is in Volume 6, on page 273.

---

4 *Ireland Births and Baptisms, 1620–1881*, index, FamilySearch (https://familysearch.org), Robert William Mcclements, 02 Apr 1867; citing 0273, LOUGHBRICKLAND,DOWN, IRELAND, reference; FHL microfilm 101145.

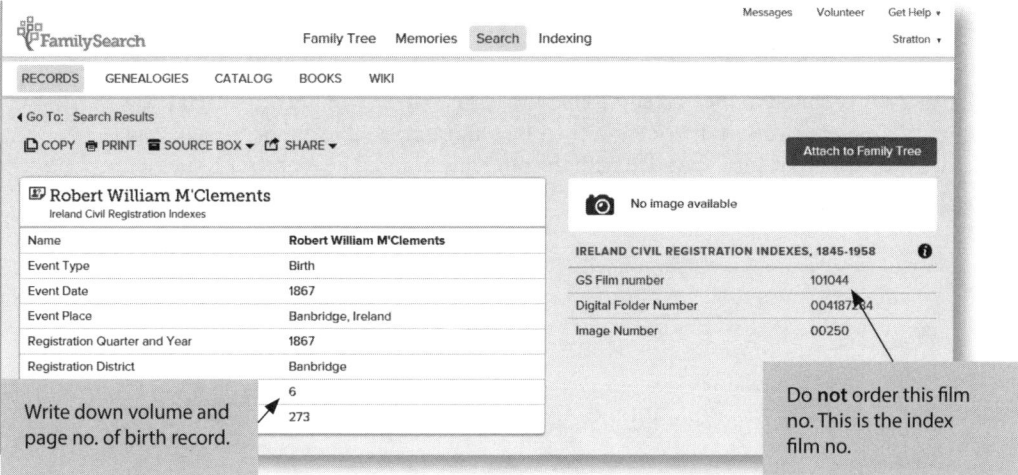

Figure 8.8. Search results page from the database *Ireland, Civil Registration Indexes,* 1845–1958, FamilySearch.org.

Note: Do not order the film number on the civil registration index page—which is the film number for the index, not the record. Order the film number 101145, as previously mentioned.

When the film arrives, we proceed to Volume 6 and go to page 273 (the printed numbers on the upper right, not the handwritten page number in the middle). The record shows the April 2, 1867, birth of Robert William McClements, son of John McClements of Bovennett and Susana McClements, formerly Moorhead. (See Figure 8.9.) His father was the informant. The townland of birth is recorded in the first column. The record also documents the residence of his father as Bovennett. A townland, as explained in the previous chapter, is the smallest geographic unit in Ireland; it often encompasses only a few hundred acres.

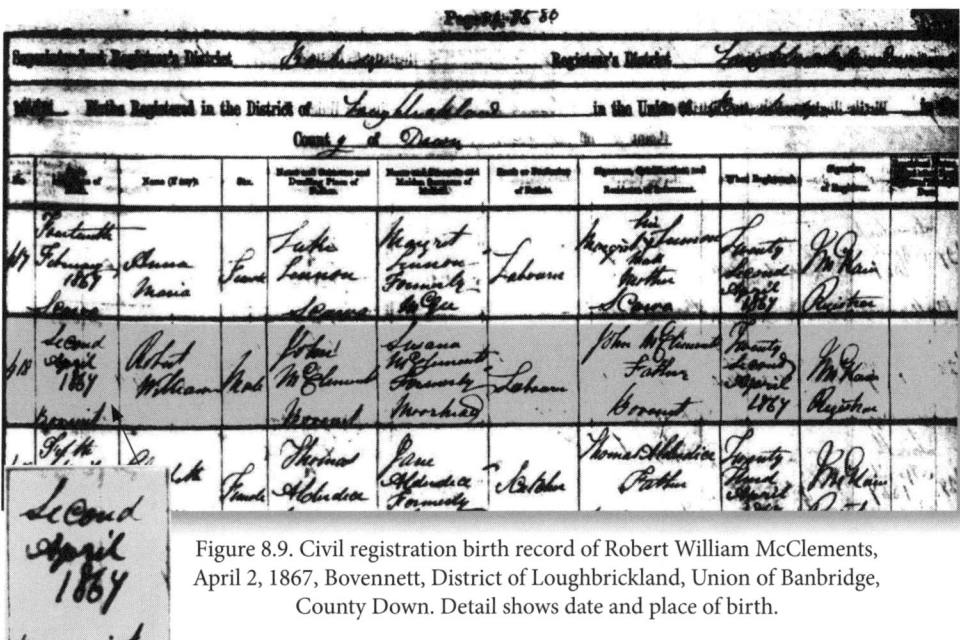

Figure 8.9. Civil registration birth record of Robert William McClements, April 2, 1867, Bovennett, District of Loughbrickland, Union of Banbridge, County Down. Detail shows date and place of birth.

Chapter 8: Irish Church Records and Civil Registrations

Bovennett is a townland in the village of Loughbrickland, parish of Aghaderg, County Down. It is located near the townland of Ballygowan.

Also as explained in the preceding chapter, Irish civil records are organized first by local area registration district and then by a more regional superintendent registrar's district that corresponded with the poor law union. Thus for the McClements family, we encounter the following:

Townland	Bovenett, County Down
Village	Loughbrickland
Civil parish	Aghaderg
Civil registration district	Loughbrickland
Superintendent registrar's district/poor law union	Banbridge
County	Down

With the name of the townland in hand, you can consult the Irish Ancestors website, www.JohnGrenham.com, to determine the relevant civil parish. Take care not to mistake the registration district for the place of birth. It can be confusing until you understand the various civil registration districts and where you can identify them. You need to see the microfilm of the original record to determine the townland of birth. In addition, you cannot search on the registration district at FamilySearch; you can search only on the poor law union. To search on all people with the surname McClements born in the registration district of Loughbrickland, you will have to enter a much wider search on Banbridge.

Table 8.1
Helpful resources for finding your ancestors in Irish civil records

Record set	Spanning years	Database	Microfilm	Which gives you
Civil registration indexes	1845–1958	FamilySearch.org Ancenstry.com Findmypast.com Irishgenealogy.ie		Poor law union (or superintendent registrar's district) plus volume and page nos.
Civil birth records, Irish Republic	1864–March 1955		FHL	townland of birth
Civil birth records, Northern Ireland	1922–1959		FHL	townland of birth
Ireland Births and Baptisms, 1620–1881	1620–1881	FamilySearch.org		civil registration district and parents' names
Ireland Marriages, 1619–1898	1619–1898 (only a few places)	FamilySearch.org		civil registration district and father's name
Ireland, Deaths, 1864–1870	1864–1870 (only a few places)	FamilySearch.org		civil registration district

The Family History Library has the microfilms for civil birth records after 1900, but they are not in a searchable database. The library does not have films of the birth records from the fourth quarter 1881 through 1900, but they do have films for the Irish Republic from 1900 through March 1955. In addition, the FHL has microfilms of birth records for Northern Ireland from 1922 through 1959. You can order the films and have them delivered to a local Family History Center. In this case, you start with the database Ireland, Civil Registration Indexes, 1845–1958, and determine the superintendent registrar's district (poor law union), date, volume, and page. Next, go to the FHL catalog. Search on the place name, Ireland, and the keyword Births. Among the results is "civil registration." After you click on this option, you will see that one of the collections is called "Quarterly returns of births in Ireland, 1864–1955, with index to births, 1864–1921." Scroll down the page to the films for 1867, and look for Volume 6. Note that the film number is 101145, the same as above. That film will be the one you need to order. To obtain certified copies of births in this time span, you will have to order them from the General Register Office in Ireland.

Use Marriage Records to Take Your Search Back a Generation

Among records of births, marriages, and deaths in Ireland, civil marriage records are the most likely to get you back another generation, since the names of the fathers of the bride and groom are documented. Ireland began recording non-Catholic marriages in 1845 and Catholic marriages in 1864. The Family History Library has entered some (not all) Irish marriages for some (not all) places into a searchable database, *Ireland Marriages, 1619–1898*.

In the case of John McClements and Susan Morehead, the parents of Robert McClements, a search in the *Ireland Marriages, 1619–1898* database at FamilySearch.org yields a transcription of their 1852 marriage record.

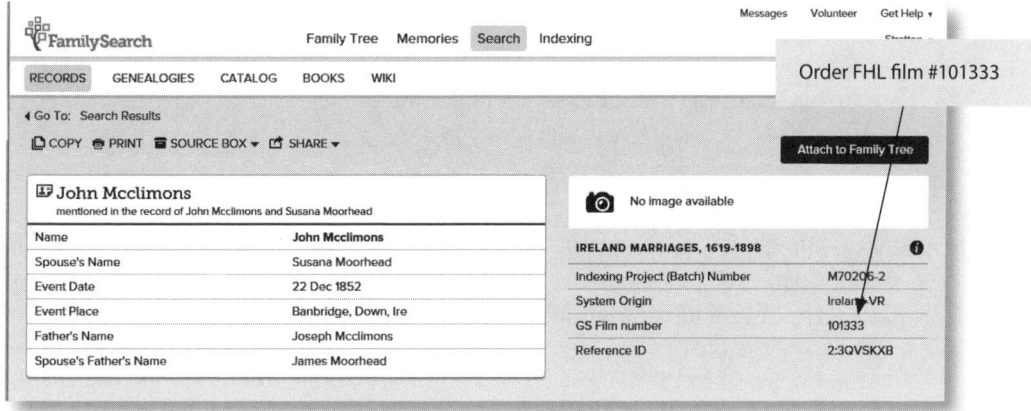

Figure 8.10. Transcription of 1852 marriage record,
John Mcclimons [sic] and Susana Moorhead.

A microfilm of the actual record can be ordered from the Family History Library. The transcription indicates that the fathers of John Mcclimons [*sic*] and Susana Moorhead were Joseph Mcclimons and James Moorhead. The registration district (poor law union) was Banbridge, County Down. Again, you need to determine the volume and page to avoid having to scan through hundreds of pages.

With this marriage record, we are back another generation in the McClements and Moorhead families. As in the case of birth records, you should access a copy of the original record to determine the townlands of residence for the bride and groom.

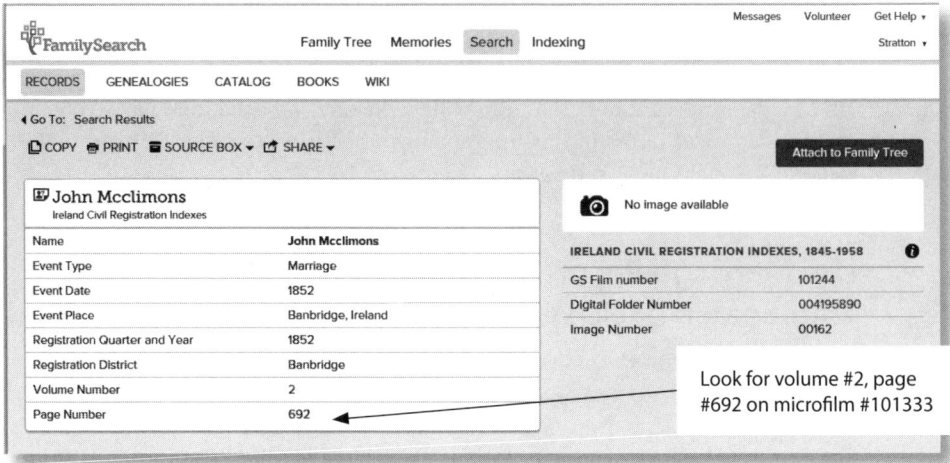

Figure 8.11. Ireland, Civil Registration Indexes, 1845–1958.

Using FamilySearch.org to locate marriage records can be unwieldy, since you have to cross reference the names of the bride and groom by making lists of the hits, writing down the volumes and pages, and comparing the two lists to identify the common volume and page number. But you can search for marriage records at Ancestry.com and Findmypast.com and see the corresponding spouse on the results page. In the case of John Mcclimons and Susana Moorhead, a search on Findmypast for Susana Morehead (checking off name variants) yields an entry for a Susana Moorhead that indicates a John Mcclimons on the same page. The results also provide the volume and page number.

The Findmypast website gives you the cross-reference so that you can verify the date, volume, and page and use this information to order the marriage record from the General Register Office in Ireland. But the website does not give you the Family History Library film number, so you will need to look up the marriage in the FHL catalog under *Marriage Records, 1845–1870, with indexes to marriages, 1845–1921, in the General Registry Office of Ireland*. The FHL does not have films of marriages after 1870. Those records you will have to order from the General Register Office of Ireland or Northern Ireland.

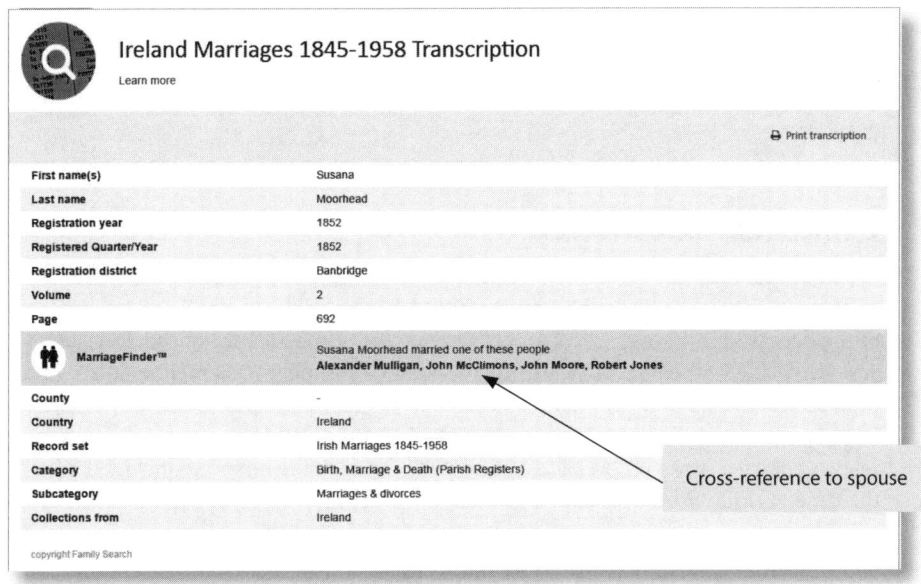

Figure 8.12. Civil registration marriage index at FindMyPast.com.

The film shows that John McClimons [sic] and Susana Moorhead [sic] were married December 22, 1852, in Banbridge. Both bride and groom were weavers and resided in the townland of Ballyvally. The marriage record also shows that John was the son of Joseph McClimons, who was a farmer; and that Susana was the daughter of James Moorhead, a labourer. Ballyvally was a townland that covered much of the town of Banbridge. So the couple probably had been working in a textile mill in Banbridge when they married. But they later moved to the townland of Bovenett in the town of Loughbrickland by the time their son, Robert, was born in 1864. Loughbrickland is located 8 miles southwest of Banbridge.

Note that there is a discrepancy between the Michigan death record and this Irish marriage record for the name of the father of John McClements. A check of the Michigan death record of Joseph McClements, a likely brother who lived next door to John McClements, shows that Joseph's father's name was Joseph.

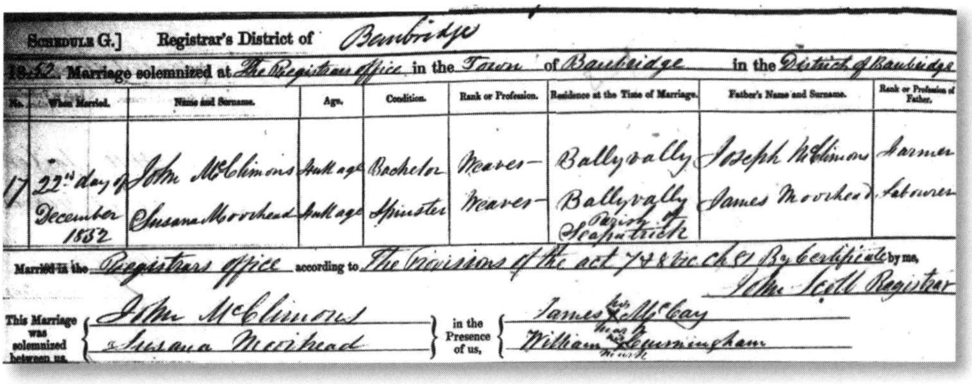

Figure 8.13. Marriage record of John McClimons and Susana Moorhead Banbridge, County Down, December 22, 1852.

Chapter 8: Irish Church Records and Civil Registrations

Furthermore, in the next chapter, we will see a Joseph McClements living in Ballygowan listed in Griffith's Valuation. So all the evidence, except John's death record, point to the name of the father of John McClements as being Joseph and not John.

Using Irish Death Records

If you are looking for Irish death records to determine the names of the parents of an Irish ancestor, you will be disappointed. The records do not list the parents of the deceased. But death records will provide the name and age of the deceased, and the place and cause of death. In the case of Joseph McClements, father of John McClements and grandfather of Robert William McClements, the Family History Library online database *Ireland, Deaths, 1864–1870* does not include any relevant entries. The FHL website explains, "Only a few localities are included and the time period varies by locality. This collection contains 51,249 records. Due to privacy laws, recent records may not be displayed. The year range represents most of the records. A few records may be earlier or later."[5] However, the FHL database *Ireland, Civil Registration Indexes, 1845–1958* shows the death of a 65-year-old Joseph M'Clements in the poor law union of Banbridge in 1866. With the volume number and page in hand, we can order a microfilm of the actual death record from the Family History Library.[6]

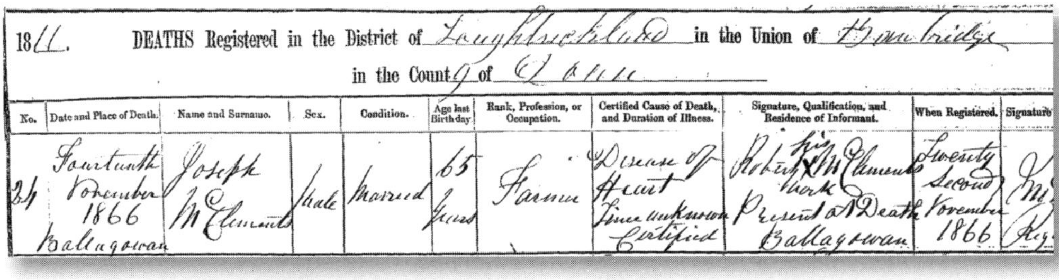
1866. DEATHS Registered in the District of Loughbrickland in the Union of Banbridge in the County of Down

No.	Date and Place of Death.	Name and Surname.	Sex.	Condition.	Age last Birthday.	Rank, Profession, or Occupation.	Certified Cause of Death, and Duration of Illness.	Signature, Qualification, and Residence of Informant.	When Registered.	Signature
24	Fourteenth November 1866 Ballagowan	Joseph McClements	Male	Married	65 Years	Farmer	Disease of Heart Time unknown Certified	Robert his X mark McClements Present at Death Ballagowan	Twenty Second November 1866	[illegible]

Figure 8.14. Death Record of Joseph McClements of Ballygowan, Loughbrickland District, Union of Banbridge, County Down, November 14, 1866.

The death record of Joseph McClements (Figure 8.14) indicates that he died in Ballygowan on November 14, 1866, of "Disease of Heart," and that he was a 65-year-old farmer. The informant was Robert McClements of Ballygowan, who may have been his son (and therefore the brother of John McClements).

Order Civil Birth, Marriage, and Death Records from Ireland and Northern Ireland

As noted above, the Family History Library does not have microfilms of all births, and there is a gap from 1881 to 1900. The FHL has marriage records for some localities from 1845 to 1870, and death records for some localities

[5] *Ireland, Deaths, 1864–1870,* database at FamilySearch.org.

[6] *Ireland, Civil Registration Indexes, 1845–1958,* database at FamilySearch.org; deaths entry for Joseph M'Clements; FHL microfilm 101583.

from 1864 to 1870. To obtain copies of these records not filmed by the FHL, you will need to order them from Ireland or Northern Ireland. If you want the information for genealogical purposes only, you should order a photocopy only, which at the time of this writing costs €4 (about $5). If you need a copy for legal purposes, such as applying for Irish citizenship, you will need to order a birth certificate—that is, a full copy—which costs more than a photocopy.

Obtaining Copies of Records

Births, Marriages, and Deaths, including pre-1922 records for the counties that became Northern Ireland

For pre-1922

- Order from General Register Office (GRO) in Roscommon.
- Download form from http://www.welfare.ie/en/Pages/General-Register-Office.aspx.
- Complete form and fax to +353(0)90 6632999 or mail to Civil Registration Office, Office of the Registrar General, Government Offices, Convent Road, Roscommon, Co. Roscommon, Ireland.
- Pay fee of €4 (about $5) by credit card.

For post-1922 (Republic)—click on "Apply for certificates online" under Online Services.

Even though you must order by mail or fax, you can request your copy via email.

Post-1922 Civil Registration Records for Northern Ireland (for all years)

- Order from the GRO for Northern Ireland, www.nidirect.gov.uk/general-register-office-for-northern-ireland.
- Pay fee of £15 (about $24) by credit card.

Note: When you are ordering pre-1922 civil registration records from Northern Ireland, the volume and page number from the civil registration indexes are not used. But ordering and paying £15 for pre-1922 civil records from Northern Ireland would be illogical when you can get the record for only €4 from the GRO in Roscommon.

Obtaining records in person in Ireland

- Obtain photocopies in person from the GRO office in Dublin (not Roscommon), on Werburgh Street, in a nondescript location at the back side of a parking lot, and adjacent to St. Werburgh Church.
- You can obtain a maximum of eight records per day.
- *Hint:* To make the best use of your visit to the GRO, research the births, marriages, and deaths online on FamilySearch.org, Ancestry.com, or Findmypast.com before arrival so that you have the volume and page numbers already identified.

Summary

To successfully research your forebears in Ireland, you must determine the names of the parents and/or the parish of origin of your immigrant ancestor in Ireland. Once you have ascertained this information, you can look for Irish records of births, baptisms, marriages, deaths, and burials. Civil registration began in Ireland in 1845 for non-Catholic marriages and 1864 for births and deaths. Even after these dates there was a considerable amount of under-registration. For records before 1864, you should search in church records for baptisms, marriages, and burials. Many church records can be accessed through online databases or on film at the Family History Library, the National Library of Ireland, or the Public Record Office of Northern Ireland. Civil registration records and many church records will provide the townland and enable you to look at census records, census substitutes, maps, directories, and estate records.

Further Reading

- Blumsom, Catherine. *Civil Registration of Births, Deaths, and Marriages in Ireland: A Practical Approach.* [Belfast?]: Ulster Historical Foundation, [1998?].
- Corish Patrick J., David C. Sheehy. *Records of the Irish Catholic Church.* Dublin, Ireland; Portland, Ore.: Irish Academic Press, 2001.
- ffeary-Smyrl, Steven C. *Irish Methodists—: Where Do I Start?* Dublin: Council of Irish Genealogical Organisations, 2000.
- Grenham, John. *Tracing Your Irish Ancestors: The Complete Guide.* Baltimore: Genealogical Pub. Co., 2006.
- Mitchell, Brian. *A Guide to Irish Churches and Graveyards.* Baltimore: Genealogical Pub. Co., 1990.
- Ó Dúill, Eileen, and Steven C. ffeary-Smyrl. *Irish Civil Registration—: Where Do I Start?* Dublin: Council of Irish Genealogical Organisations, 2000.
- Raymond Refaussé, *Church of Ireland Records.* Dublin, Ireland; Portland, Ore.: Four Courts Press, 2006.
- Ryan, James G. *Irish Church Records: Their History, Availability, and Use in Family and Local History Research.* Glenageary, Co. Dublin: Flyleaf Press, 2001.

CHAPTER 9
Using Records of Property and Valuation in Ireland

The loss of the nineteenth-century census records presents particular challenges for Irish genealogists when attempting to put families together and linking one generation to another. Thus, as a genealogist researching this time period, you will need to turn to property and valuation records as a "census substitute." These records not only identify the exact location of where an ancestor lived but, used in conjunction with other records such as parish registers, maps, civil registration records, landed estate records, and early twentieth-century census records, they can assist you in tracing the history of an Irish family in a specific location.

The most important of these is Griffith's Primary Valuation, published between 1847 and 1864. This resource is often underutilized by genealogists, yet it can serve as an entryway to nineteenth-century ancestral research. On face value, Griffith's appears to be nothing more than a list of names with descriptions of properties and unfamiliar legal terms. As you dig deeper, however, its details can help you to uncover possible family relationships, and it can assist you in piecing together clues and overcoming gaps left when records were destroyed in 1922.[1]

Irish family historians whose ancestors left Ireland before the Great Famine of 1845–1852 should not disregard these nineteenth-century property and valuation records. If you have identified your ancestor's place of origin, the information found, for example, in Griffith's and its maps will not only help you discover whether the family surname is still in the area but could very well help you locate the exact location of the ancestral home.

Historical Background

In order to use these records, it is important to understand the historical context of why they were created. In early nineteenth-century Ireland, there were two forms of local taxation: the *county cess* and the *tithes*. The county cess was a tax imposed

---

[1] James R. Reilly, *Richard Griffith and His Valuations of Ireland* (Baltimore: Clearfield Company, 2000), 48.

on occupiers of each townland. The county cess funded the local grand jury, which consisted of nearly two dozen of the largest landholders in the county. These individuals imposed the local county cess for the repair of roads and bridges and for the maintenance of buildings such as infirmaries, jails, and courthouses.[2] Each grand jury had its own unique practice for determining this tax, thus causing disproportions in the overall tax system and resentment by landowners and tenants.

The unfairness of these taxes upon the occupiers set in motion a series of land valuation surveys by the Irish government. There were three property valuations, and each produced its own set of records:

- The Townland Valuation, 1830–1840
- Tenement Valuation of 1846
- Tenement Valuation of 1852

The first property valuation in Ireland is the result of the passage of the Townland Valuation Act in 1826. A country-wide valuation was to be done on the agricultural worth of every lot of land and its buildings to determine how much each property should be taxed. By 1830, Richard Griffith, newly appointed as Commissioner of Valuation, and his team began their valuation in County Londonderry. These teams of valuators with their notebooks, surveying instruments, and maps moved from one townland to the next, progressively working their way south county by county over the course of the next seventeen years.[3] It wasn't long before Griffith realized this survey was too ambitious given the limited resources available to him, and the valuation was changed to focus only on buildings assessed at £3 or more.[4] By 1838, it was determined the survey was taking too long, and again the valuation was changed, this time to focus on buildings valued at £5 or more, thus excluding many householders in rural areas.

This initial valuation took place from 1830 to 1844 and produced two sets of records, the field books and the house books. The field books describe and measure the quality of the land and the house books note the measurement, condition, and construction of the home. The Townland Valuation taken during the years 1830 to 1838 is of particular value for those with ancestors in the parishes of the Ulster counties. As mentioned previously, the £3 threshold for assessing buildings will eliminate many of the occupiers living on farms in rural areas but it does capture many properties and householders in urban areas. Many of the notebooks classified as "field books" will contain lists of names of people living in towns and cities in places such as the city of Coleraine (Londonderry), Ballymoney (Antrim), or Downpatrick (Down). Both sets of records may have something to help you learn more about your ancestor's life in pre-Famine Ireland. The records become more valuable for two reasons. First, your ancestor may have left Ireland before Griffith's Primary Valuation was published for Ulster, which was some twenty five years after the Townland Valuation. Once Griffith completed his valuation in 1838 of the Ulster counties, he continued south and did not return until the third valuation in the late 1850s to early 1860s. Second, these records can be quite

---

[2] Reilly, *Richard Griffith,* p. 1.
[3] Reilly, *Richard Griffith,* p.13.
[4] Grenham, *Tracing Your Irish Ancestors,* p. 62.

helpful when you are attempting to piece together your ancestor's life in Ireland. The example shown in Figure 9.1 illustrates this point.

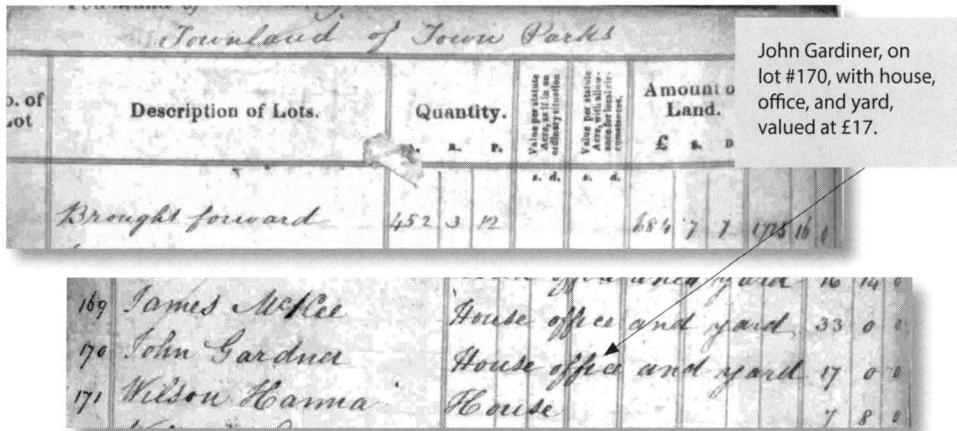

Figure 9.1. Excerpt from Townland Valuation Book at Public Record Office of Northern Ireland, Townland of Town Parks (Ballymena), Parish of Kirkinriola, County Antrim, completed January 24, 1838.

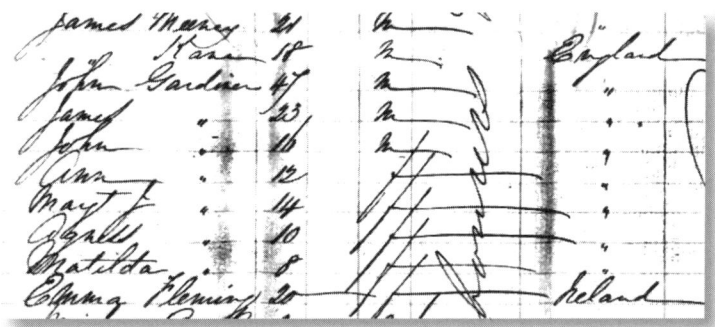

Figure 9.2. The June 1852 passenger manifest listing John Gardiner, widower, arriving at New York City on the Packet Ship *Franklin King* with his children. John and his family settled in Frankfort, Herkimer County, New York, where he purchased land in 1854.

This excerpt from the Townland Valuation Field Book of January 1838 lists occupiers in the townland of Town Parks, a townland—which, in this case, is part of town of Ballymena, in the civil parish of Kirkinriola, County Antrim. Our person of interest is John Gardiner, who immigrated to the United States in 1852 and who occupies lot 170. On his property there is a house, an office, and a yard valued at £17. ("Office" refers to another building on the property. It could be a shop or factory in an urban area. In rural areas it usually means a stable, barn, or similar structure.) Although not listed on this page of the valuation, John Gardiner lives and works on Church Street. Additional information from an 1842 business directory for Ballymena confirms that John had an "ironmongery and a delph and glass warehouse"; in other words, John was a hardware, glass, and china merchant. In documenting John's life in Ireland, we can find evidence of him in the Ballymena

Presbyterian Church marrying and having children. However, church records do not go far back enough to allow us to trace John back to a possible birth record and the identity of his parents. That is where records as the townland valuations take on greater importance: they help us fill in the blanks of our ancestor's life in Ireland.

Poor Law Act of 1838

By the 1830s a growing number of poor people in the country could no longer be supported by private organizations and the Church of Ireland. Unlike England, Ireland had no government body set up to offer relief to the poor and destitute. The Poor Law Act of 1838 established the workhouse system in Ireland. The funds to support the workhouses were to be obtained by taxing occupiers of land. The act also established the Poor Law Union Administrative Districts. The poor law union is named after the market town where the workhouse was located and includes the surrounding townlands in a ten-mile radius.

Tithe Applotment Survey ca. 1823–1838

Occupiers of an acre or more of agricultural holdings had to pay a tithe on a tenth (10 percent) on the produce of their land. This tax went to support the clergy of the Church of Ireland, the established church. Farmers of all religious denominations were required to pay the tithe. In 1823, Parliament passed the Composition Act, resulting in a revision of the way tithes were paid. Once paid in kind (with livestock or crops, not cash) by farmers, the tithes now due had to be paid in money. In order to implement this new system of taxation, a countrywide survey of all the agricultural land had to be valued. These surveys were recorded in what are known as the Tithe Applotment Books. These books are arranged by civil parish and townland. For further discussion of the Tithe Applotment Books and how to use them in your research, consult Chapter 10, Making the Most of Irish Online Records.

The Tenement Valuation Acts of 1846 and 1852

After the Poor Law Act was passed, there was growing dissatisfaction with the ongoing valuations and a widespread sense that the assessments were unfair. The country's two tax systems—poor law rates and county cess—resulted in an outcry for a more uniform system. The Tenement Valuation Act of 1842 led to a revised assessment in 1844.[5] Sir Richard Griffith and his team began the valuation in the remaining counties not yet done in the province of Munster (counties Cork, Kerry, Limerick, Tipperary, and Waterford) and included a re-valuation of Dublin.[6] In addition, the £5 threshold for valuation was discontinued and now *all* occupiers were included in the valuation. This survey proved so successful, the Tenement Valuation Act of 1852 was passed, allowing Griffith to continue the survey throughout Ireland. As these valuations were completed they were published between 1847 and 1864 and are known as *Griffith's Primary Valuation*. Beginning in the 1860s, valuators continued to return to the land every few years and recorded all changes to the value of the land, the occupier, and immediate lessor. The books that record these changes are called the

---

[5] The term *tenement* here refers to all building structures on a property and all land including bogs. Churches, schools, and hospitals were exempt from taxation.
[6] Reilly, *Richard Griffith*, p. 28.

Cancelled Land Books (or Revised Valuations). For a discussion and case study examples of how to use Griffith's Primary Valuation, its maps, and the Revised Valuations, please consult Chapter 10, Making the Most of Irish Online Records.

A Summary of Griffith's Pre-Publication Records

While many genealogical researchers have some familiarity with the printed Griffith's Primary Valuation, they may not have discovered and used the records that went into its preparation. These manuscript notebooks, frequently referred to as pre-publication records, can be quite valuable, as they can provide interesting details about the way your ancestors lived. Not all parishes have these records. However, you will want to make every effort to look at whatever has survived for the area where your ancestors lived. All these records are organized for each county by barony and parish. If using the records in Ireland, you will find them in several different repositories:

- National Archives of Ireland, Dublin, has all surviving material for the counties of the Republic of Ireland as well as some for Northern Ireland, but not a complete set.
- PRONI, Belfast, has the field and house books, along with the maps, that were created during the Townland Valuation of the 1830s for the Northern Ireland counties. A word of caution when using these records at PRONI. All records, field and house, are classified under "Field Books." When using PRONI's online catalog, it's best to use the browse feature when researching large record sets such as the valuation records. Searching on the term "val" will yield a complete listing of their valuation holdings. You can also consult a finding aid in the reading room.
- Valuation Office, Dublin, once had some of the pre-publication records in their possession, but these will be moved (if they have not been already) to the National Archives of Ireland.

The Family History Library has microfilm copies of the pre-publication records held by the National Archives of Ireland.

The good news is that the National Archives of Ireland, in partnership with Findmypast and FamilySearch, has digitized the pre-publication records in their possession. The name-searchable database, *Valuation Office Books, 1824–1856*, is available for free at genealogy.nationalarchives.ie and Findmypast.com. The valuation books on FamilySearch remain in browsable format on their library catalog and can only be accessed at their library in Salt Lake City or a local Family History Center. Genealogists take note: this online collection does not include pre-publication records recently transferred from the Valuation Office in Dublin to the National Archives. These records are being processed by the archives staff and will be digitized in the near future. Among the records of note now online is the 1837 valuation for the city of Belfast (labeled as a Quarto Book). This street-by-street valuation lists the occupier name, street address, and details regarding each property. When using the database, be mindful of spelling variations of a surname as well as the possible use of a nickname or a variant spelling to a given name. For example, Edward Hogan of Shippool, Leighmoney Parish, County Cork, can be recorded as Edward or Edmond in his children's baptismal records. He is known to be listed as a tenant in the Field, House, and Tenure books, but a search under

Edward Hogan yielded only partial results. An alternative search, using just surname and the parish, produced entries in all three valuation books.

These notebooks fall into several categories, with each providing you with different types of information about your ancestor's house and property. It's important to know the time period these books cover, what information they contain, and what parts of the country are represented, so review the descriptions for each type of valuation book before beginning any online search.

House books: Spanning the years from 1830 to the mid- to late 1850s, these books record the measurements of all buildings on a lot with occupier's name. Each structure on a lot was classified according to age, condition, and construction. "A" classifications are for new or nearly new structures built in the last 25 years; "B" represents buildings of a "medium age"; and "C" denotes buildings that are old. Within each class, a plus or minus sign represents the state of repair. The accompanying box explains these classifications further.

Field books: These books record the size of the holding as well as describe the quality of the soil. Field books done in the second valuation of the 1840s contain lot occupier names for the counties of Cork, Dublin, Kerry, Limerick, Tipperary and Waterford. Field books created in the pre-1838 valuation period list names for those in cities and towns of the counties of the province of Ulster. Consult James Reilly's *Richard Griffith and His Valuations of Ireland,* Appendix No. 3, page 70, for lists of the remaining counties and parishes with occupier names in field books.

Building classifications found in house and quarto books

1. Slated roof house of stone or brick made with lime mortar.
2. Thatched roof house of stone or brick with lime mortar.
3. Thatched roof house of stone walls with mud mortar or mud walls of best kind.

A+	Built or ornamented with cut stone, and of superior quality and finish.
A	Very substantial building and finish without cut stone ornament.
A−	Ordinary building and finish or either of the above when built 20 or 25 years.
B+	A building in sound order and good repair
B	A building that was slightly decayed, but still in good repair
B−	A building that had deteriorated and was not in perfect repair.
C+	An old building, but in repair.
C	An old building and out of repair.
C−	Old and dilapidated and scarcely habitable.

Source: James R. Reilly, *Richard Griffith and His Valuations of Ireland: With an Inventory of the Books of the General Valuation of Rateable Property in Ireland* (Baltimore: Clearfield Company, 2000), pp. 17–18.

The following notebooks were created during the second and third valuations, 1844 to late 1850s. You can find them at the National Archives of Ireland and at the Family History Library (online and on microfilm) but *not* at the Public Record Office of Northern Ireland.[7]

Tenure books: These books record the occupier's name along with amount of rent paid, whether owned property or leased, the start date of the lease, or whether the occupier is a tenant at will.

Perambulation books: These books record the value of the house, the valuator's visit to the properties, and names of all occupiers or tenants.

Quarto books: These books are just a different name for house books for large towns and cities. While they generally date from 1844 onward, there are some exceptions, such as the recently digitized quarto book for the city of Belfast, completed in 1837.

Rent books: These books are organized by landlord name and show the amounts of rents paid.

The three books you will want to consult with particular care are the field books, tenure books, and house books, with the last being the most important of the set. The house books not only provide details of the type of structure lived in, but they give us a window into the social and economic class of our Irish ancestors and bring the ancestral home to life. Since the house books predate the printed Primary Valuations, you will want to look for any changes to occupiers and land and compare it to the list of occupiers in the Primary Valuation. This is especially true of the house books created in the counties of Cork, Kerry, Limerick, Tipperary, and Waterford in the period between 1844 and about 1850, as they were the first to include all occupiers of the land. Therefore, it is very possible that changes occurred from the time the valuators were on the ground recording their findings in their notebooks to the time these valuation lists were published. Given that several years could occur between the two events (and much of this activity was during and shortly after the Great Famine), there could be a great many changes to the land and its occupiers, such as a possible death, emigration, or eviction. The example in Figures 9.3 and 9.4 illustrate the importance of looking at the pre-publication material.

The house book not only shows a revision to the lot numbers but the name of one tenant, David Leary, who was previously living on Lot #6b is crossed off, and the name of a new tenant, Daniel Coughlan, is written in. What happened to David Leary? Did he die or emigrate, or was he simply unable to pay the rent? Who is Daniel Coughlan? Could he be related to either Cornelius Desmond or David Leary? Further research is certainly needed, but if a family historian had only looked at the published Griffith's, a conclusion of "my ancestor David Leary is not in Griffith's" would have been made. The value of incorporating these manuscript materials cannot be underestimated.

---

[7] John Grenham, "What Is Griffith's Valuation?" at website Ask about Ireland, askaboutireland.ie/reading-room/history-heritage/irish-genealogy/what-is-griffiths-valuati/.

–	a	William Kerrican,		James Mahony,		House,		—			—		0 15 0		0 15 0	
–	e	Patrick Sheehan,		James Mahony,		House,		—			—		0 10 0		0 10 0	
5	a	Cornelius Desmond,		William H. Herrick, Esq.		House, offices, and land,		34	2	30	10 10 0		2 0 0		21 10 0	
–	b	Daniel Coghlan,		Cornelius Desmond,		House,		—			—		0 10 0		0 10 0	
6	a	Maurice Desmond,		William H. Herrick, Esq.		House, offices, and land,		56	1	21	35 15 0		2 0 0		37 15 0	
–	b	Denis Desmond,		Maurice Desmond,		House and garden,		0	1	25	0 2 0		0 10 0		0 12 0	
7		Thomas Palmer,		William H. Herrick, Esq.		Land,		4	2	32	1 10 0		—		1 10 0	
						Total,		235	2	13	99 1 0		10 17 0		109 18 0	

Figure 9.3. Excerpt from Griffith's Primary Valuation, townland of Ship-pool, Parish of Leighmoney, Barony of Kinalea, County Cork, published in 1851, showing Cornelius Desmond and Daniel Coughlan on Lots #5a and 5b respectively.

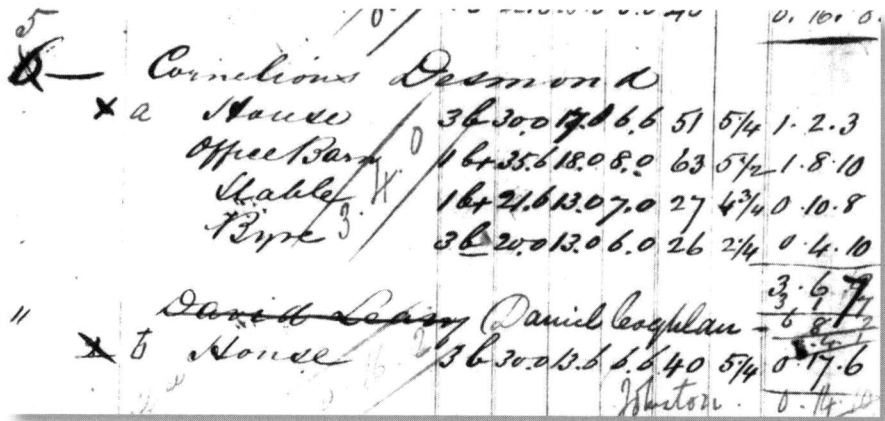

Figure 9.4. Excerpt from house book, Townland of Ship-pool, Parish of Leighmoney, Barony of Kinalea, County Cork, with changes recorded April 1, 1848.

Summary

The destruction of much of the nineteenth-century census records leaves family historians turning to a series of property and valuation records created during a tumultuous period. The bulk of Griffith's Primary Valuation was created against the backdrop of the Great Famine, with a group of surveyors and engineers traversing the nation, mapping out properties, and measuring and reporting on the value and size of the land and its structures. Sir Richard Griffith and his team assembled a great deal of records which often are underused by genealogists. From their work, three property valuations emerged, each producing its own set of records. Incorporating these records into your genealogical research, and using them with church and other records, can not only facilitate the discovery of family relationships but can make it possible to stand on the very lot your forebears once occupied.

Timeline of Key Dates Related to Nineteenth-Century Property and Valuation Records of Ireland

1800	The Act of Union was established, uniting the Kingdoms of Ireland and Great Britain, and abolishing the Irish Parliament. Governance of Ireland was now centralized in London setting the stage for future changes to methods of taxation of land and property.
1823	The passage of the Composition Act declares tithes due the established church (Church of Ireland) now had to be paid with money, no longer in kind.
1824	Ordnance Survey Office established for the purpose of surveying and mapping out administrative boundaries throughout the entire country for land valuation. Richard Griffith is appointed Boundary Commissioner.
1826	The first valuation of townlands begins with the passage of the Townland Valuation Act of 1826.
1827	Richard Griffith undertakes additional responsibility as Commissioner of Valuation.
1831	Tithe War commences, with many refusing to pay the tithes, resulting in lists of Tithe Defaulters.
1838	Poor Law Act of 1838 establishes workhouse system in Ireland. A poor law tax was instituted and the Poor Law Union Administrative division was established. The Tithe Rent Charge Act, passed the same year, abolished the tax paid by occupiers and shifted responsibility to the landowners.
1846	The second valuation of townlands begins with the passage of the Tenement Valuation Act of 1846. All occupiers are now included in the valuation.
1852	The success of the valuation of properties in the Munster counties leads Parliament to pass the third valuation of townlands. It also mandated valuators to return to the property periodically every few years to record all changes. This was carried out from the 1860s until the 1970s.
1871-1909	The various land acts passed in the late nineteenth and early twentieth century enabled tenants to purchase property from landowners. In the Revised Land Books you will be able to identify if an ancestor purchased the property by the letters L.A.P. (for Land Act Purchase) stamped on the page.
1922	The destruction of the Four Courts building in Dublin resulted in the loss of many records, including the censuses of 1821, 1831, and 1841, which predate the Famine, and the 1851 census.

Further Reading

- Grenham, John. "What is Griffith's Valuation?" At the website Ask about Ireland, askaboutireland.ie/reading-room/history-heritage/irish-genealogy/what-is-griffiths-valuati/.

- Grenham, John. *Tracing Your Irish Ancestors: The Complete Guide.* Dublin: Gill & Macmillan, 2012.

- Paton, Chris. *Discover Irish Land Records.* St. Agnes, SA, Australia: Unlock the Past, 2015.

- Reilly, James R. "Is There More to Griffith's than Just Names?" www.leitrim-roscommon.com/GRIFFITH/Griffiths.PDF.

- Reilly, James R. *Richard Griffith and His Valuations of Ireland: With an Inventory of the Books of the General Valuation of Rateable Property in Ireland.* Baltimore: Clearfield Company, 2000.

Chapter 10
Making the Most of Irish Online Census and Land Valuation Records

Once you have determined the location of your ancestor's family, and become oriented with a good background on Irish place names and administrative districts, you are ready to research further in Irish records, ideally from your home computer. In this chapter, we will look at the most commonly used sources for nineteenth- and twentieth-century research. While some guidebooks provide an in-depth description and compendium of all Irish resources, this chapter will focus more on accessing records and integrating them with other sources. To illustrate the use of the Irish records, we will feature our case studies of the Fitzgerald family of Bruff, County Limerick, and the McClements family of Aghaderg, County Down.

Search in Census Records and Census Substitutes

One of the greatest tragedies in Irish history is the loss of the Public Record Office collections in 1922. On June 30 of that year, the building in the Four Courts that housed a vast collection of historical documents dating back to the thirteenth century, was destroyed by fire. Who was to blame is still a matter of controversy, but the resulting damage to our knowledge of Ireland's past is irrefutable. The destruction included probate records, Church of Ireland parish registers, and census records. Consequently, Irish repositories have resorted to using remnants and substitutes to compensate, albeit partially, for the missing information.

Census records

The collection of population data in Ireland began with the 1821 census, which listed everyone in a household, including their ages and occupations. A census was taken every ten years after that. In the 1851 census, the names of persons who had died or were living elsewhere (including emigrants) in the previous ten years were recorded. The 1861 and 1871 census records were destroyed after they were taken, and the 1881 and 1891 census records were pulped for the paper. Except for a few remnants, the 1821–1851 census records were destroyed when the Public Record Office was blown up in the Irish Civil War.[1] The remnants that survived the fire have been scanned and are searchable on the National Archives of Ireland website, http://www.census.nationalarchives.ie.

When you see the census remnants, you will understand the magnitude of loss wreaked on the recorded history of Ireland. For instance, remnants for a good portion of County Cavan, and some parts of Fermanagh and Galway, show that the 1821 census documented not only the heads-of-household but every person in a household, and their ages and their occupations. The 1841 census detailed every person in the household at a time just before the Famine, when the Irish population was at its peak, and the remnant sheds a fascinating light on the parish of Killeshandra, County Cavan.

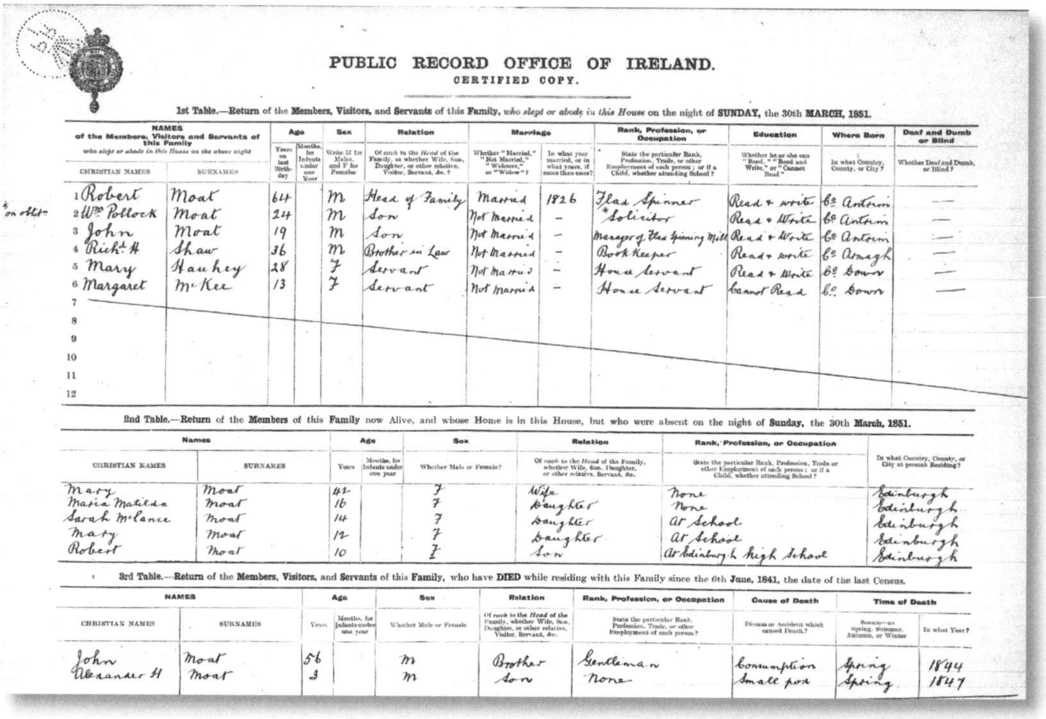

PUBLIC RECORD OFFICE OF IRELAND.
CERTIFIED COPY.

1st Table.—Return of the Members, Visitors, and Servants of this Family, who slept or abode in this House on the night of SUNDAY, the 30th MARCH, 1851.

	Christian Names	Surnames	Age: Years on last Birthday	Age: Months for Infants under one Year	Sex: Write M for Males, and F for Females	Relation: Of each to the Head of the Family, as whether Wife, Son, Daughter, or other relative, Visitor, Servant, &c.?	Marriage: Whether "Married," "Not Married," "Widower," or "Widow"?	Marriage: In what year married, or in what years, if more than once?	Rank, Profession, or Occupation: State the particular Rank, Profession, Trade, or other Employment of each person; or if a Child, whether attending School?	Education: Whether he or she can "Read," "Read and Write," or "Cannot Read"	Where Born: In what Country, County, or City?	Deaf and Dumb or Blind: Whether Deaf and Dumb, or Blind?
1	Robert	Moat	64		M	Head of Family	Married	1826	Flax Spinner	Read & write	Co Antrim	—
2	Wm Pollock	Moat	24		M	Son	Not Married	–	*Solicitor	Read & Write	Co Antrim	—
3	John	Moat	19		M	Son	Not Married	–	Manager of Flax Spinning Mill	Read & Write	Co Antrim	—
4	Richd H	Shaw	36		M	Brother in Law	Not Married	–	Book Keeper	Read & write	Co Armagh	—
5	Mary	Hauhey	28		F	Servant	Not Married	–	House Servant	Read & Write	Co Down	—
6	Margaret	McKee	13		F	Servant	Not Married	–	House Servant	Cannot Read	Co Down	—
7												
8												
9												
10												
11												
12												

*on other

2nd Table.—Return of the Members of this Family now Alive, and whose Home is in this House, but who were absent on the night of Sunday, the 30th March, 1851.

Christian Names	Surnames	Age: Years	Age: Months, for Infants under one year	Sex: Whether Male or Female?	Relation: Of each to the Head of the Family, whether Wife, Son, Daughter, or other relative, Servant, &c.	Rank, Profession, or Occupation: State the particular Rank, Profession, Trade or other Employment of each person; or if a Child, whether attending School?	In what Country, County, or City at present Residing?
Mary	Moat	42		F	Wife	None	Edinburgh
Maria Matilda	Moat	16		F	Daughter	None	Edinburgh
Sarah McLance	Moat	14		F	Daughter	At School	Edinburgh
Mary	Moat	12		F	Daughter	At School	Edinburgh
Robert	Moat	10		F	Son	At Edinburgh High School	Edinburgh

3rd Table.—Return of the Members, Visitors, and Servants of this Family, who have DIED while residing with this Family since the 6th June, 1841, the date of the last Census.

Christian Names	Surnames	Age: Years	Age: Months, for infants under one year	Sex: Whether Male or Female	Relation: Of each to the Head of the Family, whether Wife, Son, Daughter, or other relative, Visitor, Servant, &c.	Rank, Profession, or Occupation: State the particular Rank, Profession, Trade, or other Employment of each person?	Cause of Death: Disease or Accident which caused Death?	Time of Death: Season—as Spring, Summer, Autumn, or Winter	Time of Death: In what Year?
John	Moat	56		M	Brother	Gentleman	Consumption	Spring	1844
Alexander H	Moat	3		M	Son	None	Small pox	Spring	1847

Figure 10.1. 1851 census, Townland of Dunmurray, parish of Drumbeg, Upper Belfast, County Antrim. In addition to recording the population, the census logged the absent people and their location, as well as people who died in the previous ten years, the cause of death, and the date of death.

The only complete census records to survive are for 1901 and 1911, and these are available for research on the National Archives of Ireland website, http://www.census.nationalarchives.ie. The census detailed not only population data, but also descriptions of houses and outbuildings. You may be able to find an ancestor born before 1901 living with his or her family. Many young Irish men and women arrived in the United States between the 1880s and 1910s, leaving their parents

[1] History of Irish census records, National Archives of Ireland, http://www.census.nationalarchives.ie/help/history.html.

behind. Even if your ancestor emigrated from Ireland before 1901, you may be able to find his or her parents or siblings in Ireland. If you know the name of the townland, you can leave the name field blank and search on the townland. When the results are displayed, you can click on the surname heading to arrange the display alphabetically, and then go to the page with the surname of your ancestor. People with the same surname who were living in the same townland are always of interest, since they could be relatives. If you don't know the name of the townland, your search may be more difficult, since the maiden names of women are not shown, and you may find multiple couples with the same names as the parents of your ancestor. Findmypast has a 1901 census index database that allows you to cross-reference on another person in the household, thereby narrowing the search for ancestors with common names.

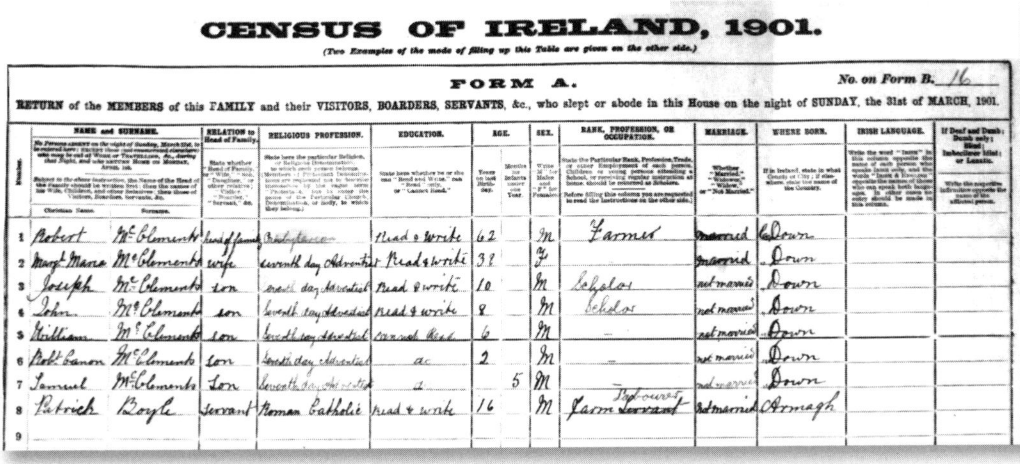

Figure 10.2. 1901 Census, Form A, Ballygowan, County Down.

To look now at one of our case studies, John and Susan (Morehead) McClements of Bovennett townland, Aghaderg parish, County Down, immigrated to Michigan in 1870, but there were likely relatives in the nearby townland of Ballygowan, where John McClements was born. In fact, we saw Robert McClements was the informant on the death record of Joseph McClements, father of John McClements, who died in Ballygowan in 1866. These relatives remained in Ireland, and the 1901 and 1911 census can be used to research and identify the relatives.

The 1901 census of Ireland had several pages or forms. Form A was a detailed population schedule listing all the members of a household, including servants, their relationship to the head of household, age, marital status, literacy, religion, county of birth, and language. Form B showed the head of household, owner, building and roof materials, numbers of windows in front, and numbers of rooms. A third schedule, Form B2, listed the farm and livestock buildings. Together, these forms provide a fascinating portrait of the homes of our ancestors.

The 1901 census for Ballygowan showed the family of 62-year-old Robert McClements with his wife and five children, as well as a farm laborer, Patrick Boyle. All but the farm laborer had been born in County Down. Form B indicates that the house of Robert McClements was made of stone, had a thatch roof, and consisted of three rooms, with three windows in front. The 1911 census showed that the house of Robert McClements had a slate roof, seven windows in front and seven rooms. So he had either built a new house or added substantially to the original house. The 1911 census also shows the farm and outbuildings. McClements had a stable, cow house, calf house, fowl house, barn, potato house, and shed.

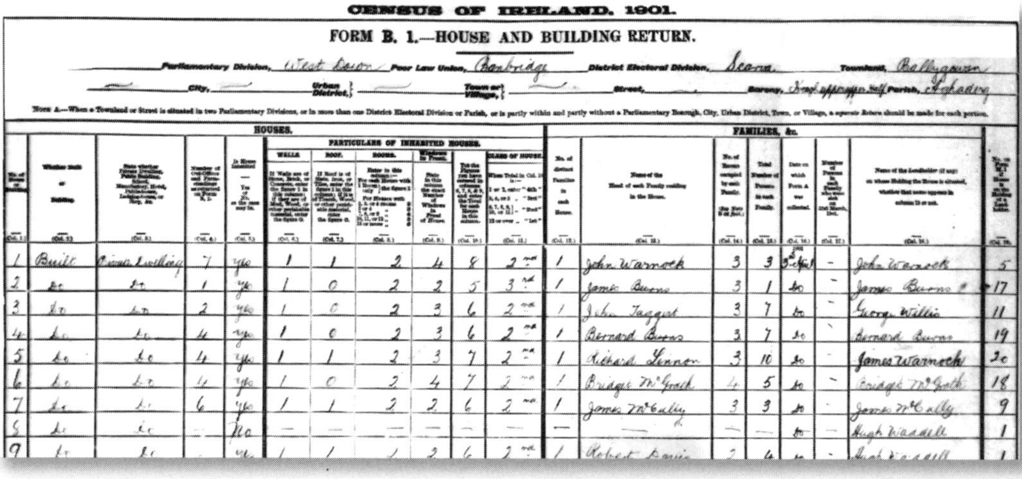
CENSUS OF IRELAND. 1901.

FORM B. 1.—HOUSE AND BUILDING RETURN.

Parliamentary Division, West Down Poor Law Union, Banbridge District Electoral Division, Seana Townland, Ballygowan

City, — Urban District, — Town or Village, — Street, — Barony, Iveagh Upper Half Parish, Aghaderg

(Col. 1)	(Col. 2)	(Col. 3)	(Col. 4)	(Col. 5)	(Col. 6)	(Col. 7)	(Col. 8)	(Col. 9)	(Col. 10)	(Col. 11)	(Col. 12)	(Col. 13)	(Col. 14)	(Col. 15)	(Col. 16)	(Col. 17)	(Col. 18)	(Col. 19)
1	Built	Private Dwelling	7	yes	1	1	2	4	8	2nd	1	John Warnock	3	3	3rd April	-	John Warnock	5
2	do	do	1	yes	1	0	2	2	5	3rd	1	James Burns	3	1	do	-	James Burns	17
3	do	do	2	yes	1	0	2	3	6	2nd	1	John Taggart	3	7	do	-	George Willis	11
4	do	do	4	yes	1	0	2	3	6	2nd	1	Bernard Burns	3	7	do	-	Bernard Burns	19
5	do	do	4	yes	1	1	2	3	7	2nd	1	Richard Lennon	3	10	do	-	James Warnock	20
6	do	do	4	yes	1	0	2	4	7	2nd	1	Bridget McGrath	4	5	do	-	Bridget McGrath	18
7	do	do	6	yes	1	1	2	2	6	2nd	1	James McCally	3	3	do	-	James McCally	9
8	do	do	—	No	—	—	—	—	—	—	—	—	—	—	do	—	Hugh Waddell	1
9	do	do	[illegible]	yes	1	1	2	2	6	2nd	1	Robert [illegible]	[illegible]	4	do	-	Hugh Waddell	1

Figure 10.3. 1901 Census, Form B, Ballygowan, County Down.

Census substitutes

Although the pre-1901 census records were destroyed, other genealogically useful records survive. The most frequently used and readily searched records are Griffith's Valuation of Ireland and the Tithe Applotment Books. These records can identify the head of household, the number of acres occupied, and the valuation of the land and buildings. In the case of Griffith's Valuation, the exact location of the household can be identified on a map and compared to modern satellite views.

Griffith's Primary Valuation of Ireland

As described in Chapter 9, Griffith's Primary Valuation of Ireland is a mid-nineteenth-century census substitute that documents the heads-of-household who were land occupiers. The valuations were published between 1847 and 1864. But the collection of the data was a massive undertaking and started earlier than the publication dates. The purpose of the survey was to establish a basis for the taxation of property or valuation. Landlords, rather than tenants, were responsible for paying the taxes on properties valued at less than £5.[2] Griffith's Valuation allows researchers to identify the exact location of their ancestor's dwelling on a map and to trace the occupancy of that dwelling forward to the twentieth century. A good article describing Griffith's Valuation by Rachel Murphy, "Griffith's Valuation as a Source for Irish Family History," appears in *Irish Roots Magazine,* 2011, Number 3.

[2] John Grenham, "What is Griffith's Valuation?" at Ask about Ireland website, http://www.askaboutireland.ie/reading-room/history-heritage/irish-genealogy/what-is-griffiths-valuati/. Also James R. Reilly, CGRS, "Is There More in Griffith's Valuation Than Just Names?" http://www.leitrim-roscommon.com/GRIFFITH/Griffiths.PDF.

Many people mistakenly believe their ancestors were too poor to appear in the valuations, but this is a misconception. The valuation recorded land occupiers, not just landowners, so even poor cottiers were documented. Griffith's Valuation assigned numbers and letters as addresses, recorded the head-of-household, the immediate lessor, the number of acres occupied, and the value of the land and buildings occupied. The immediate lessor can be a middleman or a landlord. By identifying the immediate lessor, Griffith's Valuation provides important clues in the search for estate papers.

In Bruff, County Limerick, we see a Michael Fitzgerald in the townland of Newtown, at Lot #19c. He is listed as occupying a house only, with no land, and the house was worth 10 shillings. An Edmond Fitzgerald is listed nearby at the adjacent Lot #20a. Michael Fitzgerald and four others were leasing from James Humphreys, who in turn was leasing from Frederick Bevan, Esq. Bevan was the lessor for the whole townland.

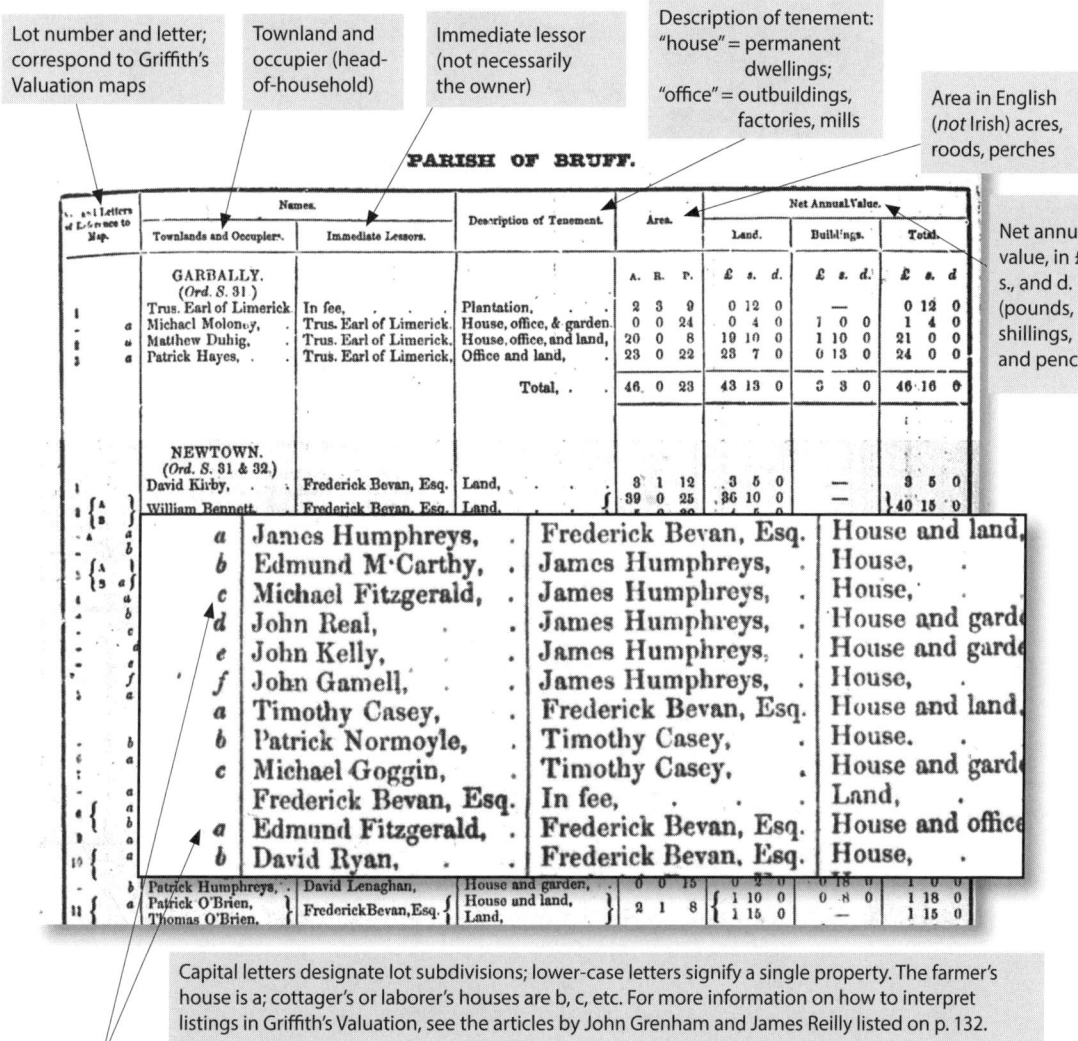

Figure 10.4. Griffith's Valuation, Townland of Newtown, parish of Bruff, County Limerick, with detail showing Michael and Edmund Fitzgerald, at Lots #19c and 20a.

Griffith's Valuation can be linked with accompanying maps that show the location of the house. The townland of Newtown lies just north of the village of Bruff. The houses are situated along the Palatine Road leading into the village and are on long, narrow lots. Two sites display the accompanying maps for Griffith's Valuation: Ask about Ireland, which is a free site, and Findmypast, which is available by subscription. Ask about Ireland displays maps that date from a later period. We see in the valuation above that Michael Fitzgerald rented house c on Lot #19. A total of six houses were on the lot. But the map shows only three houses. So three houses disappeared, probably torn down, between the time of the original valuation and the late nineteenth-century map at Ask about Ireland. Note the number 250 under the letter b on Lot 19. This number will help us identify the current location.

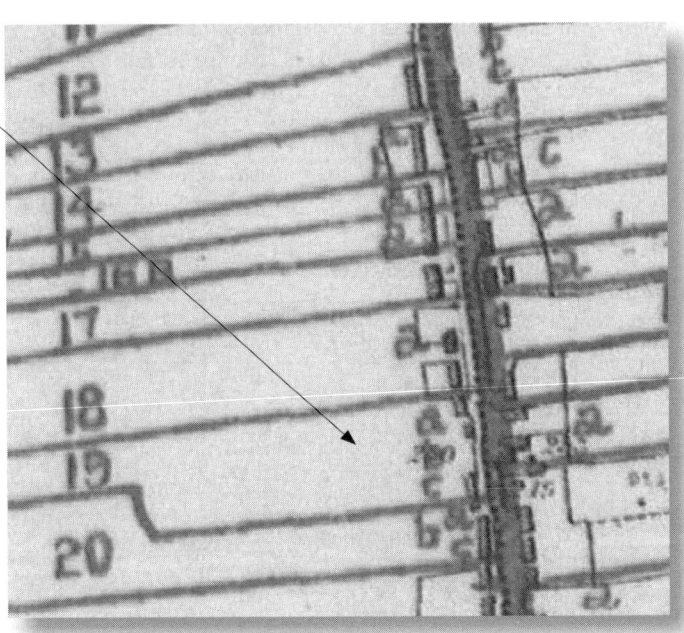

Figure 10.5. Valuation map, townland of Newtown, parish of Bruff, County Limerick.

The website Ask about Ireland has a new feature that allows you to view a parcel on a number of different maps, including a modern map. Once you have found a parcel of interest, for instance, Lot #19 in the townland of Newtown, parish of Bruff, as shown in Figure 10.5, you can access earlier black-and-white maps that may show different lot numbers and subdivisions. Michael Fitzgerald lived on Lot #19c.

In the upper right corner of the screen you will see several features, including Guide to Maps, a scroll bar from Modern Map to Historical Map, a Map version showing a range of six maps, buttons called Show Towns and Show Name Books. You can click on each of the six map versions to view other maps for the same parcel of land. Map #6 on the Ask about Ireland site shows a black-and-white map with many revisions, and may show changes from the original maps to the later color map (Valuation Map #1, Figure 10.6).

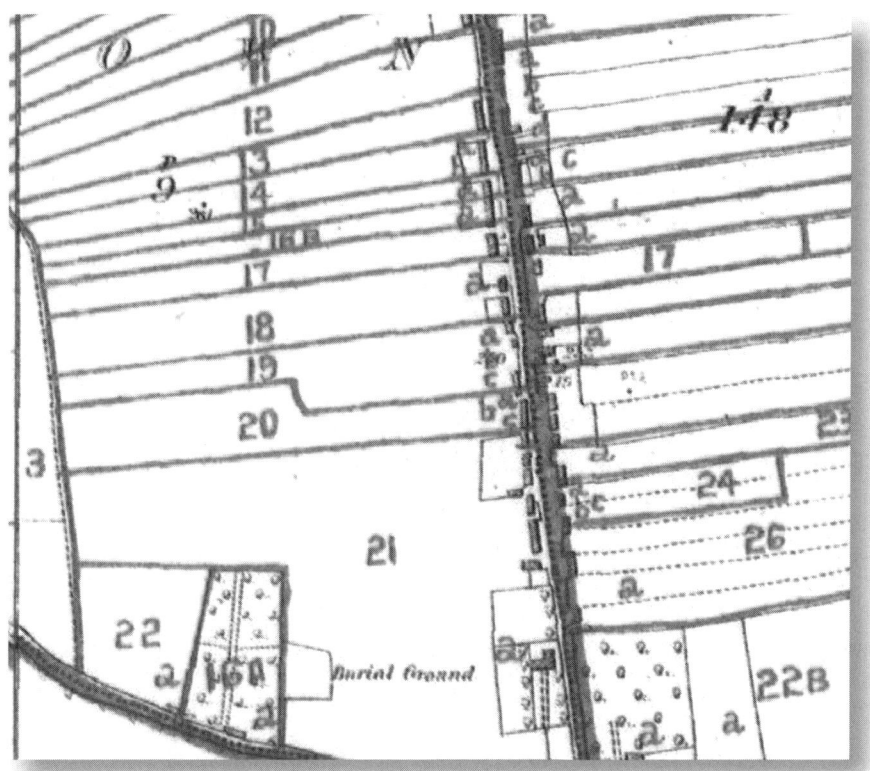

Figure 10.6. Valuation Map #1 on Ask about Ireland for Newtown, parish of Bruff.

You can also slide the bar over to the left to view the modern map. It does not have a lot of detail, but a feature on the upper left of the screen allows you to change to a satellite view. So theoretically you can stick your finger on Valuation Map #1, move the bar over to modern map, and then click on satellite view. You will now have your finger on the modern place where a house may still stand.

This website also has a feature called Find Name Books. When you click on it, a little book icon will display on the map. Click on the book icon to see a description of the townland name, gathered from various sources. The same goes for the Show Towns button, for which a small icon will appear over the town. When you click on it, a more detailed map of the town will appear.

Once you have identified the place where your ancestor lived on the valuation map and the satellite map, you can bring up the place on Google maps. Choose the satellite view on Google maps, and then use street view by dragging the little person icon to the spot where your ancestor lived. Sometimes you can find your ancestor's house still there. (See Figure 10.10.)

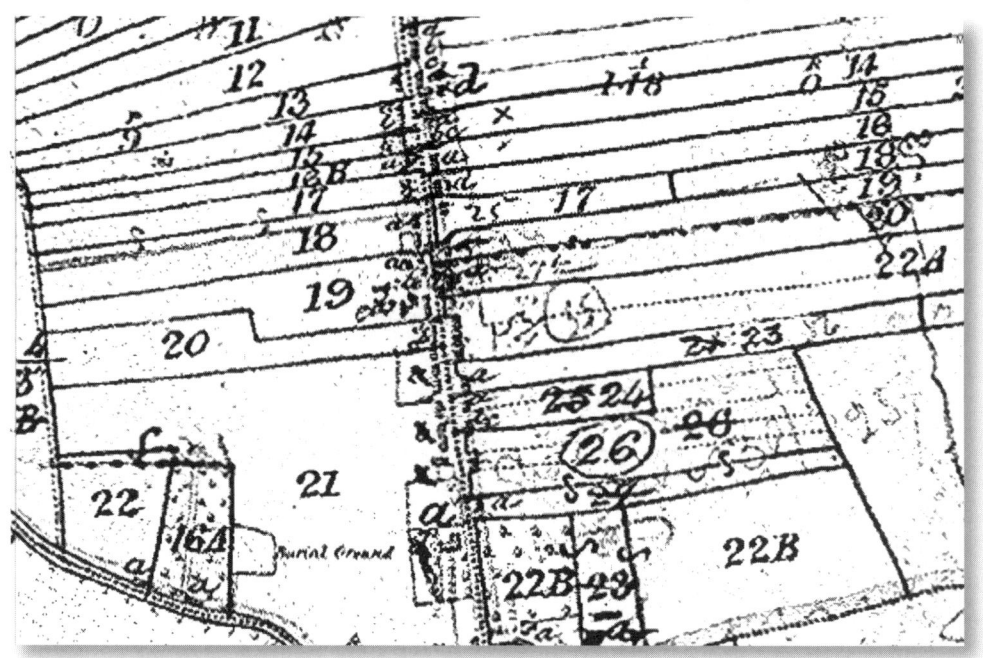

Figure 10.7. Valuation Map #6 on Ask about Ireland, Newtown, parish of Bruff.

Figure 10.8. Satellite view showing Lot #19
on Ask about Ireland, Newtown, parish of Bruff.

```
Ballycampion              -- Boundary Srs. Sketch Map   3

BAILE UI CHEAMPUIN, O'Campion's town.

Ballycampion              -- J.O'D.
Ballycampion              -- Tithe Compn. Book in possession
                             of the Revd. Mr. Massy, Bruff
                             Vicarage.
Ballycampion              -- Barony Map
Ballycampion              -- Report from the Select
                             Committee on the Survey
                             and Valuation of Ireland,
                             June 1824.

     In the N. extremity of the Parish. Bounded on
the N. by the Parish of Tullabracca, on the E. by the
Townland of Ballydoohaan, on the S. by Bruff, and on
the W. by Ballycampion. 32.

     The property of Lord Limerick, England. Containing
148 . 0 . 27. of arable Land. In the W. Boundary is
```

Figure 10.9. Name Book entry for townland of Ballycampion, parish of Bruff.

Figure 10.10. Google street view of townland of Newtown, where the Fitzgerald house once stood.

Using Griffith's Valuation to find the McClements family

We saw previously that Robert William McClements, son of John McClements and Susan Morehead, was born on April 2, 1864, in the townland of Bovennett, village of Loughbrickland, parish of Aghaderg, County Down. In Griffith's Valuation, a John McClements is listed in house #24 on Lot #10 in the townland of Bovennett, village of Loughbrickland. He does not occupy any land, only a house valued at 15 shillings. This dwelling was probably a row house along the road, across from the Gate Lodge.

VALUATION OF TENEMENTS. 63

PARISH OF AGHADERG.

No. and Letters of Reference to Map.	Names. Townlands and Occupiers.	Names. Immediate Lessors.	Description of Tenement.	Area. A. R. P.	Rateable Annual Valuation. Land. £ s. d.	Rateable Annual Valuation. Buildings. £ s. d.	Total Annual Valuation of Rateable Property. £ s. d.
	BOVENNETT—*continued.* TOWN OF LOUGHBRICKLAND.						
1 to 20	(*Valued in Townland of*	*Coolnacran.*)					
10 A 21	Robert Dixon,	Patrick Devlin,	House,	—	—	0 15 0	0 15 0
– 22	Samuel Stephenson,	Same,	House,	—	—	0 15 0	0 15 0
– 23	Anne Lennon,	Same,	House,	—	—	0 15 0	0 15 0
– – a	Patrick Devlin,	James Little,	Garden,	0 1 5	0 10 0	—	0 10 0
– 24	John M'Clements,	Mary Anne Carson,	House,	—	—	0 15 0	0 15 0
– 25		Same,	Ruins,	—	—	—	—
– 26	Hugh Brady,	Same,	House and garden,	1 1 0	2 5 0	1 10 0	3 15 0
– 27	John Monaghan,	Same,	Garden,	0 1 5	0 10 0	—	0 10 0
– 28	John Conley,	John Monaghan,	House,	—	—	0 5 0	0 5 0
– 29	John Monaghan,	Mary Anne Carson,	House, yard, & garden,	0 1 25	0 15 0	1 0 0	1 15 0
– 30	John Neill,	John Monaghan,	House,	—	—	0 10 0	0 10 0
– 31	Patrick Monaghan,	Same,	House,	—	—	0 10 0	0 10 0
– 32	Unoccupied,	Rev. Peter M'Kay,	House and yard,	—	—	1 5 0	1 5 0
– 33	John Maddock,	Same,	House and yard,	—	—	1 5 0	1 5 0

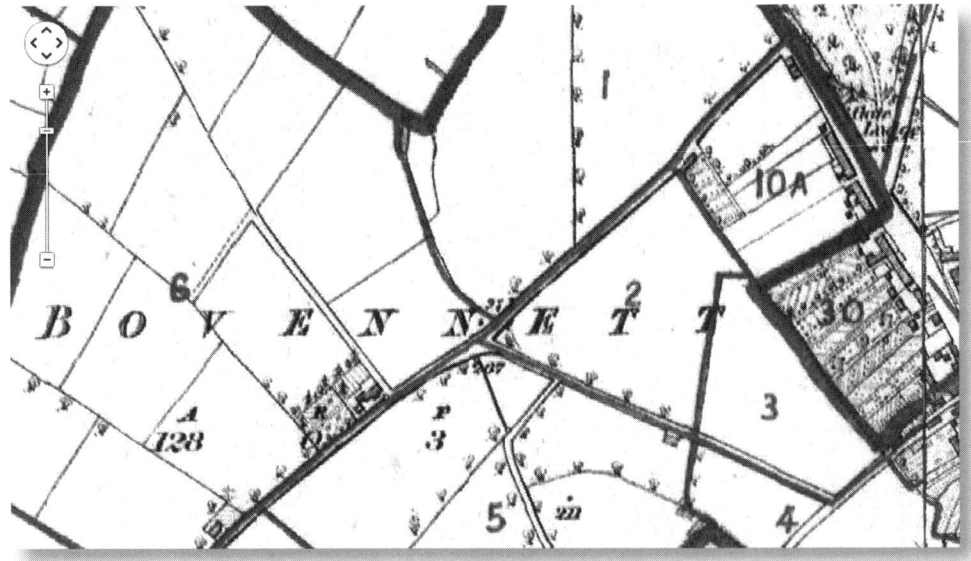

Figure 10.11. Griffiths Valuation, townland of Bovennett, parish of Aghaderg, County Down.

Figure 10.12. Lot #10A, townland of Bovennett, parish of Aghaderg, County Down.

From his 1852 marriage record, we also found that John McClements was the son of Joseph McClements, and from the 1901 death record of John McClements, we found that he had been born in Ballygowan. We also found the 1866 death record of a 65-year-old Joseph McClements of Ballygowan. That means Joseph McClements was about 50 years old when the information for Griffith's Valuation was gathered. Therefore, there is a good chance Joseph McClements will be listed in Ballygowan in Griffith's Valuation.

We find a Joseph M'Clements on Lot #19 in the townland of Ballygowan, parish of Aghaderg, County Down. He was renting approximately 11 acres of land from the Marquis of Downshire. His house and outbuildings were valued at £2

10 shillings. The corresponding valuation map shows that the map probably did not change by the late nineteenth century, since the number of lots remained the same. Also, the occupier of the adjacent Lot #20 in the townland of Coolnacran was a John McClements, who was very likely related to Joseph McClements. The map shows a house near the site of a prehistoric circular stone fort. The townlands of Ballygowan and Coolnacran were located just northeast of the village of Loughbrickland.

VALUATION OF TENEMENTS.
PARISH OF AGHADERG.

No. and Letters of Reference to Map.	Names.		Description of Tenement.	Area.			Rateable Annual Valuation.						Total Annual Valuation of Rateable Property.		
	Townlands and Occupiers.	Immediate Lessors.					Land.			Buildings.					
				A.	R.	P.	£	s.	d.	£	s.	d.	£	s.	d.
	BALLYGOWAN—*continued.*														
17 a	Richard Lackey,	Robert M'Clelland,	House and garden,	0	0	24	0	5	0	0	10	0	0	15	0
– b	Hugh Kenny,	Same,	House and garden,	0	0	25	0	5	0	1	0	0	1	5	0
– c	James Riddles,	Same,	House and garden,	0	0	21	0	5	0	0	15	0	1	0	0
18 a	William Hawthorne,	Marquis of Downshire,	Offices and land,	11	2	0	10	0	0	0	5	0	10	5	0
– b	Unoccupied,	William Hawthorne,	House,							1	5	0	1	5	0
– c	Margaret Reilly,	Same,	House,							0	10	0	0	10	0
19	Joseph M'Clements,	Marquis of Downshire,	House, office, and land,	11	1	10	10	10	0	2	10	0	13	0	0
20	James Burns,	Same,	House, office, and land,	13	0	0	12	15	0	1	15	0	14	10	0
21 A	} Robert Lennon,	Same,	} House, office, & land,	1	2	35	1	5	0				} 18	10	0
– B				2	0	0	2	0	0						
– C a)				14	1	5	12	15	0	2	10	0			
22 A	} Robert Lennon,	Same,	} House and land,	1	2	15	1	5	0				} 6	0	0
– B				4	1	5	4	5	0	0	10	0			
23	James M'Ilroy,	Robert Lennon,	House and land,	0	2	10	0	15	0	0	5	0	1	0	0
24	John Mateer,	Marquis of Downshire,	House and land,	2	0	30	2	0	0	0	10	0	2	10	0
25	Robert Hawthorn,	Same,	House and land,	8	1	0	7	15	0	1	5	0	9	0	0
26	Mary Hawthorn,	Same,	House and land,	4	0	10	4	0	0	0	10	0	4	10	0
27 A	} John Stewart,	Same,	} House and land,	1	2	30	1	10	0				} 6	0	0
– B				4	2	5	3	15	0	0	15	0			
28	Charles Stewart,	Same,	House and land,	1	3	10	1	10	0	0	15	0	2	5	0
29	James Stewart,	Same,	House, office, and land,	9	1	18	8	5	0	1	5	0	9	10	0
			Total,	431	2	8	399	5	0	77	5	0	476	10	0

Figure 10.13. Griffith's Valuation, Townland of Ballygowan, parish of Aghaderg, County Down.

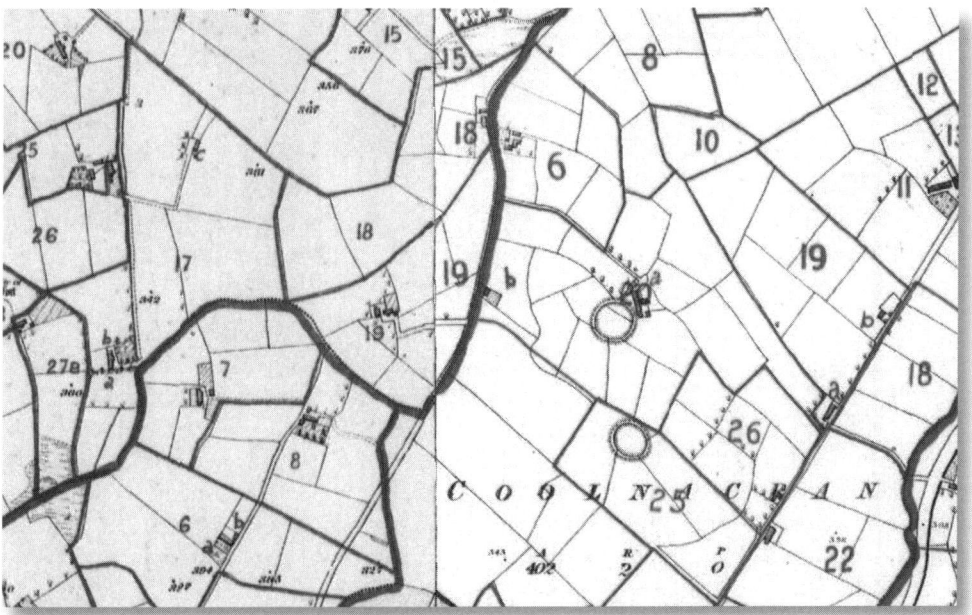

Figure 10.14. Valuation map, townland of Ballygowan and Coolnacran, parish of Aghaderg, County Down.

Chapter 10: Making the Most of Irish Online Census and Land Valuation Records

Revised valuations

The process of assessing the lands of all occupiers continued through the nineteenth and twentieth centuries. As explained in Chapter 9, the valuations were revised to show changes in occupants, lessors, lot numbers, lot sizes, and valuations. Changes were shown by crossing out the name of the former occupant and writing the new occupant's name in colored ink. The ink colors corresponded with the years the revisions took place. The index page in the beginning of each valuation record set often shows a color key for the dates. The revised valuations for the Irish Republic are available on microfilm at the Family History Library and can be borrowed. The FHL films are in black and white, however, making it impossible to discern the color coding. For Northern Ireland, the revised valuations are available online on the website of the Public Record Office of Northern Ireland (PRONI), www.nidirect.gov.uk/proni. Figure 10.15 is an example of the revised valuation for Lot #19 in the townland of Ballygowan, parish of Aghaderg, County Down. The McClements; the year of the revision was 1869. Joseph McClements's death record showed us that he died in 1866. If we had not already seen that record, the revised valuation would have suggested to us that Joseph had died or emigrated.

When doing your own research, note that even if revisions in Griffith's Valuation show that your ancestor left a certain lot, you can trace the occupancy of the lot forward to the twentieth century.

Knowing the most recently recorded occupiers will help you locate the actual land and perhaps house where your ancestor lived. When you knock on someone's door in the townland, the current residents are not likely to remember someone who lived there in 1860 and left for America. But they may remember the person who lived there in 1960.

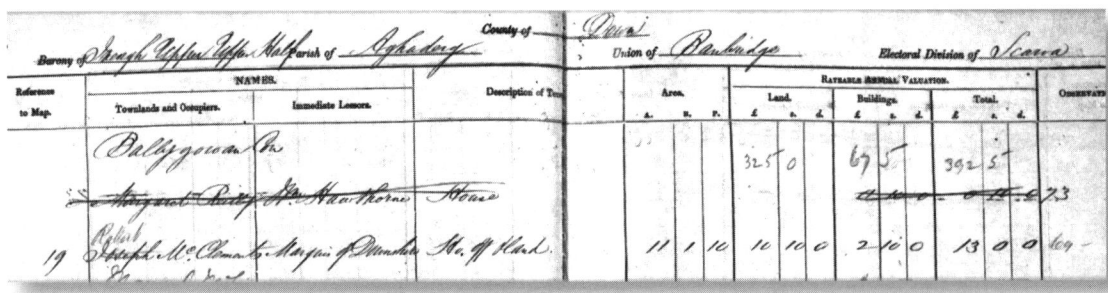

Figure 10.15. Revised valuation, Lot #19, townland of Ballygowan, parish of Aghaderg, County Down, showing transfer of the lot from Joseph to Robert McClements.

The 1901 census showed Robert McClements was 62 years old; thus he was born in about 1839. The death record of John McClements showed that he was born on February 19, 1823. Therefore, Robert could have been a younger brother of John. Tracking Lot #19 forward in time reveals the changes in occupancy and ownership. The revised valuation for 1909–1929 shows that Robert McClements was able to purchase the lot in 1915, decades after the family had been leasing the land. "In fee" means he owned the land, and "L.A.P." means he was given assistance by the Irish Land Commission to purchase the land.

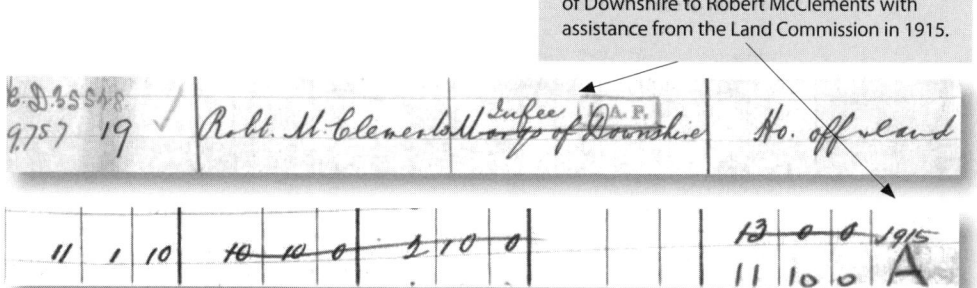

Figure 10.16. Revised valuation, Lot #19, townland of Ballygowan, parish of Aghaderg, County Down, 1909–1929.

Use Earlier Census Substitutes

With the burning of the Public Record Office of Ireland in 1922, most pre-1901 census records were destroyed. To compensate for this tremendous loss, genealogists and historians have resorted to using "census substitutes" that document the population of Ireland. We have seen Griffith's Valuation, for which the data was gathered in the mid-nineteenth century. Earlier census substitutes, such as the Tithe Applotment Books, are not as comprehensive as Griffith's Valuation, but they are still useful for finding heads of household in the early part of the nineteenth century.

Tithe Applotment Books

As stated previously, Irish census records began in 1821, but for the most part were destroyed, leaving only the 1901 and 1911 census records available for research. But census substitutes can help fill the void left by the demise of census records. Griffith's Valuation pertains to the mid-nineteenth century, from 1846 through 1852. Tithe Applotment Books can identify earlier generations, especially when the place has already been determined. Also, many people immigrated to North America in the pre-Famine period of 1820–1845 and were gone by the time the data for Griffith's Valuation was collected. Thus Tithe Applotment Books are an important tool for researching early nineteenth-century families.

The Church of Ireland was an established church, the official church of the state, until disestablishment in 1871. As a result, all households occupying more than one acre of land were required to pay tithes to the Church of Ireland, regardless of their religion. This tithe pertained to everyone, including Catholics, Presbyterians, Methodists, and others. The tithes were based on the quality and quantity of the land owned or rented. Each parish had an official tithe collector, and these officials often maintained ledgers recording the head of household and the number and quality of acres occupied. The records cover the period 1823 to 1837.[3] The Tithe Applotment Books for the Irish Republic are available on the websites of the Family History Library and the National Archives of Ireland. For Northern

---

[3] The Tithe Applotment Books, National Archives of Ireland, http://titheapplotmentbooks.nationalarchives.ie.

Ireland, Tithe Applotment Books are available on microfilm at the Family History Library and at the New England Historic Genealogical Society.

Tithes were levied on agricultural land and did not cover urban areas or include landless laborers, and they tend to under-represent the population. Also, the records for some parishes did not survive or provided no detailed list of occupiers. Nevertheless, the database on the Family History Library website includes more than 750,000 records.

Fitzgerald family

Returning to our other case study, let us look at the Fitzgerald family in the decades before the Famine in Bruff, County Limerick. We have determined that Thomas Fitzgerald was born in Bruff in 1823 and was the son of Michael and Ellen (Wilmot) Fitzgerald. So Michael was married and had one or more children in 1823, and therefore would be considered a head of household. The tithe applotment book for Bruff was recorded in 1833, so there is a good chance that Michael Fitzgerald appears in the book.

The website of the Family History Library, FamilySearch.org, has a superior search engine in comparison to the National Archives of Ireland search engine, since the FHL site will search for variant spellings. When we search for Michael Fitzgerald in Bruff, County Limerick, we get two results. The first name was abbreviated in the record as Michl. When we perform the same search for Michael Fitzgerald on the National Archives of Ireland website, we get no results, because the search did not include variants of the given name, Michael. We also found that the images for Bruff are very poor on both sites. But FamilySearch shows the images as jpeg files that can be downloaded into an image-editing program and improved by changing the contrast and brightness of the image. On the National Archives of Ireland website, the images are downloaded as PDFs, and you must

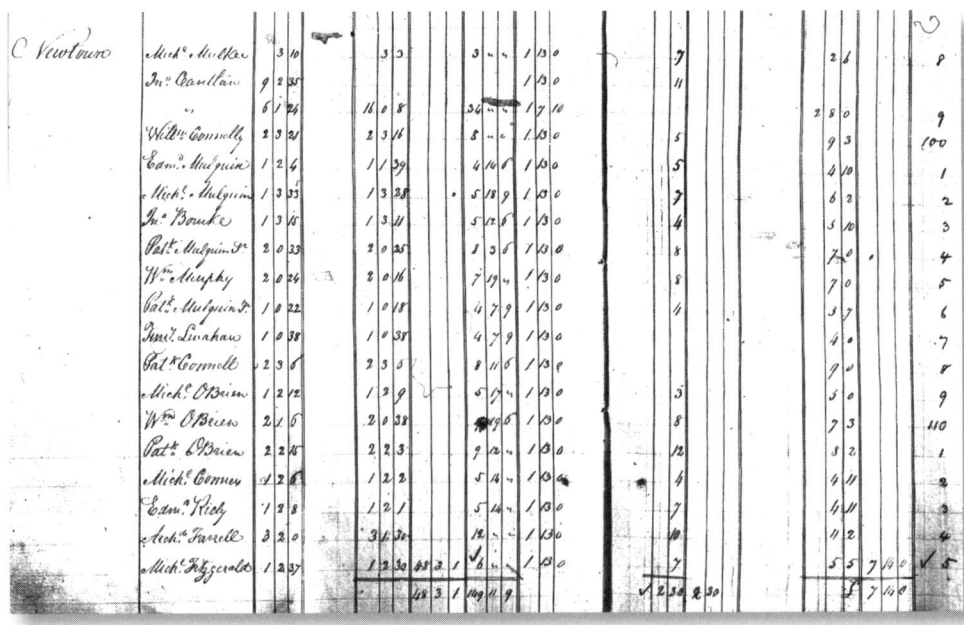

Figure 10.17. 1833 Tithe Applotment Book, Parish of Bruff, Townland of Newtown, County Limerick.

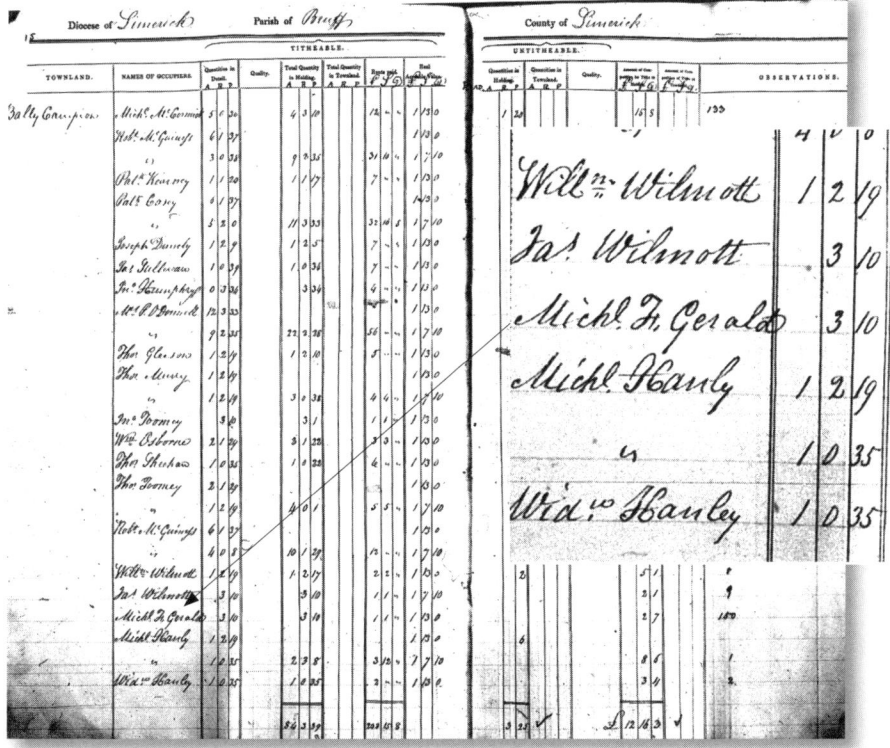

Figure 10.18. 1833 Tithe Applotment Book, Parish of Bruff, Townland of Bally Campion, County Limerick.

then copy and paste the image from there into an image-editing program. When you encounter scanned images that are unreadable, another recourse is to look at the original or the microfilm. The microfilm images for the townlands of Newtown and Ballycampion are much better, and it is apparent that the indexing for the FHL and National Archives of Ireland websites was done from the scanned images, which accounts for the mis-transcription of Newtown as Lowtown. Figures 10.17 and 10.18 were copied from the NEHGS microfilm for Bruff.

According to the Family History Library database, there were two Michael Fitzgeralds in Bruff: one in the townland of "Bally Campion" and the other in the townland of "Lowtown."[4] However, when we look at the "Lowtown" image, we find it had been mis-transcribed and was actually Newtown. (There is no townland in Bruff called Lowtown). The townlands of Ballycampion and Newtown lie on either side of the road just north of the town of Bruff. There was probably only one Michael Fitzgerald, and he occupied land on both sides of the road. He had 1 acre 2 roods 37 perches of land in Newtown, and 3 roods 10 perches (a little over 2 acres) in Ballycampion. In addition, there were a James and a William Wilmott living adjacent to Michael Fitzgerald in Ballycampion. They were very likely related to Ellen Wilmot, the wife of Michael Fitzgerald.

McClements family

---

[4] *Ireland, Tithe Applotment Books, 1814–1855,* database at FamilySearch.org, Michl Fitzgerald; FHL microfilm 256,575.

> 1 statute acre = 4,840 square yards
>
> 1 rood = ¼ acre or 1,210 square yards
>
> 40 perches = 1 rood or 30 square yards
>
> 1 Irish acre = 1.62 statute acres
>
> Note Griffith's valuation records are in statute acres, but Tithe Applotment Books are in Irish acres. For more information, see "Griffith's Valuation—Explanation of Terms," www.findmypast.com/articles/griffiths-valuation—explanation-of-terms.

As we determined in Chapter 8, Robert McClements was born in 1867 in Bovennett townland, parish of Aghaderg, County Down, and he was the son of John McClements and Susan Morehead. The 1901 Michigan death record of his father, John McClements, indicates that he had been born on February 19, 1823 and was the son of John [sic] McClements and Mary [?Brown]. We also found from the marriage record of John McClements that his father was Joseph McClements. In addition, we found John McClements in Bovennett townland in Griffith's Valuation. This person was likely to be the John McClements born in 1823.

Since John McClements was born in 1823 in Ballygowan (a townland adjacent to Coolnacran), we are looking for his father, Joseph, in the 1828 Tithe Applotment Book for Aghaderg. We scanned for anyone named McClements in Bovennett and Ballygowan. These records are not online at this time, but may be digitized at some point in the future. Right now, the Tithe Applotment Books for Northern Ireland are available on microfilm at the Family History Library, the New England Historic Genealogical Society, the National Library of Ireland, the National Archives of Ireland, and the Public Record Office of Northern Ireland.

We find that there were no other McClementses in the townland of Bovennett or Ballygowan. However, we note that there were McClementses and Moreheads in the adjacent townland of Coolnacran, which is where we found a John McClements in Griffith's Valuation. We found the following names in Coolnacran: John McClements, Samuel Moorhead, and Samuel McClements (Figure 10.19). In Griffith's Valuation, we saw that the house of Joseph McClements of Ballygowan was directly across the road from the house of John McClements of Coolnacran.

Other Records

While this book is not intended to contain a comprehensive list of sources, some valuable online repositories deserve mention. These repositories provide a variety of additional resources that can add to family histories. (For more detailed explanations of these sources, see Part 4, Online Resources.)

The Public Record Office of Northern Ireland has some important online records that cover a wide range of time periods, from the eighteenth to the twentieth centuries. These databases include probate calendars, census substitutes, lists of freeholders, street directories, and signers of the Ulster Covenant, as well as the revised valuations shown previously. In addition, PRONI has online finding guides for church records and estate records. Freeholders were people who owned or leased

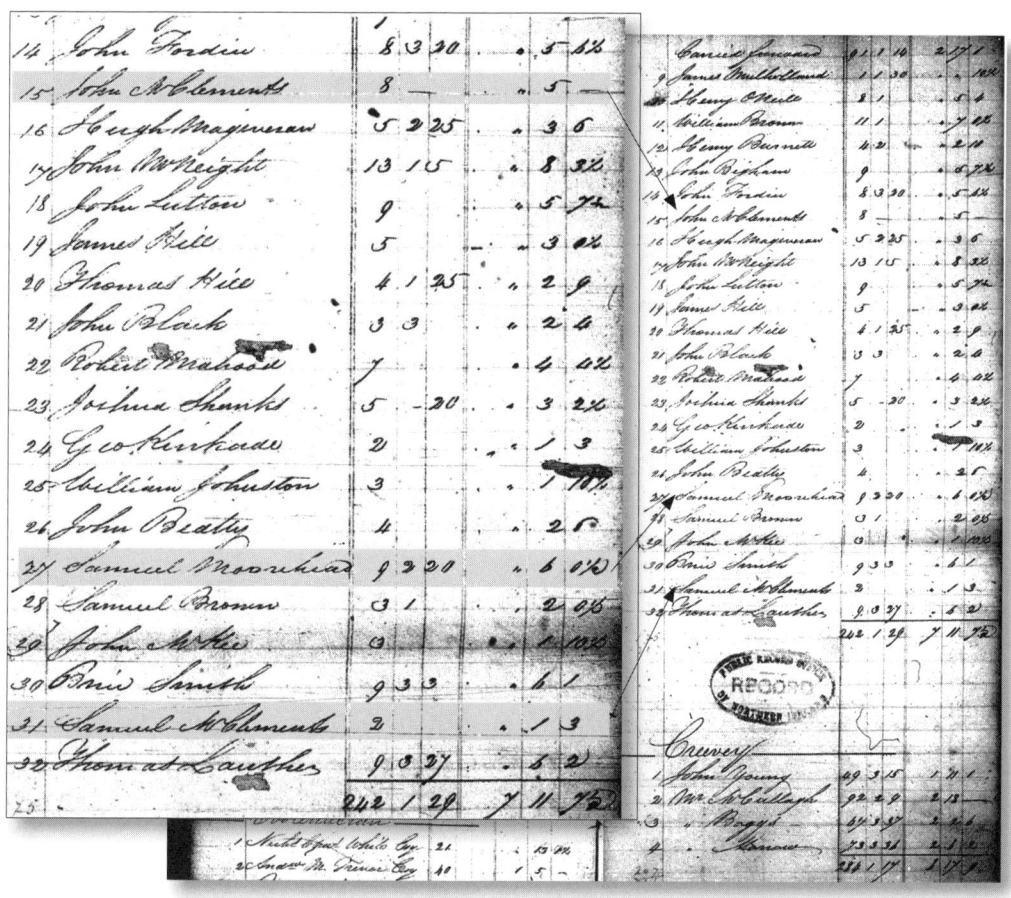

Figure 10.19. 1828 Tithe Applotment Book, Parish of Aghaderg, Townland of Coolnacran, County Down.

at least 40 shillings of land and were therefore eligible to vote. Some of these lists extend back to the eighteenth century. For the Irish Republic, the Family History Library has some lists of freeholders on microfilm, and some county libraries have digitized lists online. Figure 10.20 is an example of an 1823 freeholder list showing Samuel Moorhead of Coolnacran. The record shows the name of the landlord, John Whyte, Esq., and the names of the "three lives" listed on the rental agreement: Roger Moorhead, John Lawther, and Thomas Brown. Frequently the lengths of leases were set based upon the lives of three persons, and as long as they were alive, the lease continued.

We had seen that Joseph McClements died in Ballygowan in 1866. The probate calendar database on FamilySearch.org showed an abstract of the administration of his estate. According to the National Archives of Ireland, the wills that were recorded in the Principal Registry [Dublin] did not survive, but wills recorded elsewhere did survive.[5] Furthermore, FamilySearch.org also shows the 1890 probate calendar for Mary McClements of Ballygowan with Robert McClements as executor, and the registry was Belfast. By searching in the will calendar database on PRONI (Public Record Office of Northern Ireland), we are able to find the full copy of the will. In her will, Mary McClements of Ballygowan refers to her

---

[5] *Calendars of Wills and Administrations 1858–1920,* National Archives of Ireland, http://www.willcalendars.nationalarchives.ie/search/cwa/home.jsp.

12 BARONY OF UPPER IVEAGH.

No.	Name of Freeholder.	Place of Abode.	Situation of Freehold.	Name of Landlord.	Value of Freehold.	Names of Lives or other Tenure.	Place & Date of Registry.
553	Marshall, Patrick	Rathfryland	Rathfryland	John Chapman	40s	John Chapman and Robert Dalzell,	Rathfryland, Sept. 2, 1823.
554	Morgan, Matthew	same	Kilterriff	Earl & Countess Clanwilliam	40s.	Alex. M'Crevily, Matthew Forde & James Waddell,	same same
555	Malcomson, David	Derrydrummuck	Derrydrummuck	same	40s.	John, Robert and Joseph Lawson,	same same
556	Moore, James	Lessize,	Lessize	Countess Clanwilliam	40s.	John Pierce Meade and Thomas Percy Meade,	same same
557	May, Andrew	Rossconoor	Rossconnor	Earl & Countess Clanwilliam	40s.	William Swan, James and William Murphy,	same same
558	Morrow, George	Drumlough	Drumlough	same	40s.	John Wallace, David Lindsay & Isabella Waddell,	same same
559	Mugrans, Terence	Lenad	Lenad	Edward Magranna	40s.	Charles O'Neill,	same same
560	Magaw, Thomas	Ballymacarattymore	Ballymacarattymore	Earl & Countess Clanwilliam	40s.	John and Hugh Magaw, and William Crawford,	same same
561	Malone, Patrick	same	same	same	40s.	John Malone, Hugh I. Savage & Mary Johnston,	same same
562	Malone, Michael	same	same	same	40s.	same lives	same same
563	Magaw, Hugh	Meenin	same	same	40s.	John and Hugh Magaw, and William Crawford,	same same
564	Macken, Arthur	Drumadonnell	Drumadonnell	Countess Clanwilliam	40s.	John Pierce Meade and Arthur Macken,	same same
565	Mulligan, Gilbert	Tullyear	Tullyear	William Law, Esq.	40s.	John and George Mulligan, and Thomas Crawford,	Banbridge, Dec. 10, 1823.
566	Mulligan, Joseph	Tullyconnaught	Ballydown	John Whyte, Esq.	40s.	John and Sarah Lyon, and John Morton,	same same
567	Magiveran, Hugh	Coleneactan	Coleneactan	same	40s.	Hugh, James and Patrick Magiveran,	same same
568	Moorehead, Samuel	same	same	same	40s.	Roger Moorehead, John Lawther & Thomas Brown,	same same
569	Morgan, Charles	Daughery	Daughery	same	40s.	George Crawford and Charles Morgan,	same same

Figure 10.20. 1823 Freeholders List for the Barony of Upper Iveagh, County Down.

stepson, Robert McClements, and his sister, Anna Matilda Porter of Drumiller, as well as her nephew, William Campbell.[6] This information suggests that Robert McClements was the son of Joseph McClements and his first wife, and therefore, brother of John McClements of Brighton, Michigan. This second marriage may be fortuitous, since Joseph could have married for the second time after 1845, and more research can be done in the civil records of marriages to find this marriage. The civil record of the second marriage may show the name of Joseph's father.

Principal Registry was in Dublin and wills did not survive fire in 1922.

M'CLIMENTS Joseph.

[57] **Effects under £150.**

6 March. Letters of Administration of the personal estate of Joseph M'Climents late of Ballygawan County **Down** Farmer deceased who died 14 November 1866 at same place were granted at the **Principal Registry** to Mary M'Climents of Ballygawan aforesaid the Widow of said deceased.

Belfast wills 1858–1909 available on PRONI website

M'CLEMENTS Mary.

[346] **Effects £104.**

2 September. The Will of Mary M'Clements late of Ballygowan County **Down** Widow who died 14 March 1890 at same place was proved at **Belfast** by Robert M'Clements of Ballygowan Farmer one of the Executors.

Figure 10.21. *Top:* Will calendar showing the probate for the estate of Joseph McClements. *Bottom:* Will calendar showing the probate for the estate of Mary McClements.[7]

6 Will calendars database, *Belfast Wills, 1858–1909,* Public Record Office of Northern Ireland, http://www.nidirect.gov.uk/infrmation-and-services/search-archives-online/will-calendars.

7 *Ireland, Calendar of Wills and Administrations, 1858–1920,* database at FamilySearch.org, Mary M'Clements, 14 Mar 1890; FHL microfilm 100,991.

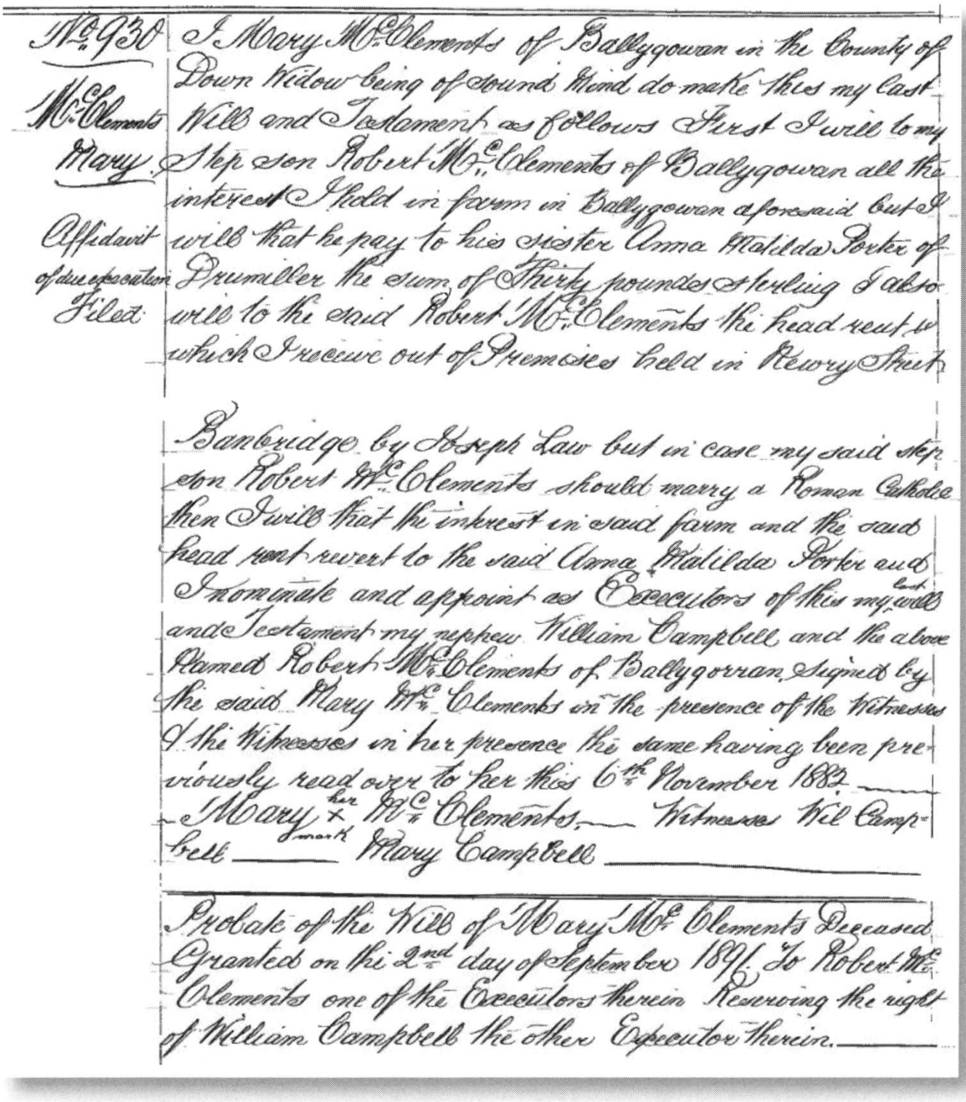
No. 930

McClements Mary.

Affidavit of due execution Filed.

I Mary McClements of Ballygowan in the County of Down Widow being of sound Mind do make this my last Will and Testament as follows First I will to my Step son Robert McClements of Ballygowan all the interest I hold in farm in Ballygowan aforesaid but I will that he pay to his sister Anna Matilda Porter of Drumiller the sum of Thirty pounds sterling I also will to the said Robert McClements the head rent which I receive out of Premises held in Newry Street Banbridge by Joseph Law but in case my said step son Robert McClements should marry a Roman Catholic then I will that the interest in said farm and the said head rent revert to the said Anna Matilda Porter and I nominate and appoint as Executors of this my last will and Testament my nephew William Campbell and the above Named Robert McClements of Ballygorran Signed by the said Mary McClements in the presence of the Witnesses & the Witnesses in her presence the same having been previously read over to her this 6th November 1882 — Mary her x mark McClements — Witnesses Wil Campbell — Mary Campbell

Probate of the Will of Mary McClements Deceased Granted on the 2nd day of September 1891 To Robert McClements one of the Executors therein Reserving the right of William Campbell the other Executor therein.

Figure 10.22. Will of Mary McClements of Ballygowan, 2 September 1891.

Other online records that can be searched are prison records and landed estate court files. Prison records and petty court session records can shed an interesting light on our ancestors, who may have been arrested for minor offenses, such as vagrancy, or major crimes. Online prison records are indexed on FamilySearch.org and are accessible at Findmypast, and in Family History Centers (sign-in required). The landed estate court records were generated when many estates in Ireland were bankrupted by the Famine. The records often detail the particulars of rentals and give a history of the tenants back to the early nineteenth century. No record could be found in prison records or landed estate records for the McClements family of Ballygowan or the Fitzgerald family of Bruff.

Lease dated 15th day of June, 1842, from James Bailie to Robert Ross for the lives of the said Robert Ross (the lessee), and James Ross, then aged 15 years, Robert Ross, junr., then aged 13 years, or 31 years, whichever should last longest, from the 1st day of November, 1836, at the yearly rent of 13s. 9d. sterling. The original of this lease is not forthcoming, but a compared copy will be handed to the purchaser. Robert Ross, the lessee, is now dead. The other two lives are still in being.

LOT No. 1—*con.*

No. on Map	Denominations	Tenants' Names	Gale Days	Yearly Rent	Quantity of Land Statute Measure	Tenure of each Tenant	Rights of Way, and other Easements preserved
				£ s. d.	A. R. P.		
			Forward	84 0 5½	18 0 24¼		
53	**Ballyhalbert** (part of)—*con.*	Robert Ross	1st May & 1st Nov	0 13 9	0 0 15½	Lease dated 15th day of June, 1842, from James Bailie to Robert Ross for the lives of the said Robert Ross (the lessee), and James Ross, then aged 15 years, Robert Ross, junr., then aged 13 years, or 31 years, whichever should last longest, from the 1st day of November, 1836, at the yearly rent of 13s. 9d. sterling. The original of this lease is not forthcoming, but a compared copy will be handed to the purchaser. Robert Ross, the lessee, is now dead. The other two lives are still in being.	
53a		Same	1st May & 1st Nov.	0 9 7	0 0 11½	Tenant from year to year, tenancy commenced on 1st November.	
54		Representative of David M'Whirr	1st May & 1st Nov.	0 11 8	0 0 16	Lease dated 28th March, 1865, from Hugh M'Kelvey and Hugh M'Kelvey to David M'Whirr, for 31 years, from 1st November, 1864, or the lives of Sarah M'Whirr, aged 42 years, wife of lessee, John M'Whirr, aged 11, and David M'Whirr, aged 9 years, or the survivor of them, at the yearly rent of 11s. 8d. Sarah M'Whirr is now dead, but the other two lives are still in being.	
55		Eliza M'Clements	1st May & 1st Nov.	1 3 4	0 0 29¼	Lease dated 1st October, 1847, from John M'Kelvey and Hugh M'Kelvey to Eliza M'Clements, for 31 years, from 1st October, last past, or the lives of Hugh M'Clements, then aged 9 years, Robert M'Clements, then aged 4 years, and Thomas Corran M'Clement, then aged 1 year. All the said lives are still in being.	
56		Gawn Thompson	1st May & 1st Nov.	2 16 10	0 1 38	Lease dated 4th November, 1856, from Hugh M'Kelvey and Hugh M'Kelvey to Gawn Thompson, for 3 lives, with covenant for perpetual renewal upon payment of a peppercorn fine if demanded.	
56a		Same	1st May & 1st Nov.	4 5 0	2 3 15	Tenant from year to year, tenancy commenced on 1st November.	
		Gross Rental - - -		94 0 7½	21 3 29¼		
		Deduct Tithe Rent-charge payable thereout - - - -		1 10 2			
		Net Rental - -		92 10 5½			

The Tenement Valuation of this Estate is £140. See Conditions of Sale and Maps annexed. 10

Figure 10.23. Example of a landed estate rental for 1883, for Ballyhalbert (on Ards Peninsula), County Down.

Estate papers can be useful in locating and possibly identifying your ancestor, especially in the pre-1840 time period, when church records and census substitutes are few. Estate papers can be held in national and county archives around Ireland, and some are still privately held. A few have been filmed by the Family History Library. For listings, you can check the general guides, such as *Tracing Your Ancestors* by John Grenham or *Irish Records* by James Ryan. The National Library of Ireland features the "Sources" database, which searches the manuscript collections of the library. The Public Record Office of Northern Ireland has online guides that can help you assess the types of materials contained in the estate papers. The Irish Genealogical Society International (IGSI) has been working with the National Library of Ireland and the National Archives of Ireland to index all of the estate records in their collections. These indexes may be purchased from the IGSI (see their blog at http://blog.irishgenealogical.org/?p=672). There is an online guide to the estate papers of the Marquis of Downshire on the PRONI website. The guide mentions that there are maps for the Banbridge estate beginning in 1720. For most estate papers, you will need to travel to the repository to examine the papers, since they are not available online.

Summary

While Irish genealogical researchers are still grappling with the impact of the 1922 destruction of the Public Record Office, many alternate sources are still being discovered, and the most useful resources have been digitized. The most important of these records are church records, civil registrations, Griffith's Valuation and the accompanying maps, and the Tithe Applotment Books. Many of these records are accessible online for free, and others are available for reasonable fees. Countless Irish American genealogists want to not only identify their forebears, but also understand the place they came from and the culture they left behind. We hope that finding our families in these sources will fulfill this quest for our Irish roots and heritage.

Further Reading

- Dooley, Terrence. *The Big Houses and Landed Estates of Ireland.* Maynooth Research Guides for Irish Local History, No. 11. Dublin: Four Courts Press, 2007.

- Grenham, John. *Tracing Your Irish Ancestors: The Complete Guide.* Baltimore: Genealogical Publishing Co., 2006.

- Mitchell, Brian. *Basic Guide to Irish Records for Family.* Baltimore: Clearfield, 2008.

- Paton, Chris. *Discover Irish Land Records.* St. Agnes, S.A.: Unlock the Past, 2015.

- Paton, Chris. *Irish Family History Resources Online, 2nd ed.* St. Agnes, S.A.: Unlock the Past, 2015.

- Reilly, James R. *Richard Griffith and His Valuations of Ireland.* Baltimore: Clearfield Company, 2000.

- Roulston, William J. *Researching Scots-Irish Ancestors: the Essential Genealogical Guide to Early Modern Ulster, 1600–1800.* Belfast: Ulster Historical Foundation, 2005.

- Ryan, James G. *Irish Records: Sources for Family and Local History.* Salt Lake City, Utah: Ancestry, 1997.

PART IV
Online Resources

Online Resources

◉ = free site; $ = subscription site

	Holdings / description	Website & URL	Notes
Web portals	Irish government web portal that can search across a variety of websites and record types	IrishGenealogy.ie ◉	
	Website providing links to more than 300,000 websites related to genealogy. There is a category for Ireland and Northern Ireland.	Cyndi's list, cyndislist.com/uk/irl/ ◉	
	Variety of records, including Griffith's Valuation and original valuation maps, civil registration indexes, will calendars, landed estate court files, prison records, and newspapers	Ancestry.com $ FamilySearch.org ◉ Findmypast.ie $	
Census records	1901 and 1911 censuses, every-name searchable (population schedules; descriptions of houses and out-buildings)	National Archives of Ireland, census.nationalarchives.ie ◉ FamilySearch.org ◉	
	Census remnants from 1821–1851	National Archives of Ireland, census.nationalarchives.ie ◉ FamilySearch.org ◉	Most census records from 1821 through 1891 were destroyed.
	Index to 1901 census	Findmypast.ie $	Allows researchers to cross-reference a second name, helping find people with common names (and helping when you are not sure of the location).
Census substitute	For Griffith's Valuation, alphabetical listing of everyone in a parish. Also Flax Growers List of 1796 and 17th-century Hearth Money Rolls.[1]	Fáilte Romhat, failteromhat.com ◉	Griffith's Valuation; parish lists useful for determining variant spellings of surnames.
	Actual images of Griffith's Primary Valuation, with links to later valuation maps. Access to all versions of Griffith's Valuation and original valuation maps.	askaboutireland.com ◉ Findmypast.ie $	Searchable database

---

[1] The Flax Growers List includes 60,000 persons who received spinning wheels from the Linen Board; the Hearth Money Rolls list those who paid taxes based upon the number of hearths in their house.

	Holdings / description	Website & URL	Notes
Census substitute (cont.)	Access to actual images of Griffith's Primary Valuation and corresponding Ordnance Survey maps (not valuation maps)	Ancestry.com $	Can perform Soundex searches, leading to more complete results.
	Tithe Applotment Books, 1823–1837 (records of land occupiers)	FamilySearch.org ⊙ National Archives of Ireland, titheapplotmentbooks.nationalarchives.ie ⊙	Variant spelling searches Browsable by townland; does not include Northern Ireland
Maps and places	Maps of poor law unions and civil and Catholic parishes	Irish Ancestors, JohnGrenham.com $	Includes information about the availability of Catholic parish registers. Has place-name search function that allows wildcard searches.
	Historic Ordnance Survey maps for all of Ireland and corresponding 2005 satellite images for the Irish Republic	Ordnance Survey Office, osi.ie ⊙	Click on CHECK OUT NAVdirect.
	Color valuation maps from late 19th century showing exact location of an ancestor's house; original b/w valuation maps that match Griffith's Valuation	askaboutireland.ie ⊙ Findmypast.ie $	Lot numbers may not match Griffith's Primary Valuation if renumbering took place.
Civil registration records	Transcription of civil birth records, 1864–1881, in the database *Ireland Births and Baptisms, 1620–1881*. Transcription of some marriages, 1864–1870, in the database *Ireland Marriages, 1619–1898*	FamilySearch.org ⊙	Allows searches by parents' names to identify all children. To easily find the databases, select United Kingdom and Ireland, then Ireland as the country.
	Index to Irish civil registration records, including 1864–1958 births, 1845–1958 marriages, and 1864–1958 deaths, but excluding index records for Northern Ireland after its creation in 1922	Ancestry.com $ FamilySearch.org ⊙ findmypast.com $	Ancestry and Findmypast cross-reference names of bridegrooms.
	Indexes for births >100 years; marriages >75 years; deaths >50 years	irishGenealogy.ie ⊙	

	Holdings / description	Website & URL	Notes
Civil registratio records (cont)	Downloadable certificate application form	General Register Office, www.welfare.ie/en/Pages/General-Register-Office.aspx ⊙	You need to have either the "Group ID" or the volume and page number of the record. Obtain the volume and page numbers from the index to Irish civil registrations at FamilySearch.org, Findmypast.ie, or Ancestry.com. Obtain the "Group ID" at www.irishgenealogy.ie.
Church records	Transcriptions of church records of many but not all counties in Ireland and Northern Ireland	RootsIreland.ie $	Can subscribe by month and day. Includes Catholic and some Church of Ireland and Presbyterian records.
Church records	Transcriptions of names in church records, including godparents and witnesses, selected counties	IrishGenealogy.ie ⊙	Allows cross-referencing of a second name. Currently covers all of Kerry and parts of Cork, Carlow, and Dublin; more records to be added in the future. Actual images for Cork.
Church records	Transcriptions of select Catholic parish registers, part of the databases *Ireland Births and Baptisms, 1620–1881; Deaths, 1864–1870;* and *Marriages, 1619–1898.*	FamilySearch.org ⊙	
Church records	Roman Catholic parish registers from the collection of the National Library of Ireland. Contain records of baptisms and marriages from the majority of Catholic parishes in Ireland and Northern Ireland up to 1880.	National Library of Ireland, http://registers.nli.ie/ ⊙	Browsable, not searchable. Allows you to enter a date to jump to section of interest. Can rotate, lighten, increase contrast, and download images.
Church records	Church of Ireland records	Church of Ireland, ireland.anglican.org ⊙	
N. Ireland records	Searchable databases of freeholders' lists; revised valuations; will calendars; street directories	Public Record Office of Northern Ireland, www.nidirect.gov.uk/proni ⊙	Also has finding guides for major estate collections and a list of parish registers on microfilm in the PRONI collections.

	Holdings / description	Website & URL	Notes
Estate & land records	Landed estate records, including tenant records, many going back generations	Findmypast.com $	80 volumes of encumbered estate records at Findmypast; FamilySearch has index only.
	Registry of Deeds records ("memorials") dating back to 1709	http://freepages.genealogy.rootsweb.ancestry.com/~registryofdeeds/index.html ⊙	Indexing and abstracting ongoing.
	Landed estates database	http://www.landedestates.ie/ ⊙	Resource guide to landed estates and historic houses in Connacht and Munster, ca. 1700–1914. Bibliography of sources listed for each estate. Maintained by NUI Galway.

Note: This list of online sources also appears online at AmericanAncestors.org/Irish-handbook, where it will be periodically updated.

Illustration Credits

Unlisted illustrations were created specifically for this handbook.

1.1, 1.2, 1.3: New England Historic Genealogical Society, AmericanAncestors.org.

2.2: 1940 federal census, Roll T627_2802; Page 9B; Enumeration District 60-29; viewed at Ancestry.com.

2.3, 2.4: 1930 federal census, Roll 1659; Page 2A; Enumeration District 0120; Image 675.0; FHL microfilm 2341393; viewed at Ancestry.com.

2.5: 1920 federal census, Roll 25_721; Page 7B; Enumeration District 165; Image 511; viewed at Ancestry.com.

2.6: National Archives and Records Administration, *Petitions and Records of Naturalizations of the U.S. District and Circuit Courts of the District of Massachusetts, 1906–1929*; Series M1368; Roll 41; viewed at fold3.com.

2.7: *Massachusetts Vital Records,* Births, vol. 630, p. 21; viewed via *Massachusetts Vital Records, 1841–1910,* database at AmericanAncestors.org.

2.8: *Massachusetts Vital Records,* Boston, Marriages, 1914, vol. 2, p. 248, #6369; viewed at AmericanAncestors.org.

2.9: 1900 Federal Census, Boston, Ward 6, Suffolk, Massachusetts; Roll 677; Page 5A; Enumeration District 1225; FHL microfilm 1240677; viewed at Ancestry.com.

2.10: *Massachusetts Vital Records,* vol. 398, pp. 106, 43, viewed via *Massachusetts Vital Records, 1841–1910,* database at AmericanAncestors.org.

2.11: *Massachusetts Vital Records,* vol. 161, p. 14, viewed via *Massachusetts Vital Records, 1841–1910,* database at AmericanAncestors.org.

2.12: 1870 federal census, Roll M593_641; Page 349A; Image 60; Family History Library Film 552140; viewed at FamilySearch.org.

2.13: 1860 federal census, Roll M653_523; Page 149; Image 149; Family History Library Film 803523; viewed at FamilySearch.org.

2.14: *Massachusetts Vital Records,* Boston Marriages, 1857, vol. 110, p. 126; available via online database *Massachusetts Marriages, 1841–1915,* FamilySearch.org.

2.15: Massachusetts State Census, 1855, database with images, FHL microfilm 953,958, viewed at FamilySearch.org.

2.16: Massachusetts Vital Records, Boston Deaths, 1885, Vol. 366, p. 146, viewed via *Massachusetts Vital Records, 1841–1910,* online database, AmericanAncestors.org.

3.1: *Massachusetts Vital and Town Records, 1620–1988,* online database, Ancestry.com.

3.2: *St. Stephen Church Baptisms 1862–1870,* p. 95, held at the Archdiocese of Boston. Used by permission of the Archdiocese of Boston.

3.3: "St. Peter's Roman Catholic Church (Manhattan)" at en.wikipedia.com.

3.4: *Baptismal Records of the Church of St. Peter's, NYC* [microform], *1797–1908,* at New York Public Library, Milstein Division.

3.5: "Table of Consanguinity," commons.wikimedia.org.

3.6: en.wikipedia.org.

4.1: 1870 Census, Boston Ward 2, Suffolk, Massachusetts; Roll M593_641; Page 349A; Image 60; Family History Library Film 552140; viewed at www.ancestry.com.

4.2: R. Stanton Avery Special Collections, New England Historic Genealogical Society, AmericanAncestors.org.

4.3: *Bergen County Declarations of Intent, 1808–1840, New Jersey, Naturalization Records, 1749–1986,* online database, www.familysearch.org.

4.4: *United States New England Naturalization Index, 1791–1906,* online database, FamilySearch.org.

4.5, 4.6: *New England, Petitions for Naturalization, 1787–1931,* online database, FamilySearch.org.

4.7: National Archives Northeast Region, Waltham, Massachusetts.

4.8: Naturalization Petition #186961, *Petitions for Naturalization from the U.S. District Court for the Southern District of New York, 1897–1944*; Series M1972; Roll 770, viewed at Ancestry.com.

4.9: *Card Manifests (Alphabetical) of Individuals Entering through the Port of Detroit, Michigan, 1906–1954.* Micropublication M1478, RG085, 117 rolls, ARC ID 4527226. National Archives, Washington, D.C. Viewed at Ancestry.com.

4.10: *New York, New York*, Microfilm Serial M237; Microfilm Roll 324; Line 30; List Number 176, viewed at Ancestry.com.

4.11: New York Passenger List, Microfilm Serial T715; Microfilm Roll 1852; Line 5; Page Number 162, viewed at Ancestry.com.

4.12: National Archives and Records Administration, Washington D.C., *Passport Applications, 1795–1905*, Collection Number: ARC Identifier 566612/ MLR Number A1 508; NARA Series M1372; Roll #375, viewed at Ancestry.com.

5.1: Photos of gravestones at Trescott, Maine; Charlestown, Massachusetts; and Waltham, Massachusetts by Marie E. Daly.

5.2: www.GenealogyBank.com.

5.3, 5.4: *Irish Immigrant Advertisements, 1831–1920 (Search for Missing Friends)*, online database, AmericanAncestors.org.

5.5: *Boston Pilot, August 5, 1843.*

5.6: *Business agent entries from Broome and Delaware Counties, New York; as shown in Victor B. Goodrich, "Sending Money Home (to Ireland), the Accounts of an Immigrant Financial Agent in Deposit, New York, 1851–1860," Tree Talks, vol. 32, Dec. 1992.*

5.7: *New York Emigrant Savings Bank, 1850–1883*, online database, Ancestry.com; original data from Emigrant Savings Bank Records, call no. *R-USLHG *ZI-815, New York Public Library.

5.8: 1836 Chap. 0253 Act to Establish the Waltham Bank, Acts and Resolves Passed by the General Court, Massachusetts, State Library of Massachusetts,: http://archives.lib.state.ma.us/actsResolves/1836/1836acts0253.pdf.

5.9: Institutional History of the Waltham Savings Bank, National Information Center, U.S. Federal Reserve System, at http://www.ffiec.gov/nicpubweb/nicweb/InstitutionHistory.aspx?parID_RSSD=936109&parDT_END=20000617.

5.10: *Massachusetts Grand Lodge of Masons Membership Cards, 1733–1990,* online database, AmericanAncestors.org.

5.11: Membership application, Massachusetts Catholic Order of Foresters, TIARA Foresters Project, tiara.ie/forest.php. Courtesy University Archives and Special Collections, University of Massachusetts Boston.

6.1: "Chapter 1, Places of Settlement," in Albert Cook Myers, *Immigration of the Irish Quakers into Pennsylvania,* 1862–1750 by Albert Cook Myers (Swarthmore, Pa., 1902), at http://www.ffiec.gov/nicpubweb/nicweb/InstitutionHistory.aspx?parID_RSSD=936109&parDT_END=20000617.

6.2: Data from Aaron Fogelman, "Migrations to the Thirteen British American Colonies 1700–1775: New Estimates," *Journal of Interdisciplinary History*, 22, No. 4, Spring 1992.

6.3: *Aghadowey, Ireland: Session Book of Aghadowey, 1702–1725,* online database, AmericanAncestors.org.

7.2: Brian Mitchell, *A New Genealogical Atlas* (Baltimore: Genealogical Publishing Co., 1986). Used by permission of the author.

7.4: Excerpt from *General Alphabetical Index to the Townlands* (Baltimore: Genealogical Publishing Co., 1984).

8.2: National Library of Ireland, registers.nli.ie.

8.3: 1870 Federal Census, Brighton, Livingston, Michigan; Roll M593_687; Page 11A; Image 25; Family History Library Film 552186, viewed at Ancestry.com.

8.4: 1900 Federal Census, Hancock, Houghton, Michigan; Roll 714; Page 18B; Enumeration District 0183; FHL microfilm 1240714, viewed at Ancestry.com.

8.5: *Michigan, Marriages, 1868–1925,* online database, FamilySearch.org, citing South Lake Linden, Houghton, Michigan, vol. 2 p. 175 rn. 32, Department of Vital Records, Lansing; FHL microfilm 2,342,518.

8.6: Death record of John McClements, Michigan Dept. of Vital Statistics, Deaths, 1901, p. 197, www.findagrave.com. Reproduced with permission.

8.7: *Ireland Births and Baptisms, 1620-1881,* online database, FamilySearch.org: Robert William Mcclements, 02 Apr 1867; citing 0273, LOUGHBRICKLAND, DOWN, IRELAND, reference; FHL microfilm 101145.

8.8: *Ireland, Civil Registration Indexes, 1845-1958,* online database, FamilySearch.org.

8.9: Quarterly returns of births in Ireland, 1864-1955, with index to births, 1864-1921, Births v. 6 1867, p. 273, FHL film 1011045.

8.10: *Ireland Marriages, 1619-1898,* index, FamilySearch.org, citing Banbridge, Down, Ire, reference 2:3QVSKXB; FHL microfilm 101333.

8.11: *Ireland, Civil Registration Indexes, 1845-1958,* index, FamilySearch.org, citing Banbridge, 1852, vol. 2, p. 692, General Registry, Custom House, Dublin; FHL microfilm 101244.

8.12: *Ireland Marriages 1845-1958 Transcription,* www.findmypast.com.

8.13: Civil marriage record of John McClimons and Susana Moorhead, Banbridge, County Down, 22 Dec. 1852, *Marriage Records, 1845-1870, with indexes of marriages, 1845-1921,* vol. 2, page 692, FHL film #101333; original record at the General Registry Office of Ireland.

8.14: Irish civil registration death record, www.groireland.ie, vol. 16, p. 125.

9.1: Townland Valuation Book, 24 Jan. 1838, Townland of Townparks, Civil Parish Kirkrinola, County Antrim, VAL/1B/177, Public Record Office of Northern Ireland, Belfast.

9.2: *New York, Passenger Lists, 1820-1957,* online database, Ancestry.com; original data from *Passenger Lists of Vessels Arriving at New York, New York, 1820-1897,* Microfilm Publication M237, NAI 6256867, Records of the U.S. Customs Service, Record Group 36, National Archives, Washington, D.C.

9.3: Richard Griffith, *General Valuation of Rateable Property in Ireland* (Dublin: Irish Microforms Ltd., 1978), County Cork, Barony of Kinalea, Parish of Leighmoney, Fiche 26, p. 61.

9.4: Great Britain, Office of the General Valuation of Ireland, "Valuation books" (microfilmed by the Genealogical Society of Utah, Salt Lake City, 2002-2004), House books, v. 636-637B, FHL film 2299730.

10.1: 1851 census Townland of Dunmurray, parish of Drumbeg, Upper Belfast, County Antrim, http://www.census.nationalarchives.ie/.

10.2: 1901 Census, Form A, Ballygowan townland, Aghaderg parish, County Down, Ireland, http://www.census.nationalarchives.ie/.

10.3: 1901 Census, Form B, Ballygowan townland, Aghaderg parish, County Down, Ireland, http://www.census.nationalarchives.ie/.

10.4: Richard Griffith, *General Valuation of Rateable Property in Ireland* (Dublin: Irish Microforms Ltd., 1978), Barony of Coshma, County Limerick, p. 31.

10.5-10.9, 10.12, 10.14: Griffith's Valuation, at www.askaboutireland.ie/griffith-valuation.

10.10: Google Street View, www.google.com.

10.11, 10.13: Richard Griffith, *General Valuation of Rateable Property in Ireland (Dublin: Irish Microforms Ltd., 1978).*

10.15: 1929, VAL/12/B/16/22A (1864-1878), Public Record Office of Northern Ireland, nidirect.gov.uk/proni.

10.16: VAL/12/B/16/22D (1909-1929), Public Record Office of Northern Ireland, nidirect.gov.uk/proni.

10.17 and 10.18: Tithe Applotment Book, parish of Bruff, County Limerick, *The Tithe Applotment Books* (Dublin: European Micropublishing Services, 1990).

10.19: *Calendar of Tithe Applotment Books (Belfast, N.I.: Genealogical* Society of Salt Lake City, 1959-1978).

10.20: Freeholders Records, Public Record Office of Northern Ireland, nidirect.gov.uk/proni.

10.21: *Ireland, Calendar of Wills and Administrations, 1858-1920,* index and images, FamilySearch.org/; Principal Probate Registry, Dublin; 100973; and Principal Probate Registry, Dublin; 100,991.

10.22: Will Calendars database, Belfast Wills, 1858-1909, Public Record Office of Northern Ireland,indirect.gov.uk/proni.

10.23: *Landed Estate Rentals,* online database, Findmypast.com.

Index

Page numbers followed by *t* or *f* refer to tables or figures, respectively.

Act of Union (1800), 67, 131
addresses
  on bank records, 69
  of banks, 70
  on birth records, 30, 114
  of churches, 36, 40
  city directories for, 36, 70
  in Griffith's Valuation, 137
  of Masonic lodges, 72
  on missing friends advertisements, 66
  on passenger arrival lists, 56, 57
  oral interviews to identify, 7
  on sick call records, 31*t*
  for transactions in business agent records
  on U.S. census records, 12, 36
  in valuation books, 127–128
administrative divisions, Ireland, 86–92, 98
  baronies and, 98
  counties and, 87
  dioceses and, 90
  electoral divisions and, 90
  Gaelic and Norman influences on, 86
  Irish language origins of, 85
  linking places of origin to, for research, 93
  McClements case study showing, 116
  parishes and, 88
  poor law unions and, 90
  Presbyterian church parishes and, 90
  probate districts and, 91
  problems in using, 85
  provinces and, 86–87
  superintendent registrar's districts and, 90–91
  to-do list for, 95
  townlands and, 91
  townland sub-denominations and, 91–92
  types of, in descending order by size, 86
advertisements
  of business agents, 68
  for missing friends. *See* missing friends advertisements
Aghadowey, County Londonderry, Ireland, session book, 80, 81*f*
Albany Evening Journal, 67
Alberta/Alberti, Maria, 57
alien (*Al*) status, on U.S. census records, 11, 14, 43, 44
Allen County Public Library, Fort Wayne, Indiana, 36
AmericanAncestors.org
  bank records on, 69
  church records on, 34
  family group sheet sample, 5*f*
  five-generation chart sample, 4*f*
  Masonic Lodge membership files, 72
  missing friends advertisements on, 65–66, 67
  newspaper obituaries on, 62
  research log sample, 9*f*
  U.S. census records on, 12
American-Canadian Genealogical Society, 36
Ancestry.com, 104–105, 157
  birth records on, 114, 116*t*, 121
  death records on, 114, 121
  Irish census records on, 158
  Irish church records on, 102, 103, 104
  Irish civil registration records on, 114, 116*t*, 121, 158
  Kennedy/Fitzgerald case study of searching, 19, 104
  marriage records on, 51, 114, 118, 121
  National Library of Ireland and, 105, 106
  naturalization records on, 47, 49, 51
  Quaker immigration records on, 76

Ancestry.com *cont.*
  Quaker meeting records on, 35
  U.S. census records on, 12, 19
  U.S. passport applications on, 57
  using "lived in" search field on, 19
  Virginia Scotch-Irish records on, 82
Andover Theological Seminary, 34
Anglican (Episcopal) churches, 33, 77.
    See also Church of Ireland
  diocesan structure of, 90
  locating church records for, 34
Anglican immigrants, 33, 88
Anglo-Irish immigrants, 75
Anglo-Irish Treaty (1922), 87
archdiocesan archives, 32, 40. *See also*
    diocesan archives
ArchiveGrid (website), 33–34, 71
archives, 11, 33. *See also* National
    Archives
  banking records in, 70, 71
  business agent records in, 68, 69
  church records in, 32, 33, 34, 35, 37,
    39, 106, 108
  college and university, 33, 34, 35,
    69, 73
  corporate, 71
  diocesan or archdiocesan, 32, 33, 34,
    37, 39, 40
  of eighteenth-century Irish immi-
    grant materials, 81, 82, 83
  of fraternal organizations, 61
  of immigrant letters, 27, 81
  Irish estate papers in, 152
  local, 68, 69, 70, 71
  newspaper, 62, 67
  orphanage records in, 40
  place name needed for using, 85
  of religious orders, 39
  state, 33, 34, 69, 70
Archive.org, 35, 75, 82
Arlington Street Church, Boston, 34
arrival, certificates of, 50
arrival, ports of. *See* ports of arrival
arrival dates
  approximate, from naturalization or
    census records, 55, 59
  date ranges ("± 2 or ± 5 years") in
    searches using, 12, 55
  on declarations of intent, 45, 51

  on naturalization petitions, 47, 48*f*,
    49, 52*f*
  on passport applications, 57
  reliability of, on naturalization
    records, 12, 45, 49, 51
arrival lists. *See* passenger arrival lists
arrival of passenger ships, newspaper
    articles on, 81, 83
Ask about Ireland (askaboutireland.ie)
  Google map street views on, 97, 139,
    141*f*
  maps for Griffith's Valuation and,
    138–139, 140*f*, 157, 158
  townland Name Books on, 95, 97,
    138, 139, 141*f*
aunts. *See also* relatives
  on family group sheets, 4–5
  oral history interviews of, 6
  on passenger arrival lists, 57

Balch Institute for Ethnic Studies, 82
Ballycampion, County Limerick,
    Ireland, townland, 141*f*, 147
Ballygowan, County Down, Ireland,
    112, 116, 120, 135–136, 142–143,
    144, 145*f*, 148, 149–150, 151
Ballymena, County Antrim, Ireland,
    Townland Valuation, 125
Bandon, County Cork, Ireland, 78
bank records, 69–71
  information kept in, 69, 70
  locating, 70
  sources for, 69, 70
banks
  determining status of, 71
  locating, 70
  state acts establishing, 70
  tracing history of, 71
baptism records, 29, 122
  age of baptism and, 29
  baptism dates on, 30, 31
  in churches, 16, 34, 35, 102, 103,
    106, 107, 122
  on Findmypast website, 104–105
  Fitzgerald case study of, 29, 30*f*, 102,
    104–105
  godparent (sponsor) names on, 29,
    30*f*, 31, 41, 65, 101, 104, 106, 157
  information included on, 31, 32

on IrishGenealogy website, 103
on RootsIreland website, 104
origins of immigrants identified
 using, 107
records helpful in locating, 59
resources for finding, 116*t*
of siblings, 29, 30*f*, 104, 106
townlands on, 104
verifying search by checking other
 family members for, 104
witnesses on, 106
years covered by, 113, 116*t*
Baptist churches, 33
church records for, 34
baronies
as administrative division, 85, 86, 88
civil parishes and, 88
General Alphabetical Index to, 93
probate district boundaries and, 91
reference works for, 93
Townland Index of, 63
when used in research, 88
beginning. *See* getting started
Belfast Newsletter, 81
Belmont, Massachusetts, 36
Bevan, Frederick, 137
biographical dictionaries, 27, 81
biographical notices, in newspapers,
 64, 67. *See also* missing friends
 advertisements; obituaries
birth certificates. *See also* birth records
ordering copies of, 121, 159
birth dates
on baptism and birth records,
 30–31, 107
date ranges ("± 5 years") in searches
 using, 12, 47, 49, 104, 110
on declarations of intent, 51
differences between naturalization
 petitions and census records
 for, 49
on family group sheets, 4
on Findmypast website, 104–105
on five-generation charts, 3–4
on naturalization petitions, 45, 47,
 48*f*, 49, 51, 52*f*
Kennedy case study of U.S. census
 record searches for, 13, 15
on passport applications, 57

reasons for exact dates not known
 for, 12
reliability of, on naturalization
 records, 45, 49, 51
birthplaces. *See also* place names, Irish;
 places of origin
on bank records, 69
on birth records, 107
on border-crossing records, 53
on declarations of intent, 45, 51
on family group sheets, 4
on fraternal organization records,
 72, 74
on gravestone inscriptions, 61, 63
of Irish-born relatives, 7
on Irish census records, 135
on five-generation charts, 3–4
McClements case study of searches
 for, 114–116
on naturalization records, 45, 46,
 48*f*, 51, 52*f*, 65, 101
of parents, on U.S. census records,
 19, 20*f*
on passenger arrival lists, 43, 54, 57
on passport applications, 57
residence not same as, 57
superintendent registrar's districts
 differentiated from, 114
on U.S. census records, 11, 12, 13
birth records, Ireland, 101, 107,
 113–117
beginning of civil registration for,
 102, 107, 113
birth and baptism dates on, 30–31
churches and, 102
date ranges used in searching, 12,
 47, 49, 104, 110
information available on, 107, 116
leaving given name field blank, to
 widen the search, 110
McClements case study of searches
 for, 110–111, 114–116
obtaining copies in person, 121
ordering certified copies of, 117, 121
ordering microfilm copies of, 114,
 115, 120–121
ordering photocopies of, 113, 121
origins of immigrants identified
 using, 107

birth records, Ireland *cont.*
  poor law unions used in, 90
  resources for finding, 116*t*
  searching for and obtaining, 110, 113–117, 122
  of siblings, 101, 102, 107, 110
  sources for, 107, 113–114
  to-do list for, 110
  townlands on, 107, 115–116
  U.S. census records used with, in searching for parents' names, 110–111
  years covered by, 107, 110, 113, 114, 116*t*, 117
birth records, United States
  arrangement by street address rather than chronologically, 30
  birth and baptism dates on, 30–31
  delayed registration in, 15
  eighteenth-century, 83
  Fitzgerald case study of, 29
  identifying previous generations using, 11, 13, 15, 17–18, 19, 25
  Kennedy case study of, 15, 18, 19
  maiden name of mother on, 15
  marriage record data used in searches for, 19, 107
  in Pennsylvania, 82
  periodic collection of data for, by canvassing, 30
  reasons for using, instead of civil records, 30
  records helpful in locating, 59
  reliability of, 30
  responsibility for reporting birth for, 30
  U.S. census record searches for, 15, 18
Bishop Loughlin's Dispensations, Diocese of Brooklyn, 1859–1866 (Silinonte), 38
bishop's registers, 31, 32. *See also* church registers
Blessing, Patrick J., 82
Books of Survey and Distribution, 88
border-crossing records, 53
  agencies responsible for, 53
  Kennedy case study of U.S. census record searches and, 14
  linking immigrant ancestors to Ireland using, 27
  McCarthy case study of, 53, 54*f*
  place of origin found using, 43
  types of information collected for, 53
  U.S. census record searches for, 14, 43
Boston, 13, 16, 18, 19, 20, 21, 22, 24, 29, 30, 33, 34, 36, 47, 49, 64–66, 67, 72, 76, 80, 101, 102
Boston Athenaeum, 70
Boston College, 70
Boston Pilot (newspaper), 29, 64–65, 67, 101
Bovennett, County Down, Ireland, 115–116, 119, 135, 141, 142*f*, 148
Boyd, William, 78
brothers. *See also* siblings
  baptism records of, 29, 30*f*
  birth records of, 15, 107
  on family group sheets, 4
  immigration stories with, 55, 69*f*, 76
  McClements case study of searches and, 112, 119, 120, 144, 150
brothers (religious orders), schools run by, 39
Brown?, Mary, 112, 148, 149–150, 151*f*
Brown, Thomas, 149
Bruff, County Limerick, Ireland, 66, 101, 102, 103–106, 133, 137–138, 139*f*, 140*f*, 141*f*, 146–147, 151
Buggy, Joseph, 25
building classifications, in house and quarto books, 128
Bureau of Immigration and Naturalization, 51
burial dates, 31
burial grounds (cemeteries), 37, 61, 62, 74. *See also* burial (cemetery) records; gravestone inscriptions
  chronological use of, 61–62
  in cities, 61–62
  family purchase of grave lots in, 62
  locating, 62, 63
  sources on, 62
burial places. *See also* burial grounds (cemeteries)
  on death notices, 62
  on death records, 61

burial (cemetery) records
   Irish, 101, 106, 122
   U.S., 31, 33, 34, 37, 61–62, 83
business agents, 67, 68–69
   finding for specific areas, 68–69
   locating records of, 69, 74
   services of, 68
business directories, 125
business records, 27, 61, 67–71, 74
   availability of, 74
   bank records and, 69–71
   business agents and, 68–69
   description of types of, 67–68
   gaining access to, 74
   sources for, 69, 70, 71
Byrne, Wm, 35

Campbell, William, 150
Canada
   crossing into United States from, 53, 54f, 57. *See also* border-crossing records
   missing friends advertisements in, 64
   repeal societies in, 67
   reasons for first traveling to, 53
Cancelled Land Books, 127. *See also* revised valuations
case studies. Fitzgerald family case study; Kennedy family case study; McClements family case study
Catholic Association of Foresters, 72–73
Catholic Church. *See also* church records, Ireland; church records, North America
   archdiocesan archives in, 32, 40
   baptism date in, 30
   dioceses in, 90
   graveyards maintained by, 61
   information included in records from, 31t
   locating church records for, 32–33, 36
   orphanage records in, 39–40
   parish system of, 88, 95, 102
   school records in, 39
   types of records kept in, 31, 32

Catholic Church in the United States of America, The (online history), 35
Catholic immigrants, 33, 36, 61, 77
Catholic Order of Foresters of Illinois, 72
Cavan (county), Ireland, 86, 87, 97, 134
cemeteries (burial grounds), 37, 61, 62, 74. *See also* burial (cemetery) records; gravestone inscriptions
   burial places on death notices and, 62
   burial places in death records and, 61
   chronological use of, 61–62
   in cities, 61–62
   family purchase of grave lots in, 62
   locating, 62, 63
   sources on, 62
cemetery associations, 37
cemetery (burial) records
   burial dates on, 31
   burial places and, 61, 62
   Irish, 101, 106, 122
   U.S., 31, 33, 34, 37, 61–62, 83
census records, Ireland, 133–136
   border-crossing records and, 53
   census substitutes used with, 123
   complete records for 1901 and 1911, 134–135
   for early twentieth-century, 123
   house descriptions on, 134, 135–136
   indexes for, 93
   leaving name field blank in searches to find relatives, 135
   loss of records from fire and other causes, 133–134
   McCarthy case study of, 53
   McClements case study of, 135–136
   poor law unions used in, 90
   records helpful in locating, 59, 122
   searching, 133–136
   search strategies for, 135
   small towns in, 23–24
   sources for, 103, 157
   townlands and, 93, 122
   years covered by, 133–134

census records, state
  ambiguity of family relationships on, 22
  existence and availability of, 23
  Kennedy/Fitzgerald case study of searching, 23
census records, United States, 11–14, 17–18
  abbreviations (codes on, 11, 14, 43
  address information in, 36
  ambiguity of family relationships on, 22
  birth, marriage, and death records searches using data from, 15
  birth date differences between naturalization petitions and, 49
  birth date estimation using, 13, 15, 17–18, 25
  changes in coverage of, over years, 11–12
  date ranges ("± 2 years") in searching, 12, 13, 17, 19
  dates of arrival guessed using, 55, 59
  death date estimation using, 25
  immigrant date searches using, 14, 20–21
  immigrant information searches in, 11–14, 17–18, 19, 43
  immigration year on, 43
  Irish civil registration records combined with, in searching for parents' names, 110–111
  Kennedy/Fitzgerald case study of searching, 12–14, 17–18, 19, 44
  marriage record data used in searches of, 19
  McClements case study of, 110–111
  naturalization data on, 11, 12, 14, 19, 44, 47
  order for searching, from most recent back to ancestors, 12, 17, 18
  person answering questions on, 43
  place of origin found using, 43
  possible birth and death of children between, 23
  range of data found on, depending on census year, 11, 12*f*, 43
  reliability of information on, 21, 43
  state census records compiled between years of, 22
  state of birth (not birthplace) used in searching, 18, 19
  to-do lists for, 15, 23
  unreliability of dates and places in, 43
  using a less common family name for searching, 13
  websites for, 12
census substitutes, Ireland, 122, 136–143, 145–148, 153. *See also* property records; valuation records
  finding townlands in, 106
  meaning of term, 123
  need to use because of fire loss of census records, 133
  searching, 136–143
  sources for, 157–158
Central New York Genealogical Society, 68
certificates of arrival, 50
certified copies of Irish birth records, 117, 121
chain migrations, 27, 80
Chalkley, Lyman, 82
Chapel Hill Cemetery, Trescott, Maine, 63
Chester County, Pennsylvania, 78, 82
Chicago Manual of Style, The, 8
children
  baptism records for. *See* baptism records
  estimating marriage date from birth of eldest, 21
  guardianships for, 24
  orphanage records for, 39–40
  parochial school records for, 39, 198
  on U.S. census records, 11, 12
Christ Church, Philadelphia, 33
Christian, Thomas, 72*f*
Christian Brothers, 39
Chronicles of the Scotch-Irish Settlement in Virginia (Chalkley), 82
church archives, 32, 34, 35, 106, 108

churches, 97. *See also* parish registers
  duplication of marriage records and, 18
  graveyards connected with, 37, 61
  identifying through marriage records, 16, 21
  locating, in cities, 36
  missing friends advertisements in newspapers of, 29, 101
  session books and, 80, 81*f*, 83, 107
Church of Ireland
  dioceses in, 90
  importance of always checking for records of, 107
  on IrishGenealogy, 103
  loss of documents from fire, 133
  online registers of, 106
  parish system of, 88
  on IrishGenealogy website, 102
  sources for records of, 103, 159
  tithe appointment survey tax supporting, 126
  vital records kept by, 108
church records, Ireland, 101, 102–107, 122, 126, 153
  on Ancestry.com, 104
  beginning of civil registration of records and use of, 102
  births, deaths, and marriages in, before civil registration, 102, 122
  burial records, 101, 106, 122
  checking image for accuracy of transcription of, 105
  on Findmypast.com, 104–105
  Fitzgerald case study using, 102, 104
  on IrishGenealogy website, 102–103
  loss of documents from fire, 133
  National Library of Ireland website, 105–106
  online finding guides for, 148–149
  property valuations used with, 130
  reliability of, 105
  on RootsIreland website, 103–104
  searching by county in, 45
  of siblings, 101
  sources for, 102, 103, 107, 122, 158
  townlands on, 122
  variations among databases holding, 102
church records, North America, 27, 29–40. *See also* baptism records; death records; marriage records; parish registers
  archdiocesan archives for, 32, 40
  baptism information in, 16
  Baptist, 34
  in Boston, 104
  burial (cemetery) records, 31, 33, 34, 37, 61–62, 83
  Catholic, 32–32
  Catholic canon law requirements on, 32
  central repository or archives for, 32
  challenges from changing immigrant population and, 33
  checking at diocesan level to locate, 32
  in cities, 36–37
  civil record gaps and use of, 27, 30, 31, 40, 102
  closed churches and, 32, 33, 34, 35
  confirmation records, 31, 37
  eighteenth-century immigrants in, 80, 83
  Episcopal, 34
  first communion records, 31, 37
  Fitzgerald case study of, 29–30, 36, 101–102
  information included in, 31
  limitations of using, 27
  linking immigrant ancestors to Ireland using, 27, 29
  marriage dispensations in, 38–39
  Methodist, 35
  ordination records, 31, 40
  orphanage records in, 39–40
  parish of origin used in, 29, 122
  parochial school records in, 39
  Presbyterian, 34
  presbytery records and histories, 80
  Protestant, 33–34
  Quaker, 34–35
  reasons for using, instead of civil records, 30, 31
  in small towns, 35–36
  types of, 31, 32
  where to find, 32
Church Record Surveys, 34

circuit courts, declarations of intent in, 44, 50, 51, 52*f*
citations. *See* source citations
cities. *See also* small towns
  banks in, 70
  business agents in, 68
  canvassing for birth information in, 30
  field books and house books with names of people in, 124
  locating church records for, 36–37
  locating graveyards in, 61–62
  repeal societies in, 67
citizenship
  courts as venue for applying for, 44, 46
  determining if and when immigrant applied for, 43
  documents generated in process of applying for, 43–44
  process of gaining, 44–45
  residency requirement for, 44, 49, 50
  standardized process (1906) of applying for, 51
citizenship records, 44, 59. *See also* declarations of intent; naturalization documents; naturalization petitions
  place of origin found using, 43
  records helpful in locating, 59
  U.S. census records compared with, 43
citizenship status
  of immigrants, from parents' status, 57
  Irish-born relatives as sources on, 7
  Kennedy case study of U.S. census record searches and, 14
  passport applications and, 57
  on U.S. census records, 11, 12, 14, 19, 43
  women's derived from husbands' status (prior to 1922), 14, 45
city directories, searching for clergy and churches in, 16, 21, 35, 36, 39, 70
civil court records, 76, 82, 83
civil parishes, 90, 92, 95, 97, 102, 116
  as administrative division, 85, 86, 88
  on birth records, 116
  counties with, 87
  General Alphabetical Index to, 93
  maps of, 95
  origins of, 88
  reference works using, 93, 126
  religious parishes and, 88, 89*f*, 102
civil records, Ireland. *See* civil registration records, Ireland
civil records, United States, 107, 110. *See also* birth records; death records; marriage records
  beginning of, 30
  church records used for gaps in, 27, 30, 31, 40
  under-registration for, 30, 122
Civil Registration, 90–91, 93
civil registration indexes, 103, 114, 115, 116, 117, 118*f*, 119*f*, 120, 121, 157
Civil Registration Office, Ireland, 121
civil registration records, Ireland, 99, 107–110, 153. *See also* birth records; death records; marriage records
  beginning of, 102, 107, 113, 122
  birth records in, 110, 113, 114–116
  census substitutes used with, 123
  church records used for gaps in, 102
  identifying previous generations using, 107
  indexes to, 103, 107, 114, 115, 116, 117, 118*f*, 119*f*, 120, 121, 157
  information available on, 116*t*
  Irish administrative divisions and, 86, 116
  Irish census records used with, 123
  Irish Townlands website and, 92
  marriage records in, 117–120, 150
  obtaining copies in person, 121
  ordering photocopies of records, 113, 120–121
  organization of, 116
  origins of immigrants identified using, 107
  poor law unions and, 90
  resources for, 116*t*
  searching, 107–110

searching for places of origin using, 111, 114, 122
of siblings, 101
sources for, 103, 107, 113–114, 116–117, 157, 158–159
superintendent registrar's districts used in, 91, 107, 110, 116, 117, 118
under-registration of, 122
years covered by, 113, 116*t*
Civil Survey (1654–1656), 88
Civil War
   Irish, 134
   U.S., 1, 50
clergy. *See also* ministers; priests
   city directories listing, 36, 39
   cooperation of, for completing civil marriage records, 31
   Irish parishes and, 88
   on marriage records, 112
   parish record maintenance by, 32
   tithe appointment survey tax supporting, 126
closed churches, records of, 32, 33, 34, 35
collateral research, 5
college and university archives, 33, 34, 35, 69, 73
common please courts, naturalization in, 44
community, researching immigrant ancestors in context of, 27, 79, 84
Composition Act (1823), 126, 131
computer programs
   footnote generation using, 8
   genealogical forms completed using, 5–6
   photocopying title pages for, 8
   source citation entered using, 8
computer storage of records
   digitized search results kept on, 5–6
   source citation records kept on, 8
confirmation records, 31, 37
Congregational Church, 33
consanguinity, degrees of, 38
convicts, immigration by, 75, 77, 84
Coolnacran, County Down, Ireland, 143, 148, 149*f*
Cork (county), Ireland, 7, 63, 76, 79, 103, 126, 128, 129, 130*f*, 159

correspondence. *See* letters
Coughlan, Daniel, 129, 130*f*
Counter-Reformation, 30
counties, Ireland. *See also specific counties, for example,* Cork (county)
   as administrative division, 85, 86, 87
   on birth records, 114, 115*f*, 116
   civil parishes and, 88
   determining location of records for, 87
   map of, 92*f*, 95
   name changes for, 87
   poor law union boundaries and, 90
   probate district boundaries and, 91
   in Ulster, 86–87
counties of origin, 46, 101. *See also* birthplaces; places of origin
   gravestone inscriptions with, 63, 74
   newspaper records with, 65
   repeal society meeting reports with, 67
countries, on naturalization records, 45
countries of origin, 46, 101. *See also* birthplaces; places of origin
county cess, 123–124, 126
county courts, naturalization records in, 44, 51, 57
county histories, 35
court records
   abstracts and microfilming or publication of, 82–83
   deeds in, 77
   landed estate, 123, 151–152, 157, 160
   petty court, 151
   researching, 76–77
courts
   criminal, 76, 82, 83, 151
   declarations of intent filed with, 49–51
   naturalization petitions filed with, 44, 46, 51–52
   naturalized status granted through, 57, 65
   petty, 151
   probate. *See* probate records
   types of, for citizenship application, 44

cousins. *See also* relatives
  marriage dispensations for, 38–39
  oral history interviews of, 6
Cox
  Philip, 21
  Rose, 19, 20–21, 104
criminal court records, 76, 82, 83, 151
Cyndi's List (web portal), 32, 62, 157

Daly, Marie, 36
dates. *See also* arrival dates; birth dates; death dates; immigrant dates; immigration dates; marriage dates; naturalization dates
  on border-crossing records, 53
  date ranges ("± 2 years") in searches, 12
  of travel. *See* border-crossing records; passenger arrival lists
death, causes of
  on death records, 107, 120
  on Irish census records, 134*f*
death age, on gravestones, 63
death certificates, 17. *See also* death records
death dates
  burial places located using, 61
  on death records, 31, 107
  on family group sheets, 4
  on five-generation charts, 3–4
  on U.S. census records, 21
death notices, 64. *See also* obituaries
  burial places usually lacking in, 62
  example of, 64*f*
death places
  on death records, 107
  on family group sheets, 4
  on five-generation charts, 3–4
  searching large towns using, 24
  U.S. census record searches for, 15
death records, Ireland, 120, 122
  beginning of civil registration for, 102, 107, 113
  causes of death on, 107, 120
  churches and, 102
  information available on, 107
  McClements case study for, 110–111, 112, 113*f*, 120, 142, 148
  obtaining copies in person, 121
  ordering microfilm copies of, 120–121
  ordering photocopies of, 113, 121
  other family members researched in, 112, 113*f*
  parents of immigrants on, 110, 120
  poor law unions used in, 90
  reliability of, 110
  searching, 120–121
  sources for, 113–114, 116*t*
  U.S. census records used with, in searching for parents' names, 110–111
  years covered by, 112, 113, 116*t*, 120
death records, United States, 17, 112–113
  burial places located using, 61
  cross reference data on with other sources, to verify accuracy, 17
  Fitzgerald case study of, 29–30, 101–102
  identifying previous generations using, 17, 22, 24, 25
  informants for data on, 17, 63, 120, 135
  information included on, 31
  Kennedy/Fitzgerald case study of searching, 19, 24
  maiden names on, 30
  parents of immigrant on, 16, 17, 22, 23*f*, 110
  reasons for using, instead of civil records, 30
  reliability of, 16, 17, 26, 63, 110
  siblings found using, 24, 102
deaths, on Irish census records, 133, 134*f*
declarations of intent, 49–51
  birth date claims on, 51
  courts as venue for applying for, 44, 46, 50, 52*f*
  date and court of, on naturalization petitions, 46
  examples of, 46*f*, 50*f*
  as first step in applying for citizenship, 44, 45
  Fitzgerald case study of, 50*f*, 51

linking immigrant ancestors to
  Ireland using, 27
naturalization petitions and court
  and date of, 51
not filing naturalization petition
  after, 51
parish or townland of birth on, 45
reasons to search for, 51
reliability of birth and arrival dates
  on, 45
residency time needed for, 49
skipping under certain circumstances, 45, 49–50
sources for searching for, 46, 51
U.S. census code Pa (first papers)
  status and, 11, 14, 43
deeds, 11
  baronies and, 88
  eighteenth-century, 78, 82, 83
  seventeenth-century, 76, 77
  sources for, 82, 160
Delaney, Henry, 45*f*
Delaware, 34, 78
delayed registration books,
  for births, 15
denization, 44
departure, ports of. *See* ports of
  embarkation
Desmond, Cornelius, 129, 130*f*
digital records
  of search results, 5–6
  source citations for, 8
directories, 97, 122
  business, 125
  city, 16, 21, 35, 36, 39, 70
  street, 148, 159
  town, 70
district (federal) courts, naturalization
  petitions in, 44, 46, 47, 48, 49*f*, 51,
  52*f*, 65
district electoral divisions (D.E.D.),
  90, 93
diocesan archives
  checking for records at, before going
    to churches, 32
  church records in, 32, 33, 34, 37, 40
  orphanage records in, 40
  school records in, 39

dioceses
  as administrative division, 90
  church structure within, 36, 38, 39,
    90, 103
  on Cyndi's List, 32–33
  histories of, 35
  locating specific churches within, 36
  on RootsIreland website, 103
dispensations. *See* marriage
  dispensations
documentation
  digitized search results kept on
    computers for, 5–6
  of oral interviews, 6
  print storage in folders or binders
    for, 6
Donegal (county), Ireland, 86, 87, 97
Donegal, Pennsylvania, 78, 80
Donoghue
  Daniel, 51–52
  Mary, 51–52
  Mary (O'Brien), 52
Downshire, Marquis of, 142, 149*f*, 152
Dunmurray, County Antrim, Ireland,
  census record, 134*f*

Earlham College Friends Collection
  and College Archives, Richmond,
  Indiana, 35
economic status, 24
Egle, William Henry, 82
eighteenth-century immigration,
  77–79
  American records as starting point
    for researching, 80
  common names and difficulty in
    researching, 80
  estimates of number of individuals
    in, 77, 79*f*
  group and chain migrations in, 80
  network of family and friends in
    researching, 80
  periods of, 78, 79
  reasons behind, 77
  transition to America after, 78–79
eighteenth-century records, 79–83
  "community" strategy when
    researching, 79, 84
  organization of, 75

eighteenth-century records *cont.*
  paucity of references on immigrants in, 80, 84
  places of origin needed for researching, 75, 79–80
  sources for, 81, 83
electoral divisions, 90, 93
embarkation, ports of. *See* ports of embarkation
entry, ports of. *See* ports of arrival
Episcopal (Anglican) churches, 33, 77. *See also* Church of Ireland
  diocesan structure of, 90
  locating church records for, 34
episcopal registers, 31, 32. *See also* church registers
estate records, 83, 122. *See also* freeholder lists; landed estate records
  Griffith's Valuation in search for, 137
  online finding guides for, 148–149
  sources for, 152, 160
  usefulness of, 152
Evernote (computer program), 9

Fáilte Romhat (failteromhat.com), 156
family bibles, 6, 47
family friends. *See* friends
family group sheets, 3
  completing, 3–4
  computer programs for completing, 5
  digitized search results kept for, 5–6
  print record storage for, 6
  sample, 5*f*
family histories, 7, 82, 103, 148
Family History Center, 114, 117, 151
Family History Library (FHL)
  barony name needed for, 88
  birth records in, 110, 113, 116*t*, 117
  church records in, 33, 34, 36, 40, 105, 107
  civil registration indexes on, 114–115, 116*t*, 122
  death records in, 113, 120
  declarations of intent in, 51
  eighteenth-century records in, 82–83
  estate papers on, 152
  Fitzgerald case study searches on, 146–148
  freeholder lists on, 149
  Griffith's pre-publication records in, 127, 129
  marriage records in, 113, 117–118
  Massachusetts Catholic Order of Foresters in, 73
  naturalization records in, 46, 47, 51
  ordering microfilm copies from, 115, 118, 120–121
  Quaker records in, 108, 109
  repeal societies notices in, 67
  research log forms from, 9
  resources available on, 148
  revised valuations in, 144
  tithe applotment books on, 145–147, 148
  townlands on, 118
  website of. *See also* FamilySearch.org
family members as sources
  for five-generation charts, 3
  oral history interviews of, 6
family network
  passage to America and, 25
  probate as information source for, 24
FamilySearch.org, 157
  birth records on, 110, 114–116, 121
  church records on, 159
  death records on, 24, 114, 116*t*, 121
  declarations of intent on, 51
  Family History Centers and, 114, 117, 151
  Griffith's pre-publication records on, 127
  image quality on, 146–147
  Ireland Births and Baptisms, 1620–1881 database on, 107, 108, 110, 113, 114, 116, 158
  Irish census records on, 157, 158
  Irish civil registration records on, 113, 114, 116*t*, 121, 158
  Kennedy/Fitzgerald case study using, 19, 24, 48, 102
  marriage records on, 18, 51, 112, 114, 116*t*, 118, 121
  Massachusetts Catholic Order of Foresters on, 73
  McClements case study using, 112
  naturalization records on, 46, 47, 48, 51–52

ordering microfilm copies from, 114, 115
prison records on, 151
repeal societies notices on, 67
research log forms on, 9
U.S. census records on, 12
U.S. passport applications on, 57
family trees, 38
fathers. *See* parents
federal census records. *See* census records
federal (district) courts, for citizenship applications, 44, 46, 47, 48, 49*f*, 51, 52*f*, 65
Federal Reserve System, 71
Federal Street Church, Boston, 34
field books, 88
    building classifications in, 128
    descriptions of, 124, 128
    excerpt from, on townland of Town Parks, County Antrim, 125
    how to use, 129
    repositories holding, 127
files and filing systems
    on computers, 6, 8
    for photocopied pages, 8
    for print records using folders or binders, 6
    for research logs, 6, 9
    for source citation records, 8
Find A Grave (findagrave.com), 62, 64, 112
Finding Your Irish Ancestors in New York City (Buggy), 25
Findmypast.com, 104–105, 157
    filtering common surnames on, 135
    Fitzgerald case study of searches on, 104–105
    Griffith's pre-publication records on, 127
    Irish census records on, 135, 157
    Irish church records on, 103, 104–105
    Irish civil registration records on, 114, 121, 158
    landed estate records on, 160
    maps on, 158
    marriage records on, 118, 121

National Library of Ireland and, 105
prison records on, 151
U.S. census records on, 12
first communion records, 31, 37
Fitzgerald
    family, 22, 29, 36, 65, 104, 106, 141*f*, 146–148
    Bridget, 24, 29–30, 101–102, 104–105
    Edmond/Edmund, 29, 49, 65, 66, 101, 104, 137
    Edward, 22
    Ellen, 22, 101, 102, 104
    Ellen (Noonan), 24, 104
    Ellen (Wilmot), 24, 30, 102, 104, 106*f*, 146, 147
    Hannah, 24, 102, 104
    Honora, 104
    James, 66
    John F., 16, 17, 18–19
    Mary, 104
    Mary J. (Hanon), 16, 17, 18–19
    Michael, 20, 21, 24, 29, 65, 101, 102, 104, 106*f*, 137–138, 146, 147
    Patrick, 24
    Rose, 13, 15, 16, 17–18, 21
    Rose/Rosa/Rosey (Cox), 19, 20–21, 104
    Thomas, 19, 20–21, 22, 23, 24, 44, 47, 48, 49, 50*f*, 51, 65–66, 101, 102, 104–105, 106*f*, 146
Fitzgerald, F. Scott, 1
Fitzgerald family case study, 133
    baptism records, 29, 30*f*, 102, 104–105
    declarations of intent, 50*f*, 51
    FamilySearch.org searches, 19, 24, 48, 102
    Findmypast.com searches, 104–105
    Griffith's Primary Valuation, 137–139
    Irish church records, 102, 104
    lack of prison records or landed estate records, 151
    state census record searches, 23
    Tithe Applotment Books, 146–148
    U.S. birth records, 29

Fitzgerald family case study *cont.*
   U.S. census record searches, 12–14, 17–18, 19, 44
   U.S. church records, 29–30, 36, 101–102
   U.S. death records, 29–30, 101–102
five-generation charts
   completing, 3–4
   computer programs for completing, 5
   digitized search results kept for, 5–6
   print record storage for, 6
   sample, 4*f*
   sources of information for, 3
Flax Growers List (1796), 83, 157
Fold3 (website), 51
format, or source citations, 8
forms
   computer programs for, 5–6
   family group sheets, 3–4
   five-generation charts, 3–4
   pedigree charts, 5–6
   research logs, 9
forty-shilling freeholders lists, 83
Four Courts building, Dublin, fire (1922), 131, 133, 134, 150*f*, 153
Fox, George, 108
Franklin King (packet ship), 125
fraternal organizations, 71–73, 74
   Catholic Order of Foresters, 72–73
   finding specific, 72
   Masonic lodges, 72
   membership applications for, 72, 73*f*
   records of, 71, 74
   sources for, 72–73
freeholders lists, 83, 148, 149, 159
Freemasonry, 72
friends
   church records and, 29, 40, 106
   as godparents or witnesses, 46, 106
   group migrations with, 80, 107
   missing friend advertisements, 29, 64–67, 74, 101
   naturalization petitions and, 46
   oral history interviews of, 6, 10
   passage to America and, 25
   widening research to include, 23
Friends Historical Library, Dublin, 108, 109
Friends Historical Library, Swarthmore College, Swarthmore, Pennsylvania, 35

Fullerton, Joseph Hea, 14, 15*f*
Fullerton, Lillian, 14
Gaelic influences, 86
Gardiner, John, 125–126
gazetteers, 95, 97
genealogical forms
   computer programs for, 5–6
   family group sheets, 3–4
   five-generation charts, 3–4
   pedigree charts, 5–6
   research logs, 9
genealogies
   importance of source citations in, 8
   tradition of preserving information in, 3
GenealogyBank (website), newspapers on, 64, 67, 81
General Alphabetical Index to the Townlands and Towns, Parishes and Baronies of Ireland, 63, 93, 94*f*
General Register Office, Ireland
   ordering copies from, 113, 117, 118, 121, 159
   superintendent registrar's districts in, 91
generation data, on five-generation charts, 3–4
geographical surveys of Ireland, 95–97. *See also* maps
Georgia, 34
getting started, 3–25
   beginning with oneself and proceeding back in time, 3
   birth records in, 15
   citing sources and keeping records in, 8
   common assumptions and mistakes in, 24–25
   computer programs for, 5–6
   death records in, 17
   digitized search results kept during, 5–6
   family group sheets in, 3–4
   five-generation charts in, 3–4
   immigrant ancestor research in, 18–20
   immigrant date research in, 20–23
   interviews of Irish-born relatives in, 7
   marriage records in, 16–17
   oral history interviews in, 6

print record storage in, 6
research log in, 8–9
starting with what you know in, 3–6
to-do lists for, 6, 7
U.S. census record searches in, 11–14, 17–18
widening focus of research in, 23–24
godparents (sponsors), on baptism records, 29, 30*f*, 31, 41, 65, 101, 104, 106, 157
Goodbody, Olive C., 108, 109
Goodfellow (ship), 76
Gookin, Daniel, 76
Google Books, 35, 109
Google maps, 97, 139, 141*f*
Government of Ireland Act (1920), 86
grand juries, and land taxes, 124
Grand Lodges, Masonic, 72
grandparents of immigrant
  alive in 1911, 7
  Irish-born relatives as sources on, 7
  naming pattern in Irish families and, 21
grandparents of researcher (yourself)
  on family group sheets, 4
  on five-generation charts, 3–4
  oral history interviews of, 6
  on U.S. census records, 12
gravestone inscriptions, 27, 61–64, 74
  checking other gravestones for related information, 62–63
  chronological use of graveyards and locating, 61–62
  church affiliation of, 37, 61
  deciphering place names on, 63
  examples of, 63*f*
  family purchase of grave lots and, 62
  finding graveyards, 61–62
  finding specific graves, 62
  keeping a wide focus in, 62–63
  not finding gravestones, 62, 101
  not finding transcribed inscriptions in sources, 64
  options after not finding (or brick wall), 101
  parish names on, 63, 88
  places of origin included on, 61, 63
  reliability of information from, 63
  reliability of information in, 63

sources for inscriptions, 62, 63–64
to-do list for, 62
websites and printed sources for, 62–64
graveyards, 37, 61, 62, 74. *See also* burial (cemetery) records; gravestone inscriptions
  burial places on death notices and, 62
  burial places in death records and, 61
  chronological use of, 61–62
  in cities, 61–62
  family purchase of grave lots in, 62
  locating, 62, 63
  sources on, 62
Great Famine (1845–1852), 63, 64, 82, 123, 129, 130, 151
great grandparents, on five-generation charts, 3–4
great-great grandparents
  on five-generation charts, 3–4
  newspapers as sources on, 65
Grenham, John, 97, 102, 107, 116, 152, 158. *See also* Irish Ancestors (website)
Griffin, Patrick, 78
Griffith, Sir Richard, 124, 126
Griffith's pre-publication records, 88, 127–130
  building classifications in, 128
  field books in, 128
  house books in, 128
  repositories holding, 127
  library catalog online searches in, 127–128
  summary of, 127–130
Griffith's Primary Valuation, 124, 136–140, 153
  example of information on, 137*f*
  Fitzgerald case study of, 137–139
  Google map street views with, 97, 139, 141*f*
  historical background for, 126–127, 130, 136–137
  land occupiers and landowners included in, 137
  locating households on maps and aerial views using, 136, 138–139, 140*f*, 143, 153, 157, 158

Griffith's Primary Valuation *cont.*
   McClements case study on, 120, 141–143
   measurements used in, 148
   poor law unions used in, 90
   records used to prepare, 127
   townlands in, 106
   value of using, 123, 136
Griffith's Revised Valuation books. *See* revised valuations
Griffith's Valuation. *See* Griffith's Primary Valuation
"Griffith's Valuation as a Source for Irish Family History" (Murphy), 136
Griffith's Valuation Cancellation Books, electoral divisions used in, 90
group migrations, 27, 33, 80
guardianships, 24
Guide to Irish Quaker Records, 1654–1860 (Goodbody), 108, 109
Guide to Massachusetts Cemeteries, A (Lambert), 63
Guilford College, Greensboro, North Carolina, 35

Hall's Index of American Presbyterian Congregations, 34
Handran, George, 95
Hanon, Mary J., 16, 17, 18–19
Harpers Ferry (West Virginia) repeal association, 68*f*
Harvard Divinity School, 34
Haverford College, Haverford, Pennsylvania
Healey Library, University of Massachusetts Boston, 73
Hearth Money Tax rolls, 83, 157
Hege Friends Historical Library, Guilford College, Greensboro, North Carolina, 35
Hibbins, Ann, 76–77
Hickey, Mary A., 16
Hill, Thomas C., 34
historical archives. *See also specific archives*
   church records in, 33
historical records, 11. *See also* federal census records; vital records

fire (1922) and loss of, 131, 133, 134, 150*f*, 153
historical registers, of Episcopal churches, 34
historical societies. *See also specific organizations*
   bank records in, 70, 71
   church records in, 34, 40, 105, 107
   family manuscript collections in, 82
Historical Society of Pennsylvania, 70, 82
History of the Catholic Church in the New England States, The (Byrne), 35
home rule, 86–87
Homes
   Robert, 78
   William, 78
house books, 88
   building classifications in, 128
   descriptions of, 124, 128
   how to use, 129, 130*f*
   quarto books and, 128, 129
   repositories holding, 127
house descriptions
   on Griffith's Valuation, 137, 142–143
   on Irish census records, 134, 135–136
   on revised valuations, 144
household information
   on Irish census records, 133, 134–135
   on Irish census substitutes, 136, 137, 145, 146
   on online Irish sources, 83
   on Protestant Householders Census (1740), 83
   on U.S. census records, 11, 12, 13, 14
   on U.S. state census records, 22
Humling, Virginia, 32
Humphreys, James, 137

Illinois, 34, 72
immigrant ancestors
   common assumptions and mistakes in, 24–25
   context of communities in researching, 27
   researching back to, 18–20
   ways of linking to Ireland, 27

immigrant dates. *See also* arrival dates; birth dates; death dates; immigration dates; marriage dates; naturalization dates
   Irish-born relatives as sources on, 7
   Kennedy case study of searching for, 20–21, 22, 23f
   researching back to, 20–23
   U.S. census record searches for, 14, 20–21
Immigration and Naturalization Service (INS), 47
immigration data
   Kennedy case study of searches for, 14
   on U.S. census records, 11, 12, 14, 15
immigration dates
   on passport applications, 57
   on U.S. census reports, 43
Immigration of the Irish Quakers into Pennsylvania, 1682–1750 (Myers), 76
immigration records, 44, 59. *See also* declarations of intent; naturalization documents; naturalization petitions; passenger arrival lists
   linking immigrant ancestors to Ireland using, 27
Immigration Service, 53
immigration year, on U.S. census records, 43
indentured servants, 84
   on court and land records, 76
   difficulties in tracing, 76, 77
   eighteenth-century immigration and, 77
   seventeenth-century immigration and, 75, 76–77
Indiana, 34, 35
informants
   for birth records, 115
   church searches based on names of, 16, 21, 36, 39
   for death records, 17, 63, 120, 135
   for marriage records, 16, 21, 31, 36
   for U.S. census records, 43
inscriptions, gravestone. *See* gravestone inscriptions
International Genealogical Index (IGI), 107
interviews. *See also* oral history interviews
   for five-generation charts, 3
   of Irish-born relatives, 7
IreAtlas Townland Database (website), 93
Ireland
   Act of Union (1800) with, 67, 131
   ancestors returning from visits back to, 57
   eighteenth-century immigration from, 77–79
   family location in. *See* origins in Ireland
   seventeenth–century immigration from, 75–76
   ways of linking immigrant ancestors to, 27
Ireland Births and Baptisms, 1620–1881 (FamilySearch.org database), 107, 108, 110, 113, 114, 116, 158
Irish American immigrants, 1
   business agents in communities with, 68
   missing friends advertisements in, 29, 64–67, 74, 101
   newspapers for, 67
   under-reporting on vital records of, 30, 40
Irish American Weekly (newspaper), 64, 67
Irish Ancestors (website, JohnGrenham.com), 97, 102, 116, 157
Irish Ancestral Research Association, The (TIARA), 72–73
Irish-born relatives
   interviewing, 7
   interview topics for, 7
   types of questions to ask, 7
Irish church records databases, 102
Irish Cultural and Heritage Center of Wisconsin, 91
Irish families
   common assumptions and mistakes about, 24–25
   family members traveling together or in stages, 54–55, 64–65
   naming pattern in, 21
   number of children in, 23, 24

Irish Family History Foundation, 103
   RootsIreland website of, 102,
      103–104, 105, 107, 159
Irish Free State, 87
Irish Genealogical Research Society, 93
Irish Genealogical Society
   International, 152
IrishGenealogy (website), 102–103,
   114, 158, 159
Irish Immigrants in the Land of Canaan
   (Miller), 81
*Irish in America, The: A Guide to the
   Literature and the Manuscript
   Collections* (Blessing), 82
Irish Land Commission, 144, 145f
Irish newspapers, sources for, 64, 67.
   See also newspapers
Irish Quakers, 108–109
Irish Townlands website, 92
Irish War of Independence (1919–
   1922), 86

Jenks, H. May, 112
Jones, Isabel, 109
"Jones Index to Quaker births, marriages and deaths in Ireland's Monthly Meetings, ca. 1606–1872" (manuscript), 109
Jurisdictional Commissions on
   Archives and History, 35

Kennedy
   Edward, 13
   Eunice, 13
   John Fitzgerald, 12–13, 15, 19, 22,
      44, 65
   Joseph, 15
   Joseph P., 12, 15, 16, 17
   Mary A. (Hickey), 16
   Nancy, 24
   Patrick J., 16
   Rose (Fitzgerald), 13, 15, 16, 17–18,
      21
   Thomas, 24
   William, 1
Kennedy family case study
   birth date searches, 13, 15
   birth records, 15, 18, 19
   border-crossing records, 14

citizenship status, 14
FamilySearch.org searches, 19, 24,
   48, 102
immigrant dates, 20–21, 22, 23f
marriage dates, 13
naturalization petitions, 14, 44, 47
parents research, 12–13, 18, 19, 22,
   101–102, 104–105
residence places, 12, 15, 18
siblings in searches, 12, 24, 29–30,
   102, 104
state census records, 23
U.S. census records, 12–14, 17–18,
   19, 44
U.S. death records, 19, 24
U.S. marriage record searches, 13,
   16, 18, 19, 21, 101
Kentucky Historical Society, 34
Kentucky State Archives, 34
Kings Chapel, Boston, 33

Lambert, David Allan, 63
Lancaster County, Pennsylvania, 78, 82
Land Act Purchase (L.A.P.), 131, 144
landed estate records, 151–152. *See
   also* estate records
   census substitutes used with, 123
   description of, 151
   example of, 152f
   indexes to, 152
   sources for, 152, 157, 160
   usefulness of, 152
landlords
   in eighteenth-century Ireland, 77
   on freeholder lists, 149
   Irish taxes and, 136
   as lessors in Griffith's Valuation, 137
   rent books organized by name of,
      129
   U.S. federal census information
      from, 43
   U.S. immigrants and, 79
land records. *See also* leases and lessors; property records; property valuations; valuation records
   civil parishes used in, 88
   eighteenth-century, 83
   sources for, 160
Lawther, John, 149

Leary, David, 129
leases and lessors
  eighteenth-century, 83
  freeholders lists, 83, 148, 149, 159
  in Griffith's Primary Valuation, 126–127, 137
  landed estate records and, 151, 152
  rent books with, 129
  in revised valuations, 127, 144
  tenure books with, 129
  in Tithe Applotment Books, 145
legislatures, state, 70
Leitrim-Roscommon genealogy website, 93
lessors. *See* leases and lessors
letters
  from immigrants, 27, 73, 78, 81, 83
  in local history collections, 82
  oral interviews using, 6
letters of administration, 91
Lewis, Samuel, 97
libraries. *See also specific libraries*
  ArchiveGrid coverage of holdings of, 33–34, 71
  business records in, 69
  church records in, 32, 33, 34, 35, 40
  gazetteers in, 97
  land records in, 149
  newspaper resources in, 62
Little, Thomas, 46*f*
local histories, 27, 35, 70, 81–82, 95
location of family in Ireland. *See* origins in Ireland
locations. *See* birthplaces; burial places; death places; marriage places; naturalization places; places of origin; ports of arrival (ports of entry); residence places
logs. *See* research logs
Londonderry, New Hampshire, 80, 81–82
Londonderry (county), Ireland, 81*f*, 86, 87, 97, 124
Londonderry Companies, 83
Loughbrickland, County Down, Ireland, 114, 115*f*, 116, 119, 120*f*, 141, 143
Louisiana, University of, Lafayette, 81

MacGregor, James, 80
maiden names
  on baptism records, 105
  on birth records, 15
  on death records, 30
  Fitzgerald case study of searches using, 105
  Irish-born relatives as sources on, 7
  on marriage records, 112
  McClements case study on using, 112
  usefulness in differentiating similar surnames, 8, 22, 101, 112
Maine, 63, 78
manifests, passenger arrival. *See* passenger arrival lists
manuscript collections
  church records, 34
  estate papers, 152
  Griffith's pre-publication records, 88, 127–128
  of Irish immigrants, 81, 82
  Quaker, 108, 109
maps, 95–97, 122, 153
  boundary identification using, 95
  census substitutes used with, 123
  gazetteers and, 97
  Griffith's Valuation linking to, 136, 138–139, 140*f*, 143, 153, 157, 158
  online resources for, 93
  Ordnance Survey maps, 86, 91, 83, 97, 131, 158
  for Presbyterian church parishes, 90
  sources for, 158
  to-do list for, 95
marriage, women's gaining citizenship at (prior to 1922), 14, 45
marriage certificates. *See also* marriage records
  Quaker, 108
marriage dates
  estimating from birth of eldest child, 21
  on family group sheets, 4
  on five-generation charts, 3–4
  Kennedy case study of U.S. census record searches for, 13
  on marriage records, 31, 107
  on naturalization petitions, 51, 52*f*

searching back from, in U.S. census records, 14, 17–18
U.S. census record searches for, 13, 18
marriage dispensations, 38–39
  degrees of consanguinity and, 38
  reasons for grant, 38, 39
  source for, 38
marriage information, on naturalization petitions, 51, 52f
marriage places
  duplication of marriage records based on two different places, 18
  on family group sheets, 4
  on five-generation charts, 3–4
  on marriage records, 51
  on naturalization petitions, 51, 52f
marriage records, Ireland, 117–120, 121
  beginning of civil registration for, 102, 107, 113
  churches and, 29, 102, 107
  cooperation of local clergy in completing, 31
  identifying previous generations using, 117–120
  information available on, 107, 119
  on IrishGenealogy website, 103
  maiden names on, 112
  McClements case study using, 110–111, 112, 117–120, 142, 148, 150
  obtaining copies in person, 121
  ordering microfilm copies of, 118, 120–121
  ordering photocopies of, 113, 121
  parents of immigrant on, 110, 117
  poor law unions used in, 90
  range of data available on, 16
  reasons for using, instead of civil records, 30
  reliability of, 110
  sources for, 113–114, 116t
  U.S. census records used with, in searching for parents' names, 110–111
  witnesses on, 106
  years covered by, 113, 116t, 117

marriage records, United States, 16–17, 112
  birth date estimation using, 19
  birth record searches based on, 19
  in churches, 34
  church records and, 16–17
  church searches from data on, 16, 21, 36, 39
  cooperation of local clergy in completing, 31
  duplication of, in two different places, 18
  identifying church on civil, 16, 21
  identifying previous generations using, 13–14, 16, 17, 19, 21, 25, 107
  informants for data on, 16, 21, 31, 36
  information included on, 31, 32
  Kennedy/Fitzgerald case study of searching for, 13, 16, 18, 19, 21, 101
  lack of, assumptions about, 31
  parents of immigrant on, 16, 17, 21, 22, 25, 31, 107, 110
  range of data available on, 16
  records helpful in locating, 59
  reliability of, 16, 22, 26, 110
  underreporting of, 16–17, 31
  U.S. census record searches for, 15, 18, 19
  using civil versus church sources for, 30, 31
  witnesses on, 31, 40
Maryland, 34
Masonic lodges, 72
Massachusetts, 35, 62
  immigration to, 76, 77, 78
  Kennedy/Fitzgerald case study using, 13–14, 15, 17, 18, 19, 20–21, 24, 29
  Masonic Lodge membership, files for, 72–73
  vital records for, 22, 104
Massachusetts, University of, Boston, 73
Massachusetts Catholic Order of Foresters, 72–73
Massachusetts Historical Society, 70, 71

Mather
    Cotton, 78
    Increase, 76
McCarthy
    John, 51, 52*f*, 53
    Mary (Donoghue), 51–52
    Mary (Ryan), 51, 53
    Nora, 53
    Patrick, 51–52, 53, 54*f*
McClements
    family, 5, 54–55, 112, 116, 118, 135–136, 144, 148, 151
    Agnes, 110
    Anna Matilda, 150
    H. John, 112
    H. May (Jenks), 112
    John, 110, 111, 112, 114, 115, 117, 118, 119, 120, 135, 141–142, 143, 144, 148
    Joseph, 110, 119–120, 135, 142, 143, 144, 148, 149, 150
    Mary (Brown?), 112, 148, 149–150, 151*f*
    Robert, 135–136, 149–150
    Robert William, 55*f*, 110, 111, 112, 114, 115, 117, 119, 120, 141, 144, 145*f*, 148
    Samuel, 148
    Susan (Moorehead), 110, 111, 112, 114, 115, 117, 135, 141, 148
McClements family case study, 133
    birthplace searches, 114–116
    birth record searches, 110–111, 114–116
    FamilySearch.org searches, 112
    Griffith's Primary Valuation, 120, 141–143
    Irish census records, 135–136
    Irish death records, 110–111, 112, 113*f*, 120, 142, 148
    Irish marriage records, 110–111, 112, 117–120, 142, 148, 150
    Irish probate records, 149–150
    lack of prison records or landed estate records, 151
    origins in Ireland searches, 110–111, 114–116
    parents search, 110–111
    passenger arrival lists, 54–55
    relatives search, 135–136
    revised valuations, 144–145
    Tithe Applotment Books, 148, 149*f*
    U.S. census records, 110–111
    wills, 149–150, 151*f*
McCulloh, Henry, 78
McGroary, Frederick, 73*f*
McQuaig, John, 63
membership applications, fraternal organizations, 72, 73*f*
membership files, 72, 82,
Methodist churches, 145
    church records for, 35, 107
Michigan, 35
    McClements case study using, 110, 111, 112, 119, 135, 148, 150
Microsoft OneNote (computer program), 9
migration experience
    family members traveling together or in stages and, 54–55, 64–65
    Irish-born relatives as sources on, 7, 25
military records, in eighteenth-century, 83
military service, and citizenship, 50
Miller, Hannah (Fitzgerald), 24, 102, 104
Miller, Kerby A., 75, 81
ministers. *See also* clergy
    on baptism records, 30
    Baptist church records and, 34
    finding church records using, 32
    Irish immigration and, 80
    on marriage records, 16, 21, 31, 36, 39
    parish information in small towns from, 35
    researching origins of, 80
missing friends advertisements, 29, 64–67, 74, 101
    example of, 66*f*
    Fitzgerald case study of, 65–66, 101
    places of origin in, 64–65
    sources for, 67
Mitchell, Brian, 90, 95
Monaghan (county), Ireland, 86, 87, 97, 103

Monthly Meetings in North America: A Quaker Index (Hill), 34
Moore
  John, 76
  Joseph, 76
Moorehead/Moorhead/Morehead
  family, 118
  Samuel, 148
  Susan, 110, 111, 112, 114, 115, 117, 135, 141, 148
Morse, Steve, 40
mothers. *See* parents
municipal courts, naturalization in, 44
municipal libraries, business agent records in, 69
Murphy
  Jeremiah W., 57
  Joseph W., 57, 58*f*
  Mary, 56, 57
  Patrick, 54, 56–57
  Thomas, 56, 57
Murphy, Rachel, 136
Myers, Albert Cook, 76

Name Books, for townlands, 95, 97, 138, 139, 141*f*
National Archives
  of Ireland, 105, 127, 129, 134, 145, 146–147, 148, 149, 152, 157, 158
  of United States, 46, 48, 51, 57
National Genealogical Society Quarterly, 37
National Information Center, Federal Reserve System, 71
National Library of Ireland (NLI), 91, 105–106
  browsing strategies on, 106
  Catholic Parish Registers at, 102
  church records on website of, 105–106
nativity, county of, 46. *See also* birthplaces; places of origin
naturalization data
  of parents, on passport applications, 57
  on U.S. census records, 11, 12, 14, 19, 44

naturalization dates
  of parents, on passport applications, 57
  on U.S. census reports, 14, 19, 59
naturalization documents, after granting of citizenship
  example of, 45*f*
  process of applying for citizenship resulting in, 45
naturalization petitions
  birth date differences between U.S. census records and, 49
  birthplaces (county or country of origin) on, 45, 46, 51, 65, 101
  birthplace used in searching, 47
  date ranges ("± 5 years") in searching for, 47, 49
  dates of arrival guessed using, 55, 59
  declarations of intent court and date related to, 51
  examples of data on, 48*f*, 49*f*, 52*f*
  Fitzgerald case study of searches for, 47–49, 101
  Irish immigrants as British citizens on, 44
  Kennedy/Fitzgerald case study of U.S. census record searches and, 14, 44, 47
  linking immigrant ancestors to Ireland using, 27
  marriage record searches based on information on, 51
  naturalization place used in searching, 47
  of neighbors, in searches for immigrant information, 14, 15*f*
  not filing, after completing declarations of intent, 51
  obtaining paper copies of, 48
  other information for narrowing searches in, 47
  other useful pieces of information on, 46
  parish or townland of birth on, 45
  post-1906, 51–52
  pre-1906, 44–46
  pre-1906 New England, indexes of, 47–49

process of applying for citizenship using, 44–45
reliability of birth and arrival dates on, 45
search strategies for, 47
Soundex codes used with, 47
sources for searching for, 46
to-do list for, 55
U.S. census record searches and, 14, 15f, 19
ways of applying for citizenship using, 44
witnesses on, 29, 46, 47, 49, 52f, 65, 66
WPA card index of, 47–48
naturalization places
in newspaper articles, 65
on passport applications, 57
searching using, 47
naturalization records. *See also* declarations of intent; naturalization petitions
county or country of nativity on, 46
dates of arrival guessed using, 55, 59
pre-Revolutionary period, 44
sources for searching for, 46
to-do list for, 55
types of courts for applying for citizenship and, 44
of witnesses, 46
naturalized citizenship
in newspaper articles, 65
on passport applications, 57
skipping declaration of intent process for granting of, 50
on U.S. census reports, as (*Na*) status, 14, 19
NEHGS. *See* New England Historic Genealogical Society
neighborhoods
changing county boundaries and histories affecting, 19
oral history interviews of, 6
researching Irish immigrants in, 70
neighbors
as godparents and witnesses in parish records, 106
group migrations with, 80
as informants on death records, 17

oral history interviews of, 6, 7
using for searches for immigrant information, 14, 15f
U.S. census record information from, 43
New England
churches in, 33
citizenship records for, 45
immigration to, 75–76, 77, 78
National Archives for, 51
pre-1906 naturalization petitions in, 47–49
New England Historical and Genealogical Society Register, 34
New England Historic Genealogical Society (NEHGS), 36, 80, 82, 97, 146, 147, 148
church records at, 80
databases at, 34, 62, 65
website of. *See* AmericanAncestors.org
New England naturalization petitions pre-1906, 47–49
Fitzgerald case study of searching, 47
strategies for searching, 47
WPA card index of, 47–48
New Genealogical Atlas of Ireland, A (Mitchell), 90, 95
New Hampshire, immigrants in, 80, 81–82
New Jersey, church records in, 34, 35
New Jersey Historical Society, 34
newspapers, 27, 61, 64–67, 74
bank information in, 70
business agent advertisements in, 68–69
eighteenth-century immigrants and shipping records in, 81, 83
Fitzgerald case study of search using, 65–66
locating burial places using, 62
missing friends advertisements in, 29, 64–67, 74, 101
obituaries and death notices in, 62, 64
range of locations covered by, 64
repeal society meetings reported in, 67
sources for, 62, 66, 81

Newtown, County Limerick, Ireland, Griffith's Valuation and maps for, 137–139, 140f, 141f
New York City, 12, 24, 33, 37, 39, 51, 53, 72
   church records in, 32–33
   Irish newspapers in, 62, 64, 67
   naturalization records for, 46
   orphanage (Foundling Hospital) in, 39, 40
   passenger arrival lists for, 54, 55f, 56, 125f
New York City Public Library, 36, 37
New York Emigrant Savings Bank, 1850–1883 (database), 69
New York Foundling Hospital, New York City, 39, 40
New York Historical Society, 40
New York State, 78
   church records for, 34, 35
New York State Archives, 34
Noonan, Ellen, 24, 104
Norman invasion (1170), 86, 87, 88
North Carolina, 33, 34, 35, 57, 78
Northern Ireland
   birth records for, 113, 116t, 117
   church registers in, 106
   counties of, 86, 87
   death records for, 113
   marriage records for, 113
   ordering photocopies of civil registration records in, 113, 121
   Ordnance Survey maps of, 97
   place names in, 93
   sources for records on, 159
Northern Ireland Placename Project, 93
note taking, during oral interviews, 6
notices in newspapers. *See also* missing friends advertisements; obituaries
   biographical, 64, 67
obituaries, 62, 74, 101
   death notices contrasted with, 62, 64
   example of death notice, 64f
   in eighteenth century, 81, 83
   locating burial places using, 62
   options after not finding (or brick wall), 101
   origin information found in, 64
   range of locations covered in, 64
   sources for, 62, 67
O'Brien, Mary, 52
O'Brien, Michael J., 77
O'Connell
   Daniel, 67
   William, 16
occupations
   on bank records, 69f
   in field books, 125
   on Irish census records, 133, 134
   on Irish death records, 120
   on Irish marriage records, 119
   on naturalization petitions, 47
   on passenger arrival lists, 56
   on U.S. census records, 11, 12
OCLC (Online Computer Library Center), 33, 71
O'Connell
   Daniel, 67
   William, 16
O'Donovan, John, 95, 97
Ohio, church records in, 33, 35
Oklahoma, 35
Old Fulton NY Post Cards (website), 67
Old Stone Bank of Providence, Rhode Island, 70
Olson, Ellen (Fitzgerald), 24, 102, 104
OneNote (computer program), 9
Online Computer Library Center (OCLC), 33, 71
oral history, 3
   gravestone inscriptions related to, 63
   local histories based on, 82
oral history interviews
   common assumptions and mistakes about, 25
   conducting, 6
   documenting, 6, 9
   five-generation charts based on, 3, 25
   how far back to ask about in, 11
   of Irish-born relatives, 7
   later searches using information from, 47, 63
   photo albums and other family keepsakes used during, 6
   possible range of people to be interviewed, 6

recording, 6
reliability of data from, 26
reluctance to talk during, 6
research log on, 9
types of questions in, 6
writing down and transcribing information from, 6, 9
ordination records, 6, 31, 40
Ordnance Survey maps, 86, 91, 83, 95, 97, 131, 158
Ordnance Survey Memoirs, 97
Ordnance Survey Name Books, 95, 97
Ordnance Survey Office, 131, 158
origins in Ireland. *See also* place history
   administrative divisions and, 86–92, 98, 116
   city origins and, 7
   importance of, for researching previous generations, 7
   Irish-born relatives as sources on, 7
   learning history of, 93, 98
   McClements case study of searches for, 110–111, 114–116
   online Irish record searches based on, 85, 133
   online resources for researching, 155–159
   oral history interviews on, 6
   place name conventions and, 85–86, 98
   places of. *See* birthplaces; places of origin
   records helpful in locating, 29, 43, 61, 75, 101–102, 123, 133
   rural origins and, 7
   ways of linking ancestors to, 27
orphanage records, 39–40
outward-bound passenger lists, for ancestors returning from visits back to Ireland, 57

Pa (first papers, declaration of intent filed) status, on federal census, 11, 14, 43
parents of immigrant
   alive in 1911 (for inclusion in Irish census), 7, 10
   on baptism records, 31, 104–105
   birthplace searches for, 18
   birthplaces of, on U.S. census records, 19, 20*f*
   on birth records, 15, 18, 107
   on border-crossing records, 53
   in church records, 17
   on death records, 16, 17, 22, 23*f*, 110, 120
   focus of research on determining, 101
   immigrant living with, in census record searches, 12, 17–18, 19, 22
   Irish-born relatives as sources on, 7
   on Irish census records, 53, 135
   on IrishGenealogy website, 103
   on Irish civil registration records, 110–111
   Kennedy case study of U.S. census record searches for data on, 12–13, 18, 19, 22, 101–102, 104–105
   on marriage records, 16, 17, 21, 22, 25, 31, 51, 107, 117, 119
   marriage record searches for, 13, 110
   married couples living with, in U.S. census record searches, 17
   McClements case study of searching for, 110–111
   need to identify to use for further research, 101, 110, 122
   on passenger arrival lists, 56–57
   on passport applications, 57
   researching records to determine, 101, 110, 122
   searching large cities using names of, 24
   state census record searches for, 22
   U.S. census record searches for, 11, 12, 13, 18–19
   U.S. census records used with Irish civil records in searching for, 110–111
parents of researcher (yourself)
   on family group sheets, 4
   on five-generation charts, 3–4
   oral history interviews of, 6
   on U.S. census records, 11, 12, 13
parishes, Ireland. *See also* civil parishes
   as administrative division, 86, 88–90
   of birth. *See* birthplaces

Index   189

parishes, Ireland *cont.*
   boundaries of, crossing other administrative units, 88, 89*f*
   on Findmypast website searches, 104–105
   General Alphabetical Index to, 93
   on gravestone inscriptions, 63, 88
   maps of, 95
   in missing friends advertisements, 66
   online histories of, 35
   Presbyterian churches and, 90
   records of. *See* church records
   Townland Index of, 63
   two types of, 88
parishes of origin, 29, 46, 122. *See also* birthplaces; places of origin
   gravestone inscriptions with, 63, 74
parish registers, 123
   Church of Ireland, 106, 133
   civil versus Catholic parishes for, 102
   Episcopal, 34
   Fitzgerald case study using, 104–105
   in libraries and archives, 34, 102, 159
   locating, 32, 36
   on microfilm, 104, 105, 107, 159
   missing or gaps in, 32, 102
   in National Library of Ireland, 102, 105, 159
   online, 102, 103, 104, 105, 106, 158, 159
   Presbyterian, 107
   Quaker, 108, 109
   search strategies for, 102, 106
   types of records in, 37
   verifying search results in, 104
   witness signatures in, 106, 159
parochial school records, 39, 198
passenger arrival lists, 54–57
   additional family information gleaned from, 57
   addresses of Irish relatives on, 57
   common assumptions and mistakes about, 25
   common stories and urban legends about families on, 55
   dates of arrival guessed for searching, 55
   date ranges ("± 2 or ± 5 years") in searching for, 55
   difficulty of locating ancestors with common Irish names on, 54
   examples of data on, 55*f*, 56*f*
   family members traveling together or solo listed on, 54–55
   Irish-born relatives as sources on dates for, 7
   linking immigrant ancestors to Ireland using, 27
   McClements case study of, 54–55
   Murphy case study of, 54, 56–57
   nineteenth-century, 56
   places of origin (birthplaces) on, 43, 54, 57
   records helpful in locating, 59
   relatives returning from visits back to Ireland on outward-bound lists, 57
   researching later arrivals in same family for information about immigrant, 57
   search strategies for, 55
   to-do list for, 55
   twentieth-century, 56
   U.S. census record searches for, 14, 43
passenger lists, outward-bound for United Kingdom, for ancestors returning from visits back to Ireland, 57
passport applications, 53, 57–58
   availability range of dates, 57
   data available on, 57
   example of, 58*f*
   Murphy case study of, 57, 58*f*
   place of origin found using, 43
   searching both for immigrants and for their children, 57
   sources for searching, 57
   U.S. census records compared with, 43
Patton, James, 78
pedigree charts
   computer programs for generating, 5
   print record storage for, 6
Penal Laws, 77, 88

Pennsylvania, 33, 34, 35, 70, 76, 78, 80, 82
Pennsylvania Genealogies: Chiefly Scotch-Irish and German (Egle), 82
perambulation books, 129
petitions for naturalization. *See* naturalization petitions
petty court records, 151
Petty's Down Survey Barony maps, 88
Philadelphia, 24, 33, 35, 40, 66
Philadelphia Archdiocesan Historical Research Center, 40
photo albums, in oral interviews, 6
photocopying records. *See also* copies of records
   source citations and, 8
physical descriptions of immigrants
   on border-crossing records, 53
   on passenger arrival lists, 57
Pioneer Irish in New England (O'Brien), 77
place history, 93–98
   administrative divisions and, 86–92, 98
   place name conventions and, 85–86
place names, Irish, 85–98. *See also* residence places
   administrative divisions and, 86–92, 98
   baronies and, 98
   counties and, 87
   dioceses and, 90
   electoral divisions and, 90
   Gaelic and Norman influences on, 86
   gazetteers for, 97
   on gravestone inscriptions, problems deciphering, 63
   Irish language origins of, 85
   linking to administrative divisions for research, 93
   maps for, 95–97
   parishes and, 88
   poor law unions and, 90
   Presbyterian church parishes and, 90
   probate districts and, 91
   problems in using, 85
   provinces and, 86–87
   references works on, 93–95
   search strategies using, 65, 66
   sources for, 63
   superintendent registrar's districts and, 90–91
   to-do list for, 95
   townlands and, 91
   townland sub-denominations (sub-townlands) as unofficial, 91–92
   using townland in searches for, 85–86
places. *See* birthplaces; burial places; death places; marriage places; naturalization places; places of origin; ports of arrival (ports of entry); residence places
places of arrival. *See* ports of arrival (ports of entry)
places of origin. *See also* birthplaces; place names, Irish
   civil registration records and, 107
   eighteenth-century record searches and, 75, 79–80
   focus of research on determining, 101
   gravestone inscriptions with, 61, 63
   Griffith's Primary Valuation in identifying, 123
   in Irish records, 101
   linking to administrative divisions for research, 93
   McClements case study of
   missing friends advertisements with, 64–65
   need to identify to use for further research, 101, 122
   networks of family and friends and, 80
   records helpful in locating, 43, 59
   passenger arrival lists and, 43, 54, 57
   repeal society meetings reports with, 67
   research in seventeenth- and eighteenth-century records and need for, 75
   searching for all immigrants from one place, 66
   travel records for determining, 43
places of worship, 97. *See also* churches

police courts, naturalization in, 44
plantation settlement programs, 77, 90
Poor Law Act (1838), 90, 126, 131
Poor Law Union Administrative Districts, 126
poor law unions
  as administrative division, 90, 91, 96f, 126, 131
  maps of, 157
  reference works for, 95, 157
  searches using, 90, 117, 118
  superintendent registrar's districts and, 91, 114, 116
Porter, Anna Matilda (McClements), 150
ports of arrival (ports of entry), 64. *See also* passenger arrival lists
  for indentured servants, 77
  interviews with Irish-born relatives on, 7
  on naturalization petitions, 47, 48f, 49, 51, 52f, 55
  on passenger arrival lists, 54
  reliability of information on, 53, 54
  trade routes influencing choice of, 75, 77, 79
ports of embarkation
  eighteenth-century immigration and, 78
  newspaper articles on, 81
  on passenger arrival lists, 54
  place of origin not related to, 54
  seventeenth-century immigration and, 77
Presbyterian churches
  parishes of, 90, 95
  registers of, 107
Presbyterian church records
  Irish, 90, 103, 107, 126, 145, 159
  U.S., 33–34, 80, 83
Presbyterian Historical Society, Belfast, 105, 107
Presbyterian Historical Society, Philadelphia, 34
Presbyterian immigrants, 33, 77, 78
presbytery records and histories, 80, 83
priests. *See also* clergy
  on baptism records, 30
  finding church records using, 32

on marriage records, 16, 21, 31, 36, 39
parish information in small towns from, 35
print records, source citations for, 8
print record storage
  folders and binders for, 6
  for photocopies of source information, 8
  for research logs, 9
prisoners, immigration by, 77
prison records, 151, 157
private organizations. *See also* fraternal organizations; social organizations
  business agent records held by, 69, 74
  estate records held by, 152
  records of, 83
probate (will) calendars, Ireland, 148, 149, 150f, 157, 159
probate districts, Ireland, 91
probate records, Ireland. *See also* letters of administration; wills
  bank information in, 70
  destruction and loss of, 133
  loss of documents from fire, 133
  locations of, 91
  McClements case study of searching, 149–150
  online databases of, 148, 149
probate records, United States, 11, 83. *See also* letters of administration; wills
  banking information in, 70
  details about ancestors available in, 24, 82
  economic status and, 24
  inventories in, 24, 70
  microfilmed originals of, 82
  in seventeenth century, 76
  U.S. census records and, 11
probate registry, Ireland, 91
property records, Ireland
  as census substitutes, 122
  historical background to, 123–127
  ways of using, 122
property valuations
  building classifications in, 128
  categories of notebooks in, 128–129
  county cess and, 124–124

field books and house books in, 124–125
historical background to, 123–127
Poor Law Act (1838) and, 126
repositories holding, 127
revised valuations for, 127, 144–145, 159
Tenement Valuation Acts (1846, 1852) and, 126–127
three types of, 124
timeline of key dates related to, 131
tithe appointment survey (ca. 1823–1838) and, 126
Townland Valuation (1830–1840) and, 124–125
Proquest (website), 81
Protestant churches, 32, 76. *See also* church records, Ireland; church records, North America; *and specific groups*
  locating church records for, 32, 33–34
  in Ulster, 86, 108
Protestant Householder Census (1740), 83
Protestant Irish settlers, South Carolina, 82
Providence Institution for Savings, 70
provinces, Ireland, 86–87
  as administrative division, 86–87
  map showing, 92*f*
Public Record Office of Ireland (PROI), 106, 134, 145, 153
  fire (1922) at, 131, 133, 134, 150*f*, 153
Public Record Office of Northern Ireland (PRONI), 81, 83, 87, 105, 106, 107, 109, 122, 127, 144, 148, 149, 150*f*, 152, 159
Puritans, 75–76

Quakers
  immigration by, 76, 77
  locating church records for, 34–35
  researching, 108–109
  sources for church records of, 107, 108–109
  sources for immigration records of, 76
  vital records kept by, 108
quarter session books, 82, 83
quarto books, 128, 129. *See also* house books
Queens University, Belfast, 93

rabbis, on marriage records, 21
Rathlin Island, County Antrim, Ireland, on gravestone inscriptions, 63
Readex (website), 81
recording oral interviews, 6
record-keeping. *See also* files and filing systems; storage of documents
  for basic genealogical forms, 5–6
  for citations sources, 8
  computer programs for, 8
  for oral history interviews, 6
  research log for, 8–9
Reformation, 88
registers. *See also* parish registers
  baptismal, 36
  burial, 37
  episcopal (bishop's) registers, 31, 32
  marriage, 38
  sacramental registers, 32
Registry of Deeds, Ireland, 88, 160
Reilly, James, 128
relatives. *See also* fathers; grandparents; mothers; parents; siblings
  bank records listing, 69*f*
  business agents working with, 68
  as godparents or witnesses on parish records, 106
  identifying, for further searches, 22, 23, 29, 59, 102
  Irish-born. *See* Irish-born relatives
  McClements case study on searching for, 135–136
  passage to America and, 25
  on passenger arrival lists, 56, 57
  oral history interviews of, 6
  people with same surname in townlands, as possible relatives, 135
  returning to Ireland to visit, 57
  starting research with relatives you know, 3
  as witness on naturalization petitions, 46, 52*f*
  on U.S. census records, 22

Index   193

religion. *See also specific churches and groups*
   of eighteenth-century immigrants and, 33, 77
   on Irish census reports, 135
   of seventeenth-century immigrants, 33, 76
religious calendars, and searching by years, 12, 45
Religious Census (1766), Ireland, 83
religious groups, in Ireland, 88, 90, 108. *See also* specific churches and groups
   cemetery affiliation with, 37, 61
   group migrations by, 33, 80
   school run by, 39
religiously affiliated school records, 39, 198
religious orders, schools of, 39
Religious Society of Friends. See Quakers
rent books, 129
repeal societies, 67, 68f, 74
   description of, 67
   newspaper reports of meetings of, 67
   sources for, 67
Representative Church Body Library, Church of Ireland, 105, 106
research
   collateral research used in, 5
   common assumptions and mistakes in, 24–25
   context of communities in, 27
   digitized search results kept in, 5–6
   print record storage in, 6
   widening number of people included in, 23, 27, 29, 110
Researching Scots-Irish Ancestors (Roulston), 83
research logs, 8–9
   downloadable forms for, 9
   filing system for storing, 6, 9
   information kept in, 8
   print record storage for, 6
   sample, 9f
residence places. *See also* house descriptions
   on baptism records, 104
   birthplace not same as, 57
   on border-crossing records, 53
   burial locations and, 62
   on civil birth records, 29, 115
   declarations of intent and, 50
   Kennedy case study of U.S. census record searches for, 12, 15, 18
   on Irish census records, 53
   on marriage records, 16, 107, 118, 119
   in missing friends advertisements on, 65–66
   most recent occupiers of, as possible resource, 144
   on naturalization petitions, 47, 53
   on online newspaper records, 65, 66
   on passenger arrival lists, 57
   in revised valuations, 144
   search strategies using, 65, 66
   townlands and, 106, 107, 115
   on U.S. census records, 12, 13, 18
residency requirement, for citizenship, 44, 49, 50
resident aliens, 34
Reunion (computer program), 5
Revill, Jean, 82
Revised Land Books, 131
revised valuations, Ireland, 144–145
   description of page markings in, 144
   historical background for, 127, 131
   McClements case study using, 144–145
   sources for, 87, 159
Rhode Island Historical Society, 70
Richard Griffith and His Valuations of Ireland (Reilly), 128
Roman Catholic Church. *See* Catholic Church
RootsIreland, 102, 103–104, 105, 159
   coverage of, 103, 107
   sample search on, 104
RootsMagic (computer program), 5
Roulston, William J., 83
rural areas
   agricultural and religious calendars in, 45
   Irish ancestors from, 7, 12, 45
   marriage dispensations in, 39
   orphaned children sent to families in, 39
   parishes in, 7
   townlands in, 91
   valuation of householders in, 124

Ruskin, John, 10
Ryan, Mary, 51, 53

sacramental records, 29, 40. *See also* baptism records; marriage records
sacramental registers, 32
St. Paul's Masonic Lodge, Boston, 72*f*
St. Peter's Roman Catholic Church, New York City, 32*f*, 37, 37*f*
St. Vincent de Paul Society, Boston, 72
sample forms
   family group sheet, 5*f*
   five-generation chart, 4*f*
   research log, 9*f*
schools
   determining who was in charge of, 39
   location of, in Ireland, 97
   parochial school records, 39, 198
Scotch-Irish Foundation Library and Archives, 82
Scots Irish immigrants, 77, 78, 80, 82, 83, 90
search strategies
   "community" strategy for eighteenth-century records, 79, 84
   context of communities in, 27
   date ranges ("± 2 or 5 years") in searches, 12, 47, 49, 55
   filtering common surnames on Findmypast.com, 135
   given name field blank in birth records searches, 110
   graveyard inscriptions, 63–64
   image quality issues, 146–147
   Irish census records, 135
   Irish church records, 102
   leaving lived-in field blank for small towns when searching Irish records, 23–24
   missing friends advertisements in newspapers, 65–66
   name field blank in Irish census records to find relatives, 135
   passenger arrival lists, 55
   place names, 65, 66
   pre-1906 New England naturalization petitions, 47
   research later arrivals in same family for information about immigrant, 57
   siblings and associates also searched, 102
   to-do lists for, 15, 23
   using a less common family name, 13
   variant spellings in search engine, 12, 102, 105, 118, 146, 158
senachies, 3
servants. *See also* indentured servants
   on civil registration records, 107
   on Irish census records, 135
   Kennedy case study of U.S. census record searches and, 14
   on passenger arrival lists, 56
session books, 80, 81*f*, 83, 107
seventeenth–century immigration
   determining religion of, 76
   estimates of number of individuals in, 75
   outline of, 75–76
seventeenth–century records, 76–77
   indentured servants in, 76–77
   organization of, 75
   paucity of references on immigrants in, 76, 84
   places of origin needed for researching, 75
   Quakers in, 108
   researching, 76–77
   sources for, 77
   town vital records used for, 76
ship names
   on bank records, 69
   on border-crossing records, 53
   general area of origin determined using, 77
   on passenger arrival lists, 54, 56
   on passenger manifests, 125*f*
   in post-1906 naturalization records, 51
shipping companies, and border-crossing records, 53
Ship-pool townland, County Cork, Ireland, property valuations, 130*f*
ships. *See also* passenger arrival lists; ports of arrival; ports of embarkation
   immigrant's choice of, 64
   in eighteenth-century immigration, 79, 81, 83

ships *cont.*
   newspapers on arrivals of, 81, 83
   in seventeenth-century immigration, 76
Shute, Samuel, 78
siblings. *See also* brothers; sisters
   assumption about immigration and, 25
   baptism records of, 29, 30*f*, 104, 106
   birth records of, 101, 102, 107, 110
   on border-crossing records, 53
   in church records, 29, 101
   death records for, 24, 102
   on family group sheets, 4
   on Irish census records, 53, 135
   Kennedy/Fitzgerald case study of searching using, 12, 24, 29–30, 102, 104
   marriage records of, 36
   on naturalization petitions, 53
   newspaper ads looking for, 64–65
   passenger arrival lists for, 55, 56
   town and townland searches for, 24, 135
   widening research on immigrant ancestors using, 23, 24, 29, 101, 102, 107, 135
   in wills, 150
sick call records, 31
signature books, for banks, 70
Silinonte, Joseph M., 38, 62
sisters. *See also* siblings
   on border-crossing records, 53
   on family group sheets, 4
   on Irish census records, 53
   Kennedy/Fitzgerald case study of searching using, 29–30, 53
   McClements case study of searching using, 150
sisters (religious orders), schools run by, 39
Sisters of Notre Dame de Namur Boston/Ipswich New England Archives, 39
slaves, immigration by, 75, 84
small towns. *See also* cities
   banks in, 70
   business agents in, 68

clusters of immigrants leaving from, 24
leaving lived-in field blank when searching, 23–24
locating church records for, 35–36
locating graveyards in, 61
locating places of origin for immigrants to, 66
networks and immigration to, 80
repeal societies in, 67
researching other immigrants with same surname from, to locate specific family immigrant, 24
Smith, James, 1
Smith, John, 76
social organizations, 71, 74. *See also* fraternal organizations
Society of Friends. *See* Quakers
Society of Friends Library, Lisburn, County Antrim, Ireland, 108–109
Soundex codes, 47, 93, 158
source citations, 8
   computer programs for recording, 8
   digitized search results on computers for, 5–6
   documenting interviews for, 6
   example of, 8
   generating footnotes for, 8
   importance of keeping, 8
   for photocopies, 8
   rationale for using, 8
   styles for, 8
   for vital records, 8
   for web pages, 8
South Carolina, 33, 35, 78, 82
starting. *See* getting started
state archives, 33, 34, 69, 70
state courts, declarations of intent in, 51
state legislatures, 70
state libraries
   business agent records in, 69
   church records in, 33, 34
states, Masonic Lodge membership files for, 72
storage of documents. *See also* files and filing systems
   digitized search results on computers, 5–6
   print storage in folders or binders, 6

street directories, 148, 159
sub-denominations of townlands (sub-townlands), 91–92
superintendent registrar's districts
  birthplaces differentiated from, 114
  on birth records, 114, 115f, 116
  civil registration records and, 91, 107, 110, 116, 117, 118
  indexes for, 93, 117
  Irish civil records using, 91, 116
  as administrative division, 90–91
  poor law unions and, 91, 114, 116
superior courts, naturalization in, 44, 57
supreme courts, county, naturalization in, 44
Swarthmore College, Swarthmore, Pennsylvania, 35

taxation system, in Ireland, 131, 136. *See also* property valuations
  two forms of local taxes in, 123–124
  workhouses supported by, 126
tax lists, United States, 78, 82, 83
tax records, civil parishes used in, 88
tax valuation records, Ireland, 88
Taylor, George, 1
tenant right, 77
tenants. *See* leases and lessors
Tenement Valuation Acts (1846, 1852), 124, 126–127, 131
tenure books, 129
theological school libraries, church records in, 34
Thornton, Matthew, 1
Tithe Applotment Books, 145–148, 153
  Fitzgerald case study using, 146–148
  historical background for, 126, 145–146
  information available in, 136
  McClements case study using, 148, 149f
  measurements used in, 148
  sources for, 145–146, 158
  years covered by, 145–146
tithe appointment survey (ca. 1823–1838), 126
tithes, in local taxation, 123, 131, 145–146
Tithe War (1831), 131
to-do lists, 6, 7, 39, 55, 62, 95, 110
Tombstones of the Irish Born: Cemetery of the Holy Cross, Flatbush, Brooklyn (Silinonte), 62
Topographical Dictionary (Lewis), 97
town directories, 70
Townland Index, 63
townlands
  as administrative division, 86, 91
  on Ask about Ireland website, 139
  on baptism records, 104
  of birth, 45, 46. *See also* birthplaces; places of origin
  on birth records, 107, 115–116, 122
  on church records, 122
  critical for searches, 85, 91
  electoral divisions with, 90
  General Alphabetical Index to, 93, 94f
  on gravestone inscriptions, 63, 74
  in Griffith's Primary Valuation of Ireland, 137, 138, 139
  in Irish census records, 134f, 135
  Irish census record searches using, 135
  Irish language origins of, 85
  on marriage records, 118, 119, 122
  maps of, 95, 97
  poor law unions of, 90, 126
  sources for finding, 91–92
  standardized spelling of names of, 97
  sub-denominations (sub-townlands) of, 91–92
  Townland Index of, 63
  towns differentiated from, 91
  usefulness in handling individuals with the same surnames, 91
Townlands in Poor Law Unions (Handran), 95
Townland Valuation (1830–1840), 124–125, 127, 128
Townland Valuation Act (1826), 124, 131
Townland Valuation Field Book, 125
townland valuations
  church record gaps covered in, 126
  field books and house books used in, 124–125

Town Parks (Ballymena), County Antrim, Ireland, field book, 125
town records, seventeenth-century, 76
towns. *See also* cities; small towns
  banks in, 70
  eighteenth-century immigration to, 78–79
  field books and house books with names of people in, 124–125
  maps of, on Ask about Ireland, 139, 140*f*
  townlands differentiated from, 91
Tracing Your Irish Ancestors (Grenham), 107, 152
trade routes, and immigration, 75, 77, 79
travel records, 53, 59, 74. *See also* border-crossing records; passenger arrival lists; passport applications
  linking immigrant ancestors to Ireland using, 27
  paper trail left in, 53
Tree Talks (Central New York Genealogical Society), 68
Trinity College, 92
Ulster (county), Ireland, 86
  complexity of researching, 86
  counties in, 86–87
  field books for, 128
  Presbyterian immigrants from, 77, 78
  Quakers in, 108
  sources for, 83, 97, 103
  townland names in, 93
  Townland Valuation for, 124
Ulster Covenant, signers of, 148
uncles. *See also* relatives
  on family group sheets, 4–5
  oral history interviews of, 6
undertakers
  burial grounds and, 37
  death records and, 16, 17, 61, 63
United Kingdom
  Act of Union (1800) and, 67, 131
  early Irish settlers considered citizens of, 44
  home rule struggles with, 86–87
  outward-bound passenger lists from, for ancestors returning from visits back to Ireland, 57
  plantation settlement programs backed by, 77
United Methodist Church General Commission Archives and History, 35
U.S. Catholic Sources: A Diocesan Research Guide (Humling), 32
U.S. Federal Reserve System, 71
U. S. Immigration Service, 53
U. S. National Archives, 46, 48, 51, 57
university archives. *See* college and university archives

Valuation Books, in Griffith's pre-publication records, 127–129
  building classifications in, 128
  categories of notebooks in, 128–129
  repositories holding, 127
Valuation Office, Dublin, 87, 127
valuation records, Ireland
  as census substitutes, 122
  historical background to, 123–127
  timeline of key dates related to, 131
  types of property valuations and, 124
  ways of using, 122
Vermont, Catholic Church in, 36
Vermont French-Canadian Genealogical Society, 36
veterans, and applications for citizenship, 50
Virginia, 33, 35, 75, 78, 82
Virginia Company, 76
Virginia State Library Archives, 34
vital records, Ireland. *See also* birth records; death records; marriage records
  church records used for gaps in, 102
  seventeenth-century, 76
  under-registration for, 30, 122
vital records, United States, 11, 15–23. *See also* birth records; death records; marriage records
  church records used for gaps in, 27, 30, 31, 40
  citing sources for, 8
  eighteenth-century, 83

Waltham Bank, Massachusetts, 70
Waltham Savings Bank, Massachusetts, 71
Webb, Morrison deS., 108–109
Webb, Thomas Henry, 109
"Webb Pedigrees" (manuscript), 109
web pages, source citations for, 8
web portals, resources on, 157
websites. *See also specific websites*
   date ranges ("± 2 years") in searching, 12
   for U.S. census records, 12
Wells Fargo Bank, 71
Whyte, John, 149
will (probate) calendars, Ireland, 148, 149, 150*f*, 157, 159
Williams
   Andrew, 101
   Bridget (Fitzgerald), 24, 101, 102, 104
wills
   bank information in, 70
   eighteenth-century, 83
   example of, 151*f*
   McClements case study of, 149–150, 151*f*
   probate districts for, 91
   sources for, 103
Wilmot
   Ellen, 24, 30, 102, 104, 106*f*, 146, 147
   William, 147

Wilson, Shane, 93
Winthrop, John, 76
witnesses
   on baptism records, 106
   on church registers, 106, 159
   on marriage records, 31, 40, 106
   on naturalization petitions, 29, 46, 47, 49, 52*f*, 65, 66
wives. *See also* maiden names
   on citizenship petitions, 52*f*
   citizenship status derived from husbands' status (prior to 1922), 14, 45
   on husband's naturalization petition, 51, 52*f*
   Irish census forms including household information about, 135
   missing friends advertisements and, 64
women
   citizenship status derived from husbands' status (prior to 1922), 14, 45
   immigration by, 75, 80, 107, 134–135
workhouses, 90, 126, 131
Work Progress Administration (WPA), 33, 47–48
World War II military service, 50

About the Authors

Marie E. Daly is Senior Genealogist at the New England Historic Genealogical Society. Formerly Director of NEHGS Library Services, she has been researching, lecturing, and writing about Irish genealogy since 1976 and is the past president and co-founder of TIARA (The Irish Ancestral Research Association). She is particularly interested in old Irish graveyards and has transcribed the tombstone inscriptions in several Irish cemeteries in the Boston area.

Judith Lucey is Archivist at the New England Historic Genealogical Society, having joined the staff in 2003. Her research interests include Irish, Italian, and New England family research and nineteenth- and twentieth-century genealogical research. Judy has been researching her own Irish-Italian ancestry for more than fifteen years; in her spare time she continues to seek her elusive Lucey ancestors in County Cork, Ireland.